Mind and Religion

COGNITIVE SCIENCE OF
RELIGION SERIES

Series Editors: Harvey Whitehouse
and Luther H. Martin

The Cognitive Science of Religion Series publishes research into the cognitive foundations of religious thinking and behavior and their consequences for social morphology. The emphasis of the series is on scientific approaches to the study of religion within the framework of the cognitive sciences, including experimental, clinical, or laboratory studies, but works drawing upon ethnographic, linguistic, archaeological, or historical research are welcome, as are critical appraisals of research in these areas. In addition to providing a forum for presenting new empirical evidence and major theoretical innovations, the series publishes concise overviews of issues in the field suitable for students and general readers. This series is published in cooperation with the Institute for Cognition and Culture at Queen's University Belfast.

TITLES IN THE SERIES
Modes of Religiosity
A Cognitive Theory of Religious Transmission
By Harvey Whitehouse

Magic, Miracles, and Religion
A Scientist's Perspective
By Ilkka Pyysiäinen

Why Would Anyone Believe in God?
By Justin L. Barrett

Ritual and Memory
Toward a Comparative Anthropology of Religion
Edited by Harvey Whitehouse and James Laidlaw

Theorizing Religions Past
Archaeology, History, and Cognition
Edited by Harvey Whitehouse and Luther H. Martin

How the Bible Works
An Anthropological Study of Evangelical Biblicism
By Brian E. Malley

Mind and Religion
Psychological and Cognitive Foundations of Religiosity
Edited by Harvey Whitehouse and Robert N. McCauley

FORTHCOMING TITLES
The Evolution of Religion
By Harvey Whitehouse

God from the Machine
By William Sims Bainbridge

Mind and Religion

Psychological and Cognitive Foundations of Religiosity

Edited by
Harvey Whitehouse
and
Robert N. McCauley

ALTAMIRA
PRESS

A DIVISION OF
ROWMAN & LITTLEFIELD PUBLISHERS, INC.
Walnut Creek • *Lanham* • *New York* • *Toronto* • *Oxford*

ALTAMIRA PRESS
A division of Rowman & Littlefield Publishers, Inc.
1630 North Main Street, #367
Walnut Creek, CA 94596
www.altamirapress.com

Rowman & Littlefield Publishers, Inc.
A wholly owned subsidiary of The Rowman & Littlefield Publishing Group, Inc.
4501 Forbes Boulevard, Suite 200
Lanham, MD 20706

PO Box 317
Oxford
OX2 9RU, UK

British Library Cataloguing in Publication Information Available

Library of Congress Cataloging-in-Publication Data

Mind and religion : psychological and cognitive foundations of religiosity /
edited by Harvey Whitehouse and Robert N. McCauley.
    p. cm. — (Cognitive science of religion series)
    Includes bibliographical references and index.
    ISBN 0-7591-0618-5 (alk. paper) — ISBN 0-7591-0619-3 (pbk. : alk. paper)
    1. Psychology, Religious.   2. Whitehouse, Harvey.   I. Whitehouse, Harvey.
II. McCauley, Robert N.   III. Series.

BL53.M555 2005
200'.1'9—dc22   2004029723

Printed in the United States of America

To Richard English and Mark Burnett, in appreciation of your abiding friendship and intellectual stimulation, and to Ellen Amanda McCauley—"Thou wast that did preserve me."

Contents

Preface

This volume arises from a conference on the Psychological and Cognitive Foundations of Religiosity that took place at Emory University (Atlanta, Georgia) in August 2003. The conference brought together scholars from ten nations and six disciplines (psychology, anthropology, religious studies, biology, philosophy, and cognitive science) for the dual purpose of presenting new developments at the interface of the cognitive sciences and religion and of examining Whitehouse's theory of "modes of religiosity." The papers that make up this volume are those that focused particularly on Whitehouse's work. The conference was made possible by generous funding from the Emory University Subvention Fund, the John Templeton Foundation, the British Academy, the Emory Cognition Project, the Emory Department of Philosophy, and the Emory Center for Humanistic Inquiry, for which we are profoundly grateful. This was the third of three conferences initiated through the Modes of Religiosity Project, funded by a British Academy Networks Grant. The first two conferences occurred at Kings College, University of Cambridge (December 2002) and at the University of Vermont (August 2002). They resulted, respectively, in *Ritual and Memory: Toward a Comparative Anthropology of Religion*, edited by Harvey Whitehouse and James Laidlaw (2004), and *Theorizing Religions Past: Archaeology, History, and Cognition*, edited by Harvey Whitehouse and Luther Martin (2004). The first of these volumes brings together criticism and commentary concerning Whitehouse's modes theory from the perspective of ethnographers and cultural anthropologists. The second volume is a collection that examines the theory from the perspectives of researchers in the history of religions and in archaeology. For a period of two years from September 2003, Harvey

Whitehouse was the recipient of a British Academy Research Readership, relieving him of teaching obligations and greatly facilitating his work on this and other volumes arising from the Modes of Religiosity Project and related research activities.

Harvey Whitehouse
Robert N. McCauley

Introduction

Robert N. McCauley

In a series of books and papers that have appeared over the past fifteen years, the cognitive anthropologist, Harvey Whitehouse, has developed an elaborate theory of two alternative modes of religiosity (e.g., Whitehouse 1992, 1995, 2000, 2004). The theory has attracted considerable attention from scholars across a host of fields (e.g., Whitehouse and Laidlaw 2004; Whitehouse and Martin 2004; McCauley and Whitehouse 2004; Martin and Whitehouse 2004; Martin and Whitehouse 2006). This volume contains eleven papers by theorists and experimentalists in the cognitive science of religion that address Whitehouse's theory.

Whitehouse's modes theory is one of a number of theories in the cognitive science of religion that has arisen over the past fifteen years. Cognitive scientists of religion have advanced assorted theoretical proposals about an array of different religious phenomena. What they all have in common is that they champion the promise of the methods and findings of the cognitive sciences for enhancing our understanding of those phenomena. The earliest works in this field looked to theoretical strategies from the various cognitive sciences, including linguistics (Lawson and McCauley 1990), evolutionary psychology (Boyer 1992, 1994), and cognitive psychology (Guthrie 1980; Whitehouse 1992, 1995), in order to formulate new theories about a wide range of religious materials, including religious ritual, religious representations, and, of course, modes of religiosity. Works exploring the consequences of these theories and advancing additional cognitive theories about these and other religious phenomena soon followed. Examples of the former include experimental work in psychology (Barrett, Richert, and Driesenga, 2001; Bering and Bjorklund, in press) and anthropology (Malley and Barrett 2003) as well as attempts to test these theories cross-culturally (Abbink 1995)

and historically (Vial 2004). Such work has generated new proposals about
the nature of ritual transmission (Barth 2002; Bloch 2004), sacred texts
(Pyysiäinen 1999, 2004; Malley 2004), the connections between religion and
morality (Hinde 1999; Boyer 2001), and the character of religious belief and
theology (Barrett 2004; Slone 2004).

Like many other researchers in the cognitive science of religion, Whitehouse adopts a selectionist perspective on religious transmission. In order
to be passed on, religious concepts and practices must achieve a certain
level of psychological fitness. Some religious representations are naturally
"catchy." For instance, simple notions of supernatural agency (Boyer
2001), conceptions of the forms of rituals as actions (McCauley and Lawson 2002), and certain aspects of mythological narrative (Turner 1996) may
be acquired somewhat automatically, due to relatively fixed and generic
features of our evolved cognitive architecture. These "cognitively optimal"
features of religion recur over time and space regardless of the varied social and cultural contexts in which people happen to be raised. Whitehouse emphasizes that many religious traditions *also* involve the transmission of more complex and cross-culturally diverse concepts and practices
that present a major challenge to adherents' cognitive systems. For instance, a theological system may postulate elaborate logical or temporal
connections between dogmas and cosmological events and processes. And
religious authorities may insist that only certain versions of an extensive
belief system are allowed. Getting the story straight can be a matter of life
and death in traditions intolerant of heretics or blasphemers. Why do religious beliefs become complex and challenging? And why is it so important
to adherents that their own particular versions of the Truth should tran-
scend all others? Whitehouse's answer begins with the strengths and limitations of human memory.

People obviously cannot remember everything they see and hear. Two
factors greatly increase the chances that knowledge will be recalled. One is
repetition. If you take in a piece of information on numerous occasions, you
are more likely to remember it than if you only hear it once. The other is
arousal. If an event is shocking, upsetting, euphoric, or disturbing, then you
are more likely to remember it than if it is dull and unremarkable. But these
two routes to remembering give rise to rather different kinds of recall. Repetition produces what psychologists call "semantic memory": the capacity to
recall general knowledge (London buses are red, Paris is the capital of
France, etc.) without being able to say when or where one first acquired that
information. Arousal, by contrast, tends to be associated with "episodic
memory": the capacity to recall specific events in one's life experience (one's
first kiss, the day John F. Kennedy was assassinated, etc.) According to
Whitehouse, religious traditions exploit these two kinds of memories in ways
that have considerable consequences for the way religious concepts are

formed and transmitted and for the way religious traditions, as social institutions, are organized and spread.

Whitehouse's starting point is that all religious traditions are constructed around ritual behavior. Ritual, he argues, is a special kind of behavior insofar as it does not originate in the intentional states of the ritual actor and is irreducible to a set of technical motivations. (See Humphrey and Laidlaw 1994.) Rituals are actions that are stipulated in advance, and there is no intuitive causal connection between the acts and their presumed outcomes. So who decided that the ritual procedure should be done this way, rather than that? And why? These are natural questions about the intentions behind ritual—but since the ritual actors are not the creators of their acts, we cannot assume that they will know the answer. If we are to learn the meanings of ritual actions, we either have to be told about their symbolic properties from some trustworthy source (e.g., religious authorities) or we have to exercise our own imaginations. This is where memory becomes important.

If rituals and their meanings are frequently repeated, we are capable of both learning a great deal of very complex exegesis and dogma and storing that knowledge in semantic memory. Because the knowledge is continually reviewed, it becomes easy to spot deviations and, therefore, to maintain orthodox versions. Since the knowledge is codified in language, it is relatively simple to transport, by a small number of gifted orators (gurus, prophets, messiahs, disciples, priests, missionaries, evangelists, etc.) The association of authoritative doctrine with designated leaders facilitates the growth of centralized hierarchy and the standardization of the creed over wide areas. Whitehouse refers to this complex of features as the "doctrinal mode of religiosity."

Doctrinal transmission implies downward flow of information, from experts to laity. It tends to discourage people from developing their own interpretative frameworks and cosmologies. If, however, people participate in rare and shocking ritual activities, a rather different pattern of religious thinking emerges. For a start, people will recall the rituals as very distinctive episodes in their life experience. People who have undergone terrifying initiations or participated in shocking behaviors like ritual cannibalism, human sacrifice, or ritualized warfare will never be able to forget the acts they have performed or the things that were done to them. Whitehouse maintains that for years to come they will ruminate on the meanings of their experiences—from Mithraism in ancient Greece to diabolists in modern England, from male fertility cults in New Guinea to West African secret societies, spontaneous exegetical reflection (SER) lies at the core of all varieties of mystical religion. Whitehouse refers to this as the "imagistic mode of religiosity." Traditions based on this kind of religious transmission tend to be small-scale or fragmentary. In part this is because they create intense cohesion among coparticipants. People remember their experiences episodically, so they can tell you who went through the rituals with them (and consequently who did not). Such ritual groupings, once formed, cannot be expanded to embrace newcomers. Moreover, the tradition cannot be spread by orators, since the esoteric knowledge is not codified in language. The only way to gain access to these cultic mysteries is to undergo the rituals and embark on a private revelatory journey of one's own. In consequence, these traditions spread inefficiently, if at all. Whitehouse has tabulated the main differences between doctrinal and imagistic modes as a set of basic contrasts in their psychological and sociopolitical features (see table 1).

This book contains three parts. The first, entitled "Theoretical Context," includes chapters that focus on various details of the modes theory, frequently offering alternative accounts of the phenomena to be explained.

Pascal Boyer's chapter suggests that Whitehouse's two modes of religiosity do not explain diverging religious arrangements so much as they organize and describe two prominent patterns in need of explanation. Boyer argues for construing Whitehouse's modes theory as delineating two "bundles of features" (as, in effect, ideal types), rather than as providing a "causal nexus" that explains those patterns in the way that Whitehouse's treatments of the theory sometimes maintain. Boyer then lays out what he terms a "reductionistic" account of prominent features of Whitehouse's two modes that, he holds, is more economical and more in keeping with the "standard model" of theorizing and investigation within the cognitive science of religion. (I will refer to theories of this sort as "standard theories" hereafter.) Whitehouse's approach looks at how the interaction of cognitive processes

Table I.1.   Contrasting Modes of Religiosity

Variable	Doctrinal	Imagistic
Psychological Features		
1. Transmissive frequency	High	Low
2. Level of arousal	Low	High
3. Principal memory system	Semantic schemas and implicit scripts	Episodic/flashbulb memory
4. Ritual meaning	Learned/acquired	Internally generated
5. Techniques of revelation	Rhetoric, logical integration, narrative	Iconicity, multivocality and multivalence
Sociopolitical Features		
6. Social cohesion	Diffuse	Intense
7. Leadership	Dynamic	Passive/absent
8. Inclusivity/exclusivity	Inclusive	Exclusive
9. Spread	Rapid, efficient	Slow, inefficient
10. Scale	Large scale	Small scale
11. Degree of uniformity	High	Low
12. Structure	Centralized	Noncentralized

with particular historical and cultural circumstances results in specific religious systems and various types of overt understandings. By contrast, the standard theories aim to account for the recurrent features of mostly unconscious mental representations on the basis of the selection of minor variants on the operations of common cognitive mechanisms. Testing such theories turns on examining how they square with actual representations that arise within human groups and with experimental findings about those mechanisms. Boyer asserts that theories that operate within this standard framework are general, probabilistic, and "experience distant" and that they tend to "fractionate" and "deflate" religion. In addition to his own work, Boyer includes, as examples of theories and research that operate within the framework of the standard model, such works as Lawson and McCauley (1990), Barrett (1996), and Pyysiäinen (2001).

Boyer wields Occam's razor decisively. He holds that his alternative proposals are more economical than Whitehouse's since they appeal to psychological mechanisms and social configurations that (a) are more fundamental and more ubiquitous than anything specifically religious and (b) involve no appeal to what Whitehouse refers to as "revelations" (a notion Boyer regards as unhelpfully ambiguous and peculiarly connected with the so-called "world" religions). With respect to the imagistic mode, Boyer surveys evidence that imagistic rituals do not stimulate revelations in any systematic or principled way. He argues that their distinctive features probably have much more to do with processes of selection enlisting dispositions of the human mind concerned with contagion avoidance and the formation of coalitions. Boyer offers even more ambitious proposals concerning the doctrinal mode. He suspects that familiar social and cognitive dynamics, which operate in a variety of domains in addition to the religious, generate guilds of religious specialists concerned with brand management in large-scale polities that possess the tools of literacy. Boyer argues that they not only explain the prominent features of the doctrinal mode that Whitehouse notes but additional features that he unveils as well. He suggests that while recognizing the importance of the two constellations of phenomena Whitehouse's work highlights, a cognitively informed anthropology of religion should eschew explanatory constructs such as "revelation" and avoid the needless causal speculations that Whitehouse's reification of the two modes prompts.

If Boyer's take on religion is reductionistic, Robert Hinde's is just the opposite. Hinde, who brings the insights of a researcher who works at the interface between biology and psychology to bear on the cognitive science of religion, advocates an approach that does justice to the myriad complications that the analysis of complex systems, like religions, entails. He argues that we obtain a richer understanding of such complex systems, whether biological or psychological, when we take up three tasks that consider, respectively, (1) their components and those components' interactions, (2) their contexts, and (3) their diachronic dimensions (both developmental and evolutionary). (See Craver 2001 also.) He offers both strengths and shortcomings among the work of Whitehouse, Boyer, and McCauley and Lawson to illustrate many of his methodological observations.

The first task, viz the study of a system's components and their interactions, begins with careful description. Hinde maintains that in the case of religion this involves attention to at least six components: (1) structural beliefs, (2) narratives, (3) ritual, (4) moral codes, (5) religious experience, and (6) relations between participants. It also involves attention to their interactions. So, for example, Hinde faults Whitehouse and McCauley and Lawson for their neglect of the connections between ritual and a community's more general rules for behavior. The second task Hinde stresses requires that cognitive scientists of religion explore the causal interactions of religious cognition with the larger systems in which it occurs. These progressively broader contexts include individuals' general psychological economies, their webs of interpersonal relations, their religious systems, and their cultures, at least. The third task, examining complex systems' diachronic dimensions, immediately implicates functional as well as structural analyses of mechanisms. In both his paper and its appendix, Hinde argues that religious systems may prove functional in ways that Boyer is reluctant to acknowledge. Hinde largely agrees with Boyer's various arguments that no single functional consideration seems capable of making sense of the wide array of religious systems. He holds, however, that it is unnecessary to demonstrate the pervasive influence of a single factor for functional analyses to offer causal insights. (See McCauley and Lawson 1984.) When pondering the role of evolutionary considerations in the genesis of pancultural psychological traits, Hinde warns of the need for researchers to marshal independent forms of evidence in order to avoid what has sometimes been deemed the "adaptationalist fallacy" (Gould and Lewontin 1979).

Otherwise, Hinde explores what he describes as a "heterogeneous" collection of issues. He registers concerns about the conceptual clarity, the explanatory power, and the causal fecundity of various psychological proposals that populate prominent cognitive theories. Specifically, he raises questions, like Boyer, about the revelations occasioned by imagistic ritual, but the questions he raises are of a different sort. He suggests that the psychological underpinnings of Whitehouse's proposals about SER are difficult to understand, as is the character of the putative revelations.

Thomas Lawson's chapter takes issue with only one part of the modes theory, viz Whitehouse's contention that the levels of sensory pageantry in rituals are inversely proportional to the frequency with which they are performed, which McCauley and Lawson (2002) have dubbed the "ritual frequency hypothesis." Otherwise, Lawson seems to envision the modes theory and his and McCauley's (1990) theory of religious ritual competence as compatible. The chapter's first part sketches McCauley and Lawson's alternative account of these matters in terms of a corollary of their theory, the ritual form hypothesis. The theories agree that both enhanced episodic memory for a ritual (at least if supplemented by subsequent cultural support) and increased motivation to transmit the accompanying religious representations are more likely to ensue when rituals are infrequent and emotionally arousing. The two hypotheses differ, however, about *which* rituals include the high levels of sensory pageantry likely to prove emotionally arousing.[1] The ritual frequency hypothesis maintains that these will be rituals that are infrequently performed.[2] Lawson and McCauley, by contrast, point to what they argue is an underlying cognitive variable, viz., participants' representations of rituals' forms, that determines, among a host of features that the modes theory leaves unaddressed, a ritual's level of sensory pageantry. They hold that *special agent rituals*, those rituals whose cognitive representations portray the rituals' most immediate connections with a god by way of the element in those rituals' agent slots, are the ones possessing *comparatively* higher levels of sensory pageantry and, thus, are the ones that are more likely to elicit stronger emotional responses and vivid episodic memories. Lawson also argues that participants' tacit knowledge of these rituals' forms contributes to their interest in transmitting the associated religious representations. This account picks out all of the rituals Whitehouse has in mind but avoids designating additional rituals that his formulation in terms of frequency incorrectly picks out as well (even *within* the more restricted set of religious actions that McCauley and Lawson's theory count as religious rituals).

As Boyer indicated, McCauley and Lawson's theory of religious ritual competence falls within the standard framework, in that (1) its predictions are both comparative and probabilistic, (2) it appeals to a general cognitive mechanism for the representation of action that is "experience distant" (as its emergence does not turn on explicit instruction, its facility does not turn on increasing exposure, and its operation does not turn on explicit representations), and (3) it fractionates religious phenomena by virtue of concentrating not only on religious actions but on only a subset of those that the theory designates, on a variety of independent measures, as religious rituals proper. In Lawson's summary of the ritual form hypothesis' implications for ritual innovation and its place both in the reinvigoration of religious systems and in the instigation of new religious movements, he recounts three psychological obstacles that constrain any lasting options, viz., the dangers associated with tedium and habituation (on which Whitehouse has written too), as well as those associated with sensory overload. He then briefly reviews his and McCauley's treatment of *balance* within religious ritual systems, various ways religious ritual systems can achieve some comparative stability, and the further hazards that either *insufficient or excess conceptual control* can wreak on such stability—a topic and a treatment that are echoed and amplified in others' chapters in this volume, including those of Tremlin, Pyysiäinen, Sorensen, and Slone.

McCauley and Lawson's (2002) discussion of the comparative merits of the two hypotheses focuses overwhelmingly on naturalistic and ethnographic evidence.[3] In the second part of Lawson's chapter, he underlines the crucial role of experimental evidence in adjudicating competing hypotheses, and he declares the advent of experimental research a sign of a progressive science. He extols the experimental studies in Richert, Whitehouse, and Stewart's chapter in this book (which he is not above mining for evidence to support the ritual form hypothesis!)

Todd Tremlin also advances a hypothesis that fits snugly within the framework of Boyer's standard model. He argues that a dual-process theory—of the sort to which psychologists appeal to explain a wide variety of psychological phenomena from memory to attention—will not only organize a host of findings about religious cognition but will also serve as a springboard for clarifying its connections with many features of religious systems. On this view, the stability of public religious systems is rooted in the same cognitive constraints that regulate individuals' religious thought. To the extent that Tremlin envisions a dichotomous arrangement that looks to underlying cognitive variables, his proposal resonates with Whitehouse's modes theory, but it seems safe to say that they diverge on many details.

Tremlin's dual-processing model of religious cognition contrasts "explicit" and "implicit" processing. Explicit processing involves operations that are conscious, serial, and slow and deals with representations that are explicit, abstract, and emotionally removed. Implicit processing consists of operations that are automatic, effortless, parallel, and fast and traffics in representations that are unconscious, practical, and emotionally charged. At the psychological level, Tremlin's thesis is that the latter regularly trumps the former. Tremlin argues that this is because implicit processing has advantages of both utility and relevance; the ease with which it is engaged, the wealth of inferences it affords, and the evocativeness of its emotional coloring make it the more *natural* mode of cognitive operation. Tremlin maintains that this dual-processing scheme and the psychological priority of implicit processing make sense not only of findings concerning theological correctness (Barrett 1999, 2004; Barrett and Keil 1996) but of what Boyer (2001) has called "the tragedy of the theologian." Try as they might, theologians and, especially, ecclesiastical leaders are unable to inhibit participants from introducing variations on received religious formulae. (See too Slone 2004.) Finally, Tremlin argues, these cognitive dynamics also make sense of a variety of features of religious systems at the sociocultural level. The forms of religiosity associated with Tremlin's explicit processing arise in tandem with sociopolitical constraints on what Whitehouse would describe as doctrinal systems. These are forms of processing and types of constraints that Boyer has argued turn on dynamics that are not unique to religious systems. Appealing to such dynamics, Tremlin identifies the conditions that are likely to generate religious innovations as well as those that result in the comparative stability of religious systems.

Matthew Day concurs with Boyer's assessment that on some fronts Whitehouse's modes theory stands apart from the standard model. Day, however, thinks that this is a crucial advantage. At times, Day, in his "self-appointed role as agent provocateur," openly paints standard theories with a very broad brush in order to spotlight the issues that interest him. Examples include when he suggests that most standard theories construe religious cognition on an analogy with the development and exercise of our linguistic capacities (as opposed to regarding it as "a haphazard by-product of our evolved cognitive architecture") and, bluntly, when he proposes *any* "forecast" that religious systems will prove little more than "the minimalist affairs of modestly counterintuitive, easily acquired concepts that [for example] Boyer's cognitive optimum hypothesis . . . " describes.

Day cites concerns that traditional researchers in religious studies raise about the cognitive approach. Standard theories advance compelling explanations about the psychological foundations of cultural forms and, thus, about features that recur in all of the clear cases. At least so far, what they fare less well at, however, is explaining many of the details of specific religious systems (in their ecological, historical, and cultural settings)—details that so often absorb scholars in religious studies. Day holds that, finally, cognitive theories should offer insights about these matters and that building more bridges across this gap between the psychological bases for recurrent features of religious systems and the host of questions about particular religious actors' conduct and beliefs in particular religious systems in particular sociohistorical settings deserves ongoing attention. Here is precisely where he thinks that Whitehouse's modes theory stands apart among cognitive theories by virtue of its promise to address "religion in the round."

Along with Whitehouse, Day underscores that religions are both more than and much more elaborated than what the accounts, which most cognitive theories offer, might seem to suggest. In addition to the representations and conduct that cluster around the various cognitive optima that those cognitive theories explicate, religions often include "unnatural," cognitively difficult materials as well. Day argues that the question of how these esoteric representations and behaviors surface and persist is just as important as questions about recurrent forms that standard theories address. Diverging from Tremlin, who implies that such cognitively challenging materials appear overwhelmingly in the doctrinal mode, Day maintains that such representations can arise in both modes and that Whitehouse's theory accounts for this. Day and Whitehouse concur with Durkheim that cultural particularities can interfere with, reverse, or even inundate influences born of psychological commonalities. Day praises Whitehouse for envisioning an account of cognition that resonates with the work of theorists such as Hutchins (1995), Clark (1997), and Tomasello (2000). All accentuate the critical role that our deliberate structuring of the external world plays in human cognition. Humans devise tools and practices that provide scaffolding for all sorts of intellectual and practical accomplishments that would be impossible for their bare brains, which is to say impossible for the sorts of idealized, theoretically isolated cognitive subsystems that often populate theories in cognitive science and what I have been calling "standard" theories in the cognitive science of religion. Most human cognition takes place in settings finely appointed with a vast array of cognitive prostheses—from pencils, computers, and banking systems to rituals, vestments, and holy books. Day is betting, first, that satisfactory explanations of many of the details of the thoughts and behaviors of religious people that do not reside near the cognitive optima will require appeal to just these sorts of mind tools and, second, that Whitehouse's modes theory seems readily suited to incorporate such considerations.

The second is the smallest of the book's three parts. Titled "Testing the Modes Theory," it comprises two chapters that address some of the theory's empirical consequences.

Justin Barrett's account differs from Day's in two ways. First, although he positions Whitehouse's modes theory along the same line of sight (from the perspective of standard theories), he apparently employs a different metric, since he seems to situate the modes theory much *closer* to the standard model than Day does. Second, at various points Barrett seems less sanguine about the putative advantages that accrue even to this less remote location—though, like Lawson, he emphasizes throughout his paper that these are thoroughly empirical matters.

Barrett concurs with Day about the principal point of contention that defines that line of sight, viz., the modes theory's commitment to the view that religious people's cognitively recondite beliefs and activities play a prominent role in explaining religious phenomena overall. This is the fourth of four foundational claims to which the modes theory is committed, and the only one that Barrett, in contrast to Day, regards as controversial among cognitive theorists. On Barrett's analysis, standard theories share the first three foundational commitments with Whitehouse's theory, viz., (1) that religious traditions are "materially constrained," (2) that they take the shapes they do as the result of processes of selection, and (3) that context influences the results of these processes. He does note, however, in the spirit of Day's account, that the modes theory, compared with standard theories, gives far more attention to the third. The resulting picture portrays Whitehouse's theory as inclusive, since it generally does not contest the positive accomplishments of the standard theories, but also as more ambitious, since it seeks to account for a wider range of phenomena than the standard theories, except, perhaps, for Boyer's theory and that of Atran (2002), which echoes it.

Barrett points out that most of the experimental evidence pertaining to the fourth foundational claim is not particularly congenial. He stresses, however, that the amount of available evidence is meager, that experimental evidence is not the only kind of evidence obtainable, and that this foundational claim and at least sixteen other consequences of the modes theory (eight per mode) that he reviews will submit to a wide variety of additional experimental, naturalistic, and ethnographic (including historical and archaeological) tests. Barrett inventories these sixteen testable consequences. The inventories include assessments of (a) these various consequences' centrality to the modes theory and, thus, of the relative priority the investigation of each merits, (2) the current status of the evidence bearing on each, and (3) the probabilities in each case that studies of different sorts will prove enlightening. Concerning these sixteen consequences, Barrett severally registers enthusiasms, worries, counterexamples (both real and hypothetical[4]), and, sometimes, specific proposals about possible future studies.

The second among the testable consequences of Whitehouse's claims concerning the imagistic mode that Barrett lists is the hypothesis that episodic memory for religious events (presumably rituals with high levels of sensory pageantry especially) promotes SER. Barrett notes that Whitehouse's own study (1995) of the Dadul-Maranagi splinter group offers some ethnographic evidence for this claim, but he foresees formidable obstacles—concerning ecological validity, in particular—to studying this hypothesis experimentally. Nonetheless, Barrett thinks experimental tests of this hypothesis should be a high priority since this claim is "not obviously true and fairly fundamental to the dynamics of the Imagistic Mode." Only adding to this imperative is Boyer's comments in his chapter about the lack of evidence both for this claim and the claim that any resulting reflection will have any coherent or principled effects.

Undaunted, Rebekah Richert, Harvey Whitehouse, and Emma Stewart have undertaken experimental studies of both the hypothesis that imagistic rituals will provoke SER and another closely related one, viz., that over time participants with strong emotional reactions to a ritual will engage in more SER and deeper SER than participants who react less intensely. They report on these experiments in their chapter. To carry out any experiments of this sort requires measures of both the quantity and depth of SER. Richert and her colleagues gather data about SER from interviews with participants two and a half months after they participated in the experimental ritual in the first study and both immediately afterward and then one month after they participated in the experimental ritual in the second study. Quantitative measures of SER concern the number of actions in each of the studies' rituals about which participants offered commentary about their possible meanings. Each commentary about an action was given a score of 1 unless it contained an analogy (such as noting that shoving a stone into the ground with a stick suggested the planting of a seed), in which case it received a score of 2. Total scores for each participant's protocols yielded a measure of the depth of SER.

In Richert's first experiment (the "Propagation Ritual Experiment"), participants, who went through the experimental "ritual" with a group in either a high- or a low-arousal condition, reported on their emotional responses on an emotion rating form administered immediately after the study. The subsequent interviews two and a half months later indicated that participants who reported (then and there) experiencing stronger emotional reactions to the ritual exhibited significantly greater volume and depth of reflection than those who found the experimental ritual less emotionally stimulating. In order to corroborate participants' reports about their emotional responses in the second "Altar Ritual" experiment, Richert and her colleagues not only solicited those responses on the emotion rating form, but they also monitored participants' galvanic skin responses at two points in the "ritual." Those two points involved musical stimuli that varied on a host of fronts (including volume, intensity, spatial distribution, and more). These variations along with different lighting conditions again yielded high- and low-arousal conditions for different subsets of the participants. Unlike the first experiment's design, participants in the second experiment participated in this "ritual" individually rather than with a group. Participants' self-reports of emotion correlated significantly with the findings about their galvanic skin responses. In this second study, comparisons of participants' reports about SER immediately following the experimental ritual and after one month revealed that, as predicted, participants who experienced higher levels of emotional arousal showed a significantly greater *increase* in the volume and depth of SER over the subsequent month.

Richert and her colleagues acknowledge some of the limitations of this research. For example, although it addresses the hypotheses that rituals in Whitehouse's imagistic mode will prompt SER and that the amount and depth and the increase in SER over time will correlate with higher levels of emotional arousal, the experiments do not speak to questions (which worry Lawson) about whether or not more profound SER (issuing, perhaps, in the "revelations" that Boyer and Hinde query) will move participants to transmit the associated religious representations. Like Barrett, Richert and her colleagues worry about the experiments' ecological validity but propose that this consideration probably works to their advantage, since the studies yielded positive findings even though participants in their contrived experimental rituals surely did not find these experiences of any consequence personally. One feature of these studies raises a different problem for Whitehouse's theory. In both experiments, Richert and her colleagues could distinguish between two groups of participants that experienced high and low levels of emotional arousal, but these groups did *not* correspond to the high- and low-arousal conditions in the experiments, contrary to the theory's assumptions. These findings suggest that different participants have different thresholds for what they take to be emotionally arousing, as Lawson claims and as McCauley and Lawson (2002) argue in their discussion of what they call different cultures' (and individuals') "baselines." A related question concerns the amount of variance within these post hoc divisions of the participants.

The book's final part, entitled "Wider Applications," includes three additional chapters and Whitehouse's comments and replies to all of the contributors. All four pieces concern either clarifications (or modifications), resonances, or extensions of the modes theory.

As is true with almost any extended theory developed over the course of nearly two decades, Whitehouse's modes theory has undergone substantial elaboration and gradual evolution. Ilkka Pyysiäinen is less concerned with canonical interpretation of the theory than he is with simply bringing the theory's resources to bear on familiar religious phenomena—in this case, conversions. Like Boyer, Pyysiäinen prefers to see the modes theory as delineating two ideal types, neither of which may ever be fully realized in the comings and goings of the real world of religious thought and action. Doing so retreats from stronger and more readily testable causal interpretations of Whitehouse's theory that some of his discussions seem to suggest, but it also enables Pyysiäinen to carry out a wide ranging exploration of the possible insights into conversion that the theory may have to offer. His aim is to map the varied types of conversions and their features across the entire span of possibilities that Whitehouse's two modes encompass. This, however, inevitably generates problems for what seem to be the most straightforward readings of the modes theory. So, for example, Pyysiäinen remarks that "somewhat paradoxically" conversions seem to require both intense group cohesion *and* dynamic leadership. That is, they seem simultaneously to demand conditions that Whitehouse identifies as paradigmatic features of the imagistic and the doctrinal modes, respectively. Pyysiäinen ponders the possibility of resolving the paradox, which linking this pair of features occasions, by weakening their conjunction to a disjunction.

Pyysiäinen proceeds systematically, surveying the promise of the dual moments of each of twelve modal variables that Whitehouse's theory catalogs for illuminating the varied phenomena that count as religious conversions. Pyysiäinen does not pretend that the notion of conversion is either well understood or well defined. For example, after commenting on different methodological weaknesses of many of the studies in question, Pyysiäinen, in an informal meta-analysis of the experimental literature on whether conversion experiences enhance or detract from the mental health of the converted, perceptively observes that overall the findings do not seem to vary much from chance.

His tentative verdict concerning conversion returns to what is by now a familiar theme, viz., the inability of religiosity born of explicit processing (to use Tremlin's terminology) to fully contain and control religiosity born of implicit processing. Pyysiäinen's treatment, though, articulates that theme *within* the universe of the modes theory's descriptive resources. His initial qualifications about fruitful interpretations of the theory notwithstanding, Pyysiäinen regards conversion as basically an imagistic reaction, at both the psychological and the social levels, to the heavy hand of what Whitehouse would identify as doctrinal forms and practices. This seems yet another manifestation of the persistent resurgence of online, implicit processing in religious cognition that standard theories spotlight, but by fashioning it as a reaction to doctrinal forms, Pyysiäinen's take on conversions requires the *interplay* of imagistic and doctrinal religiosity. Pyysiäinen proposes that the most stable attractor within the space of possible religious arrangements involves both doctrinal and imagistic elements. (See Tremlin's and Lawson's chapters in this volume and McCauley and Lawson, 2002.) The modes theory on his account provides tools for analyzing the interdependence of the psychological and social variables.

In the second half of his chapter, Pyysiäinen points out, in passing, resonances between Whitehouse's theory and Weber's on these counts, construing conversions as imagistic responses to the abstract, esoteric representations that doctrinal codification produces—responses that restore religious representations' relevance and motivational force. Jesper Sørensen's chapter explores related resonances between Whitehouse's work and that of Weber.

He explores how Weber's account of religious innovation and change in terms of oscillations between traditional and charismatic leadership can illuminate the relationship between Whitehouse's doctrinal and imagistic modes. Sørensen suggests that the dominance of one of the modes' practices and forms gradually creates conditions that occasion the appeal of the other mode's practices and forms. Weber's theory of charismatic religious authority holds that religious innovation relies primarily on imagistic practices but that the resulting religious expression is unstable at best and often uncontrollable. To persist, such charismatically inspired religious manifestations need to be routinized and coordinated with everyday activities (to insure subsistence at the very least) or confined and circumscribed to established times and places. Taming these imagistic forms of religious expression, in effect, requires instituting processes of religious regularization that have the characteristic earmarks of Whitehouse's doctrinal mode, from increased codification and integration of beliefs to concentrated, hierarchical authority to more restrained, less stimulating, but frequently performed rituals. Sørensen's point, of course, is that it is precisely the consolidation of such traditional, doctrinal forms and the resulting tedium for participants that such forms produce that sews the seeds of yet another cycle of resurgent charismatic leadership. Boring, repetitive rituals and difficult-to-process religious representations dampen participants' enthusiasms and stifle their quests for inferential relevance. Sørensen maintains that under such circumstances participants will seek opportunities for emotional arousal, the influence of which will seep back into these doctrinal systems anywhere it can, which can prompt, in reaction, new, heightened levels of control from the priestly guild, which will provoke even greater incentive for new kinds of stimulating religious experience, and so on.

Sørensen's chapter looks at one part of this cyclical process in greater detail. His particular interests concern three related phenomena associated with the broadly imagistic side of this oscillation, viz., (1) charisma, its marks, their psychological underpinnings, and its role in new religious developments, (2) the pivotal role that ritual plays in certifying charisma, and (3) the interpretive problems that rituals present. Concerning the first, Sørensen notes that human beings throughout the world seem to recognize charismatic qualities in some people, that they tend to regard charismatic individuals as possessing some hidden essence, and that they are particularly prone to deploy such essentialist conceptions about persons in religious authority (even contrary, sometimes, to doctrinal systems' explicit proscriptions against such attributions). Ritual is one of the principal means through which individuals' charismatic authority is authenticated. Sørensen investigates why. Rituals fail to square with humans' standard conceptions of agents and their actions. Typically, humans view agents as possessing internal *force*, which has physical, psychological, and social manifestations in their actions (Talmy 2000). Unlike everyday actions, rituals are disconnected both from ordinary instrumental assumptions and from the intentions of the individuals who perform them (Humphrey and Laidlaw 1994). How do rituals incorporate such agentive force, if, as so often is the case, their overt agents do not supply it? In accord with the findings reported in Richert, Whitehouse, and Stewart's chapter, the arousing rituals charismatic leadership inspires reliably incite speculations about their aims, their forms, and the authors of each, as well as about their sources of force, and charismatic leaders (and their pronouncements and actions) reliably surface as prominent candidates. Such attributions introduce the question of what participants make of these rituals. Sørensen sees two major options here, viz., the "magical" and the "symbolic." Magical interpretations focus on the ritual act itself, its immediate context, their perceptually available properties, and the ritual's putative purpose. Magical interpretations permit greater latitude than do symbolic interpretations, which, by contrast, attend to rituals' positions within overarching doctrinal systems. Thus, symbolic interpretations invariably trade in the abstruse representations of doctrinal systems that bring stability but bring it at the price of what Sørensen calls a "triviality effect," which seems the conceptual analog of Whitehouse's tedium effect. Lawson explains this emerging sense of the triviality of these religious representations that Sorensen detects in terms of religious hierarchies exerting excessive conceptual control.

On Boyer's account of the position of the modes theory relative to standard theories, Jason Slone's chapter may pose as direct a challenge as any of the book's chapters to the spirit of Whitehouse's theory (if not its letter). Yet, on Day's and Whitehouse's view of things, it may, rather, constitute a spring-board for developing just the sort of "layered" approach to religious cognition that Whitehouse endorses in the final chapter. On the basis of the considerations that inform the standard model, cognitivists, according to Slone, have been wary of many scholars' penchant for overestimating the differences among religions by fastening onto the explicit, recondite, theological formulations that proliferate in doctrinal systems. Appearances, however, can be deceiving.[5] And Slone argues that cognitivists concede too much. Contrary to the prevailing views within both religious studies and cultural anthropology about the rich diversity and intricacy of religious forms and systems, Slone insists that _even at the level of the explicit processing of esoteric theologies_ religious systems in the doctrinal mode exhibit numerous recurrent features. He scrutinizes the persistent appearance of free-will problems.

Slone argues that it does not take much explicit rumination on religious themes before inevitably spawning problems associated with the "ambiguity of agency." This, in short, is the problem of who is in control. Do powerful gods influence and control events (and human events in particular), or are human beings free agents (too)? Slone surveys a swarm of problems this ambiguity of agency begets across the four most widespread religious systems currently. Even this partial tally displays this conundrum's indifference to whether a religious system is monotheistic or polytheistic and the chronic reappearance (in all of these religions) of three sorts of proposals for managing agency's ambiguity.

Slone's analysis may pose a serious challenge to Whitehouse's view because, finally, Slone proposes to explain the ambiguity of agency, the myriad problems it introduces (in elaborated religious systems), and the highly restricted set of theological proposals for handling those problems in terms of "universal generic cognitive architecture." Appealing to the work of developmental psychologists (e.g., Rochat 2001), Slone highlights the rapidity with which infants gain expertise about causal relations with respect to three salient domains, viz., the actions of other agents, the interactions of objects, and their own actions. In fact, these cognitive capacities are sufficient to generate plenty of ambiguity about agency by themselves (Bloom 2004). That ambiguity typically goes unnoticed, though, since the systems in question operate unconsciously for the most part and in comparative isolation from one another. On the hoof, humans are prone to disregard the utterly partial and sometimes inconsistent accounts of causal relations that these systems regularly offer up.[6]

Religious representations populate the world with additional agents, and given the sorts of agents they are, easily drawn inferences counsel taking them and their possible influences on us and our affairs quite seriously. Slone contends that the growth and spread of doctrinal systems requires gods whose influence and power must be increasingly pervasive. It is only when humans must slug their ways logically and conceptually through the ambitious but cognitively burdensome projects with which philosophers and theologians have truck that the inconsistencies get spotlighted; pondered; and, by the vast majority of us the vast majority of the time, routinely neglected, forgotten, or swamped in the face of the ongoing pronouncements of our implicit cognitive capacities as we make our ways in the world. Like Tremlin, Slone holds that online, implicit processing reliably prevails in its collisions with the radically counterintuitive representations of intricate theologies. So, for example, no matter what the doctrines say, humans cannot shake the intuition that they are usually in control of their actions. This is why, among other things, Calvinists still evangelize.

Rather than summarizing Whitehouse's responses to these discussions in the book's final chapter, I will let him speak for himself. He has consistently been the first to acknowledge the many ways in which his research has benefited from the demands of theoretical competition and from such probing commentary and criticism. What Whitehouse's theory, his response, and the eleven other chapters in this book most obviously demonstrate is the vitality and insight of the debates that the cognitive approach to the study of religion has engendered.

NOTES

1. McCauley and Lawson's "sensory pageantry" has emerged as the preferred term in the literature for referring to the various ways in which rituals can produce emotional arousal in participants. Although this usually involves incorporating means for stimulating (either positively or negatively) the various senses, it is also presumed to include such measures as sexual arousal, mind-altering drugs, and more.

2. McCauley and Lawson (2002) point out that it is incumbent upon advocates of the ritual frequency hypothesis to supply a criterion for gauging rituals' performance frequencies. They then argue at length that the only viable criterion depends *fundamentally* upon considerations of ritual form.

3. See Justin Barrett's chapter for an account of the principal forms of evidence available to researchers in the cognitive science of religion.

4. Since one includes his good humored, speculative counter-example about the group cohesion that might result from a marathon canasta tournament on a resort island, I feel compelled to mention my reservations about his suggestion that " . . . for people who have often visited restaurants, typically little effort is made to engage the

server as an individual." These reservations are based on my knowledge of a real counter-example, viz., the meetings of my father's Tuesday morning retirees' breakfast gang over the past eight years (in Pittsburgh) and their *considerable* knowledge about the lives of the staff members who serve them.

5. In the first paragraph of the final chapter, Whitehouse emphasizes (correctly) that constants cannot explain variables, but, of course, that is only one way of telling the story about the role of theories in science. Another is to headline the appearance-reality distinction. Successful theories often reveal that what *appears* to be variable, for example, apples falling from trees, cannon balls, baseballs, and soccer balls' trajectories, and the orbits of satellites, moons, planets, and comets, are, from the standpoint of a penetrating theory, often instances of *the same type of phenomenon*, conforming to the same underlying principles.

6. Their incompleteness and inconsistency have kept the philosophy of mind in business for more than two millennia.

REFERENCES

Abbink, J. 1995. Ritual and Environment: The *Mosit* Ceremony of the Ethiopian Me'en People. *Journal of Religion in Africa* 25: 163–90.

Atran, S. 2002. *In Gods We Trust*. Oxford: Oxford University Press.

Barrett, J. L. 1996. Anthropomorphism, Intentional Agents, and Conceptualizing God. Ph.D. Dissertation, Cornell University.

———. 1999. Theological Correctness: Cognitive Constraint and the Study of Religion. *Method & Theory in the Study of Religion* 11: 325–39.

———. 2004. *Why Would Anyone Believe in God?* Walnut Creek, CA: AltaMira Press.

Barrett, J. L., and F. C. Keil. 1996. Conceptualizing a Nonnatural Entity: Anthropomorphism in God Concepts. *Cognitive Psychology* 31: 219–47.

Barrett, J. L., R. A. Richert, and A. Driesenga. 2001. God's Beliefs versus Mom's: The Development of Natural and Non-Natural Agent Concepts. *Child Development* 72: 50–65.

Barth, F. 2002. Review of *Arguments and Icons*. *Journal of Ritual Studies* 16: 14–17.

Bering, J. M., and D. F. Bjorklund. In press. The Natural Emergence of Reasoning about the "Afterlife" as a Developmental Regularity. *Developmental Psychology*.

Bloch, M. 2004. Ritual and Deference. In *Ritual and Memory: Toward a Comparative Anthropology of Religion*, ed. Harvey Whitehouse and James Laidlaw. Walnut Creek, CA: AltaMira Press.

Bloom, P. 2004. *Descartes' Baby*. New York: Basic Books.

Boyer, P. 1992. Explaining Religious Ideas: Outline of a Cognitive Approach. *Numen* 39: 27–57.

———. 1994. *The Naturalness of Religious Ideas*. Berkeley: University of California Press.

———. 2001. *Religion Explained*. New York: Basic Books.

Clark, A. 1997. *Being There*. Cambridge: MIT Press.

Craver, C. F. 2001. Role Functions, Mechanisms, and Hierarchy. *Philosophy of Science* 68: 53–74.

Gould, S. J., and R. C. Lewontin. 1979. The Spandrels of San Marco and the Panglossian Program: A Critique of the Adaptationalist Programme. *Proceedings of the Royal Society of London* 205: 281–88.

Guthrie, S. 1980. A Cognitive Theory of Religion. *Current Anthropology* 21: 181–203.

Hinde, R. 1999. *Why Gods Persist.* New York: Routledge.

Humphrey, C., and J. Laidlaw. 1994. *The Archetypal Actions of Ritual: A Theory of Ritual Illustrated by the Jain Rite of Worship.* Oxford: Oxford University Press.

Hutchins, E. 1995. *Cognition in the Wild.* Cambridge: MIT Press.

Lawson, E. T., and R. N. McCauley. 1990. *Rethinking Religion: Connecting Cognition and Culture.* Cambridge: Cambridge University Press.

Malley, B. 2004. *How the Bible Works.* Walnut Creek, CA: AltaMira Press.

Malley, B., and J. Barrett. 2003. Can Ritual Form Be Predicted From Religious Belief? A Test of the Lawson-McCauley Hypotheses. *Journal of Ritual Studies* 17: 1–14.

McCauley, R. N., and E. T. Lawson. 1984. Functionalism Reconsidered. *History of Religions* 23: 372–81.

———. 2002. *Bringing Ritual to Mind: Psychological Foundations of Cultural Forms.* Cambridge: Cambridge University Press.

McCauley, Robert N., and Harvey Whitehouse, eds. 2004. The Psychological and Cognitive Foundations of Religiosity. Special issue, *Journal of Cognition and Culture* 4, no. 3.

Martin, Luther H., and Harvey Whitehouse, eds. 2004. The Cognitive Science of Religion. Special issue, *Method and Theory in the Study of Religion* 16, no. 3.

Martin, Luther H., and Harvey Whitehouse, eds. 2006. History, Memory, and Cognition. Special issue, *Historical Reflections/Reflexions Historiques* 32, no. 1.

Pyysiäinen, I. 1999. Holy Book—A Treasury of the Incomprehensible: The Invention of Writing and Religious Cognition. *Numen* 46: 269–90.

———. 2001. *How Religion Works: Towards a New Cognitive Science of Religion.* Leiden: Brill.

———. 2004. *Magic, Miracles, and Religion: A Scientist's Perspective.* Walnut Creek, CA: AltaMira Press.

Rochat, P. 2001. *The Infant's World.* Cambridge: Harvard University Press.

Slone, J. 2004. *Theological Incorrectness: Why Religious People Believe What They Shouldn't.* New York: Oxford University Press.

Talmy, L. 2000. Force Dynamics in Language and Thought. In *Toward a Cognitive Semantics,* ed. L. Talmy. Cambridge: MIT Press.

Tomasello, M. 2000. *The Cultural Origins of Human Cognition.* Cambridge: Harvard University Press.

Turner, M. 1996. *The Literary Mind: The Origins of Thought and Language.* Oxford: Oxford University Press.

Vial, T. 2004. *Liturgy Wars: Ritual Theory and Protestant Reform in Nineteenth-Century Zurich.* London: Routledge.

Whitehouse, H. 1992. Memorable Religions: Transmission, Codification, and Change in Divergent Melanesian Contexts. *Man,* n.s., 27: 777–97.

———. 1995. *Inside the Cult: Religious Innovation and Transmission in Papua New Guinea.* Oxford: Clarendon Press.

———. 2000. *Arguments and Icons: Divergent Modes of Religiosity.* Oxford: Clarendon Press.

————. 2004. *Modes of Religiosity: A Cognitive Theory of Religious Transmission*. Walnut Creek, CA: AltaMira Press.

Whitehouse, H., and J. Laidlaw, eds. 2004. *Ritual and Memory: Toward a Comparative Anthropology of Religion*. Walnut Creek, CA: AltaMira Press.

Whitehouse, H., and L. Martin, eds. 2004. *Theorizing Religions Past: Archaeology, History, and Cognition*. Walnut Creek, CA: AltaMira Press.

I

THE THEORETICAL CONTEXT

1

A Reductionistic Model of Distinct Modes of Religious Transmission

Pascal Boyer

Interaction with imagined nonphysical agents (gods, spirits, ghosts, etc.) is a puzzling cultural universal, as it is of no straightforward adaptive value, indeed is often costly to individuals or groups. One promising research strategy is to evaluate to what extent religious concepts and norms may be a by-product of evolved brain function (Boyer 2003). Indeed, in the past fifteen years, a variety of anthropologists, psychologists, and religious scholars have demonstrated that the apparently complex and variable domain of religious concepts and behaviors could be better understood in terms of the cognitive processes involved (see surveys in Barrett [2000], Boyer [2003], and Pyysiäinen [2001]).

This has led to a common or standard model of religious concepts and norms (presented in more detail below) that is extremely general in its scope. It describes mental states and processes found in most people in most religious contexts most of the time, without providing descriptive or explanatory models for those features that distinguish one religious tradition from another.

Starting from this general model, there are two ways to progress in the explanation of religion. One is to provide more and more sophisticated, empirically tested descriptions of the underlying processes that make religion in general possible and probable in human minds. Another one is to describe how these cognitive processes interact with specific historical circumstances, producing specific religious systems. In a series of recent books and articles, Harvey Whitehouse has offered a major contribution to this latter enterprise. Starting from his description of "modes of religiosity," I will try to outline the potential and pitfalls of this move toward greater specificity.

In particular, I want to delineate two stages in this process of making the cognitive model more historically or culturally specific. At first, we should do what Whitehouse did, that is, take into account the fact that religious systems seem to come in different *types*, in different packages of correlated features that Whitehouse called "modes of religiosity." Religious systems with priests and organized theologies also seem to comprise frequent, repetitive, and less-than-altogether-thrilling rituals; systems with inspired individuals seem to focus on rare, exciting, and conceptually ambiguous rites (Whitehouse 2000; McCauley and Lawson 2002). A thorough description of the correlated features in these two modes, such as that offered by Whitehouse, should then lead, in my view, to a second stage where we can jettison some unnecessary assumptions of the "modes" model and propose a *stepwise model* of particular features of religious systems, for which we can for now provide only a very rough, programmatic outline based on Whitehouse's own model.

A STANDARD MODEL OF RELIGIOUS THOUGHT AND BEHAVIOR

Cognitive accounts of religion share two important features that may explain their attractiveness to many social scientists (and perhaps their repulsiveness for others). First, cognitive models *fractionate* the domain of religion. That is, they demonstrate that there is no unified "cognitive domain" of religion organized by a single set of principles. Rather, different domains of religious thinking and behavior (e.g., religious rituals, metaphysics, morality, affiliation, etc.) are informed by different cognitive principles. Second, cognitive explanations also *deflate* religion. What we observe in aspect of religion can be explained in terms of human propensities that would be there, religion or not. Religious ritual is constrained by ordinary representations of agency (McCauley and Lawson 2002). Religious ontology (gods, spirits, magical objects, etc.) is based on minor "tweaking" of ordinary ontological intuitions (Boyer 1994a). The organization of larger-scale religious narratives and conceptual systems is constrained by human memory capacities (Barrett and Keil 1996). Religious morality is a slight variation on early-acquired moral intuitions that do not require religion (Boyer 2001).

In the past fifteen years, various accounts of specific features of religion (Lawson and McCauley 1990; Boyer 1994b; Barrett 1996; Pyysiäinen 2001; Atran 2002; Boyer 2001) have converged to constitute what could be called a common or "standard" model of religious thought and behavior, which can be summarized as follows:

1. The background of the argument is a "selectionist" view of human cultural evolution, as presented in theories of meme transmission and cultural epidemics (Sperber 1996; Boyd and Richerson 1985). Religious

concepts and norms that we find widespread in human cultures are those that resist the eroding, distorting influence of individual transmission better than others. Equally important, the existence of roughly similar versions of some thought in different brains is not the outcome of a replication of cultural "memes." It is a consequence of similar inferences, on the basis of cultural or natural input, produced in brains with massively similar conceptual architectures, composed of functionally distinct capacities specialized in different types of objects and problems (Sperber 1996). The fact that mental systems comprise different conceptual tools, handling different kinds of problems, is a result of evolution by natural selection (Cosmides and Tooby 1994). Religious concepts are widespread the world over, not because they are an adaptation of human minds, but because they are an optimally salient and inferentially rich *by-product* of normal brain function (Boyer 2003).

2. There is a limited catalog of supernatural concepts, a subset of which is found in religious systems. Supernatural concepts (found in religion but also in fantasy, dreams, "superstitions," etc.) are informed by very general assumptions from domain concepts such as person, living thing, man-made object. A spirit is a special kind of person, a magic wand a special kind of artifact, a talking tree a special kind of plant. Such notions are salient and inferentially productive because they combine (1) specific features that violate some default expectations for the domain with (2) expectations held by default as true of the entire domain (Boyer 1994a; Barrett 1996). These combinations of explicit violation and tacit inferences are culturally widespread and may constitute a *memory optimum* (Boyer and Ramble 2001; Barrett and Nyhof 2001).

3. A subset of this supernatural repertoire consists in religious concepts proper, which are taken by many people as, firstly, quite plausibly real and, secondly, of great social and personal importance. These concepts generally describe *intentional agents* so that all standard agency assumptions are projected onto them (Lawson and McCauley 1990). Concepts of gods and ancestors require minor but consequential "tweaking" of the standard theory of mind (Barrett and Keil 1996).

4. Religious morality is parasitic upon evolved moral intuitions that are there, religion or not. Nonphysical agents are associated with moral intuitions in that the agents are construed as "interested parties" in decision making. The ancestors know, for instance, what you are up to, know you feel bad about it, and know that it is bad; the spirits know that you are generous, know how proud you feel, and know that that is praiseworthy (Boyer 2000).

5. Religious rituals are constrained by agency assumptions, such that the presence of superhuman agents as presumed actors or patients in rituals predicts a number of intuitions about the positions of other elements

such as instruments and human participants (Lawson and McCauley 1990; Barrett and Lawson 2001).

6. Religious concepts are connected to concepts and theories about death that derive from nonreligious sources. A great deal of religious elaboration centers on notions of souls and spirits of dead people that naturally result from animacy systems and theory-of-mind systems found in all normal human minds (Boyer 2003). Religious concepts of this kind also receive an additional boost from perception of dangers (and risk of mortality) associated with predation and risk in environments of human evolution (Atran 2002).

7. Religious concepts are optimally suited for the building of coalitional affiliation, as they provide easily recognizable group-membership markers (Bacharach and Gambetta 2001) and shared commitment to costly activities (Atran 2002). In both cases, the religious concepts are parasitic upon human coalitional capacities that are also found outside religion.

What is this "standard model" a model of? It aims to describe the recurrent features of *mental representations* held in roughly similar forms by most people in particular groups. The different authors who built this general model used a simple strategy. They started with those structures that we already knew could be found in human conceptual frames the world over. They then hypothesized that religious concepts could be produced by minor "tweaking" of such widespread concepts. This produced hypothetical descriptions of religious ontology, religious moral feelings, ritual form, or purity emotions that could be tested against the evidence in terms of (a) predicting the actual representations found in human societies and (b) being based on experimentally demonstrated mechanisms.

As I emphasized above, this model is largely about thoughts and processes that are not accessible to conscious inspection. For that reason, it is also not directly about those explicit contents that most ethnographers work on, in the absence of experimental techniques. The model aims to describe actual cognitive processes underlying their religious concepts, which is not necessarily captured by their explicit understandings of those concepts. In the domain of religion, as in syntax, people's effortless production is made possible by implicit principles they rarely know.

More importantly, the model describes untutored religious concepts and emotions, which may be (in fact generally are) rather distant from official understandings of religion. In many cultures in the world—but specially so in large societies with states and literacy—there are official accounts of what religion is, what the beliefs are, and what the practices ought to be. Most anthropologists have reported that people's actual practices and concepts (inasmuch as field techniques allow such inferences) generally deviate from officially sanctioned ones. This is sometimes described as "theological incorrectness" in the literature (Barrett and Keil 1996; Slone 2004).

To sum up, then, the "standard model" described here amounts to a description of (a) most people's actual representations in oral tradition societies and (b) most people's untutored, spontaneous religious thoughts in literate societies and groups with organized religious communities.

GENERAL PROBABILISTIC MODELS AND THE PULL OF HISTORY

All the propositions of the standard model are *general, probabilistic,* and *experience distant.*

They are "general" in the sense that they could apply to any cultural milieu. Indeed, most explanatory accounts of religious concepts in cognitive terms make very little mention of the particular norms or practices that make one religious community different from the others. The way superhuman agency is derived from ordinary assumptions about agency, for instance, is a cognitive process that may be found in Italian Catholics and Korean shamans.

Cognitive accounts are "probabilistic." The fact that a given religious concept is easily acquired and recalled, salient and inferentially rich, explains why, all else being equal, there is some likelihood that such a concept will be imagined and, once imagined, successfully transmitted in a particular cultural milieu.

Cognitive accounts are "experience distant"—using a common anthropological term for explanatory accounts whose terms do not easily map on to people's own experience. We describe religious concepts (gods, spirits, etc.) as only partly accessible to conscious inspection (Boyer 1992). The processes that make them salient or memorable, and lead the mind to particular expectations, are also outside awareness (Barrett and Keil 1996). The logic that governs our intuitions about ritual actions is not a conscious phenomenon, no more than the principles of syntax (Lawson and McCauley 1990).

Some social scientists may consider that we should also strive to make the model more historically specific. What this would mean, in practice, is this. We would take some predictions of the general cognitive models and see to what extent the presence of particular cultural or historical factors changes likelihoods, makes certain outcomes more probable than others. For instance, we could make a contrast between two behaviors that make supernatural agency more palpable, through a medium's trance or through an initiation rite. We could then specify political conditions under which each of these is more likely, and measure the success of such predictions against observed religious institutions. More generally, what we would do is gradually add factors to the general likelihood function of religious concepts and norms, and measure to what extent each addition reduces the overall behavioral variance to explain.

This, too, is a sound strategy in all empirical sciences, particularly in their more applied domains. In the case of religion, this enterprise is all the more necessary as there is a clear social value in understanding, not just why there is religion in the first place, but also why it often takes forms that make social interaction difficult, dangerous, or impossible. One could not be content with theories of religion that explain the attraction of superhuman agency but have nothing to say about why people spend time and effort in rituals, why many people in the world are so concerned about other people's beliefs, and why some are prepared to oppress or massacre others on apparently religious grounds.

MODES OF RELIGIOSITY:
BUNDLES OF FEATURES OR CAUSAL NEXUS?

How does one progress toward such empirically more specific models? The general recipe adopted in other empirical sciences is to start with the general explanatory models and add one additional variable at a time, measuring the reduction of variance achieved with each additional factor, stepping back and sideways to consider other variables if there is no improvement in the theory's explanatory power. This *stepwise* method may not always be available or practical in the social sciences, which is why we often proceed in a more roughshod way, taking a few empirical cases as a starting point, evaluating what is *not* explained by the general models available, and putting forward some more detailed account. This, to some extent, is what Whitehouse did in his accounts of Melanesian cults (Whitehouse 1995), more recently extended to religious transmission in general (Whitehouse 2000).

For Whitehouse, the crucial variable in the dynamics of religious systems lies in *transmission*. Like other anthropologists interested in mapping and explaining the dynamics of selective transmission, Whitehouse stresses the causal role of individual *cognitive* processes. No concept or norm could get transmitted unless it was acquired, stored, and transmitted by individual minds in a way that preserves its essential features. A crucial task, therefore, is to study the ways in which acquisition and memory favor specific kinds of concepts and conceptual organization.

The psychology of memory is crucial to the argument, for there are really only two principal ways in which relatively complex sets of concepts and norms, such as those found in religious systems, could be successfully transmitted from one individual to another. One is a form of intellectual training, accumulating a great number of relevant and explicitly connected propositions. The other one is through rare but exceptionally salient experience, so striking that its details remain engraved in memory. Each cognitive route is more appropriate to a specific kind of mental content and has specific effects on the nature of religious affiliation. The "doctrinal" mode requires constant communication of relatively intelligible and explicitly articulated material, therefore high-frequency exposure. "Imagistic" effects require highly salient occasions, therefore low-frequency rituals. Doctrinal practices constantly run the risk of generating as much boredom as conceptual clarity, while imagistic ones can become so incoherent that most conceptual content is lost.

Whitehouse argues that a whole range of social, political, and conceptual aspects of religious systems are associated with these two distinct "modes." The doctrinal and imagistic modes result in different types of ritual meaning (learned vs. generated), social cohesion (diffuse vs. intense), leadership (dynamic vs. passive), spread (rapid vs. slow), potential scope of the religious community (universal vs. ethnic), degree of uniformity (high vs. low), and organization (centralized vs. decentralized).

So far, the model emphasizes what could be called two *bundles of features*. In the same way as feathered animals tend to have a beak and furry ones a mouth, features of religious systems go together to constitute distinct "packages." You do not observe all possible combinations of all features— far from it. The model does not stop there and offers a penetrating analysis of the way these two ways of doing religion are ultimately based on different ways of activating human memory systems.

However, in several places, Whitehouse has argued that the model should be taken further, to provide not just two contrasted ideal types but also a *causal* nexus that explains their constitution (Whitehouse 1995; Whitehouse 2000; Whitehouse 2004). The argument proceeds in several distinct steps, which I will enumerate for further reference:

[1] Whitehouse points out that the "standard model" as described above may seem to miss some motivational aspects of religion. That is, even though some concepts and norms are described by the model as likely to be easily acquired and communicated, this may not be sufficient to explain people's obvious commitment to maintaining and keeping intact their religious traditions.

[2] The source of motivation for maintaining and preserving what are often costly rituals certainly lies in the cognitive and emotional effects of these rituals.

[3] Both "doctrinal" and "imagistic" modes of religion provide what Whitehouse calls *revelations*, that is, new conceptual frames that inform non-religious experience. Although the way revelations are produced is very different in the two modes, it is this effect of religious ritual and performance that explains people's commitment.

[4] The "choice" of one mode or another (Whitehouse, like most anthropologists, does not think that it is a matter of deliberation—one's rituals happen to be in one mode or the other) is the "prime mover" that explains all the other features listed above. For instance, once a particular group has its religious revelations delivered in the doctrinal mode, this lays the foundation for learned ritual meaning, diffuse social cohesion, dynamic leadership, rapid spread, universal orientation, high degree of uniformity, and centralized organization.

This last point is the core of the causal interpretation of religious "modes." In the following pages, I would like to suggest that this causal interpretation is most likely misleading—indeed, that it might hinder a proper interpretation of the differences in religious transmission so clearly analyzed by Whitehouse himself.

To anticipate, I will try to show that the "bundles-of-features" interpretation is far more likely. The reasons why the features of religious transmission are bundled together lie outside religious concepts proper, and certainly outside the domain of possible "revelations." I will focus on two points to illustrate this. First, imagistic rituals do not provide revelations in any principled sense, and the explanations for their peculiar aspects probably have little to do with their conceptual content. Second, most features of doctrinal systems are easily explained in terms of well-known social and cognitive dynamics that are effective in many domains besides religion. So we should be able to take advantage of all the useful features of Whitehouse's model without committing ourselves to unnecessary causal speculation.

IMAGISTIC RITUALS: PUZZLING REVELATIONS

The "imagistic" mode includes a variety of rituals with relatively high "sensory pageantry," to use McCauley and Lawson's ingenious term (McCauley and Lawson 2002). These include trance and possession rituals (to the extent that they are ritualized), as well as many initiation and sacrificial rites. One general point about these rituals, noticed for as long as anthropologists bothered to consider them, is that—to be rather blunt—they do not seem to make much sense at all. At least, it seems difficult to extract a coherent "lesson" from them, regardless of one's familiarity with the cultural environment in which they take place. Indeed, the participants themselves are often reduced to arguing that the rituals simply *have* to be performed the way they are; that they certainly *do* have some effects, although these are impossible to describe; and that it would be extremely *dangerous* to change them, although why that is so is not always clearly explicated. This insistence on perfect performance without clear conceptual rationale can be seen as a hallmark of *traditional* religion (Boyer 1990).

So this domain is particularly challenging for a theory that sees *revelations* as the main cognitive effect and motivational foundation of religious rituals. "Revelation" is a rather ambiguous term, being derived as it is from organized world religions. It seems particularly difficult to transpose the concept to imagistic rituals. Herdt described these rituals as creating "focal imagery for subsequent reflection" (cited by Whitehouse 2000, 30). In his account of Baktaman initiation, Barth talked of "analogical codes" that associated different elements of the rituals and objects of everyday life (Barth 1975). Whitehouse himself considers that the rituals provide "lasting revelations" and that their ultimate meaning is constructed through "speculative exegesis."

But is that really the case? What is the actual evidence that Baktaman initiation for instance has coherent cognitive effects? Barth argued that the main cognitive effect of the rituals was to promote an "epistemology of secrecy," that is, the intuition that knowing more is always dangerous and painful (Barth 1975). But that notion is triggered by the rite as a whole, by the succession of painful ordeals followed by the disappointing revelation that . . . the revelation will only come after the *next* ordeal. Such a thin conceptual lesson cannot provide the motivation for ritual ordeals. In a more psychological vein, Whitehouse writes that after initiation "everyday objects [. . .] come to be seen in a radically new light," but that is certainly insufficient as a description of cognitive effects. What "light" is that? How are everyday objects conceived of as an effect of the ritual? True, some objects or substances have become potential reminders of a novel and salient context (fur and fat, for instance, may now remind you of the instruments the elders used to torture you), but I do not see any evidence that this has modified people's conceptual knowledge of everyday objects in any *principled* way. Perhaps imagistic rituals trigger conceptual associations that are so unpredictable and idiosyncratic that they have little in common between any two participants, except the sense that the ritual must be performed again in a similar way. I see little evidence in the ethnographic literature that would rule out this minimalist interpretation.

Accepting this, however, leaves us with all sorts of unsolved questions: Why are rituals fascinating and compelling, when their conceptual contents seem opaque or simply vacuous? Why do people feel they *should* perform these rituals again? Why are some of them, particularly male initiations, punctuated by gruesome ordeals? Why would anyone want to join such clubs at such a price? Answering these would certainly require more than this chapter, but I would like to offer some suggestions here and argue that phrasing the questions in terms of "revelation" is probably an impediment to a satisfactory model.

COMPULSIVE RITUALS

The "modes" theory suggests that imagistic rituals transmit a revelation, that this is fundamental to people's identity, so that they transmit it. But most steps in this causal chain are hypothetical. More parsimoniously, one might say that imagistic rituals are such that people just feel compelled to reiterate them as they occurred (or rather, as they think they occurred) the last time around. After all, in many other domains, transmission of a group's culture is independent of people's motivation (Boyer 1992). Instead of assuming that people repeat rituals because they want to reestablish revelation (which requires a rich interpretation of people's usually vague utterances on the topic), we could start from what people actually say: that there is a perceived *danger* in not performing the ritual or performing it in a different way, that they often cannot really explain what that danger is or why nonperformance would make it real.

This is not the only context where we find such intuitions of possible danger that strongly motivate people's behavior and have the same inexplicable contents. As I mentioned above (see the "standard model" description), the themes of religious rituals are strikingly similar to those of neuropsychological conditions like obsessive compulsive disorder (OCD) (Dulaney and Fiske 1994). A preoccupation with limits, boundaries, special colors or special numbers, but above all a concern with *purity, cleanliness,* and possible *pollution* are central themes in both domains. Also, in both domains people are strongly motivated to reiterate the behaviors in question, feeling that there is some undefined but imminent danger in not performing them. Finally, in both domains this compulsion is *not* accompanied by any clear conceptual framework that would justify it. People just *feel* they have to perform the sequence of actions in the way they performed it before.

Although the similarity had been noted by psychologists and anthropologists for a long time, they usually framed it as the question, whether religious ritual was a collective obsession, or obsessions were private religious rituals, or perhaps both (Freud 1922, 1928). Since none of these statements is anything but hopelessly vague and metaphorical, they do not get us any closer to a satisfactory explanation. It may be more promising to connect these two domains to a third situation where we know that similar intuitions are produced, those of contagion and contamination.

Discovery of this specialized inference system stemmed from psychologists' studies of the puzzling features of *disgust* in humans (Rozin et al. 1993). Disgust is one of the "basic emotions" (Ekman 1999) and certainly a very ancient reaction to possible ingestion of dangerous substances. It is no surprise that the most common sources of violent disgust are decaying corpses or putrefying wounds, excrement, other people's blood or saliva, and the like. However, experimental studies of disgust also show that humans blithely overextend the domain of disgusting stimuli. Subjects who understandably resist drinking from a glass of water that contains a live cockroach show the same reluctance if the cockroach is dead and sterilized, and even if it is a plastic model (Rozin et al. 1993). Why should that be the case? Disgust is driven by an inference engine that specifies causal links between a given object and a possible danger according to principles of "magical thinking" (Nemeroff 1995). Specifically, three major principles are involved here: (1) that sources of danger are generally invisible (what is bad about rotten meat, or maggots for that matter, is not visible), (2) that all modes of contact are equally dangerous (sharing food with a sick person is dangerous, but so is touching them, kissing them, wearing their clothes, etc.); (3) there is no "dose effect" (you'll get sick after eating rotten corpses, no matter how little you ate; you'll catch the person's disease, no matter how few kisses you exchanged). These principles make sense if we think of disgust as an evolved computational engine, the function of which is to provide strong motivation to avoid common sources of toxins and pathogens (Cosmides and Tooby 1999). The pathogen-avoidance interpretation makes good sense, not just of the usual targets of disgust (excrement and festering bodies are indeed extremely dangerous sources of pathogens), but also of the principles themselves. For most pathogens are invisible, they invade organisms in a variety of different ways, and they multiply inside organisms (so that the initial dose is irrelevant).

Neuropsychological and neuroscientific evidence suggests that the impairment responsible for OCD pathology is distributed around networks that are usually activated by perception of danger and plans to avoid danger (Adler et al. 2000; Rauch et al. 2001; Sacchetti et al. 1999). The intuition of danger that most OCD patients report at the idea of not performing their rituals might just be an exaggerated (or rather noninhibited) version of danger intuitions and precaution plans that are entertained by most normal minds in situations of possible, invisible contamination risk. The pathology seems to combine an excessively low threshold for the production of such intuitions, an abnormally high motivation for danger avoidance, and an inability to eliminate the intuition of danger after taking precautionary measures (hence the repetition). The respective role of these three factors is still unclear, although the neuropsychology of the condition is making great progress.

It is the normal, usually fairly mild reaction to possible invisible danger that religious rituals seem to activate. Consider all the ritual precautions and seemingly arbitrary selections of symbols listed by Fiske and colleagues (Dulaney and Fiske 1994; Fiske and Haslam 1997). The description of unseen dangers, of undefined "pollution" and "cleanliness," all belong to what psychologists would call the "input format" of the contagion-avoidance system. With hindsight, this set of ritual themes now appears as a fiendishly clever way to trigger the kind of anxiety about precaution and invisible dangers that normal brains are equipped with and that impaired brains run amok with. But there is of course no cleverness here, and no deliberate selection of stimuli. It is only the hidden hand of cultural selection that makes such rituals somewhat more compulsive and motivating than rituals that would use fewer of these conceptual elements.

The consideration of contagion systems offers, in my view, a parsimonious explanation of some important aspects of imagistic rituals. It explains the compulsion of performance, the anxiety at incorrect or missed performance, as well as the conceptual opacity of the ritual elements. There are no "lessons" to be found in most religious rituals. Whatever meaning people find in ritual actions consists in interpretations of these actions rather than content transmitted by these actions. The explanation is parsimonious also because the psychological mechanisms it requires have been independently established in another domain of behavior. Since we know that humans have contamination-avoidance systems, and the principles organizing this domain are extraordinarily similar to those involved in religious rituals, it would be perverse to think that these two domains have completely independent origins.

VIOLENCE AND INITIATION

The notion of hidden danger only explains part of the variance here. Many imagistic rituals also include gruesome ordeals, over and above the usual ritual themes. This is most impressive in male initiation rituals. If anything, initiation rituals *should* be explainable in terms of transmitted "revelations." After all, a familiar rationale for initiation is that young boys must acquire the secret knowledge and skills that define real manhood. However, going though initiation is very far from either attending college or going to summer camp. The secret knowledge is more often than not either vacuous or paradoxical. In many rites the candidates are taught that the secret of the rite is precisely that there is no secret at all, or that they will not be told what it is until they reach a further stage of initiation. The rites seem to promote what Barth called an "epistemology of secrecy," a notion that knowledge is intrinsically dangerous and ambiguous. The few who reach the end of the cycle have not learned much, except that secret knowledge consists in a series of recursive secrets, probably with no clear end point (Barth 1975). Initiation rites seem conceptually "inchoate" (Fernandez 1982).

The rites also seem to boost this conceptual confusion by making use of constant paradoxes. In the Beti male initiation in Cameroon, boys are for instance told to wash in mud puddles. If they oblige, they are beaten up for getting dirty; if they refuse, they are of course beaten up for staying unwashed. They are instructed to hunt in the forest, but they are the ones stalked and attacked by the elders. Houseman argues that such paradoxical events, which create a kind of cognitive blur, are central to male initiation (Houseman 1993).

So there is no clear conceptual content that could match the compulsion and personal cost characteristic of these rites. Initiation does not transmit much in terms of skills either. Although the rites are sometimes said to turn immature boys into competent hunters or warriors, nothing of great use is acquired during these long periods of seclusion. Military drills or strategy, when present, are clearly not the most important aspect of the ceremonies. Indeed, many initiation rites comprise long series of painful ordeals and episodes of torture that do not at first sight seem to enhance much the fighting capacities of young boys. Having one's penis grated or one's toes dislocated may do wonders to focus the mind, but it could hardly count as preparation for serious engagement.

INITIATION AND COMMITMENT

A satisfactory account of violent initiations would have to make sense of this combination of violence and seemingly vacuous conceptual associations. Perhaps a starting point would be to emphasize four features that are left aside when we consider initiation as a form of religious "revelation." First, the violent ordeals are generally typical of *male* initiations. Second, they typically occur in cultures where men engage in *dangerous* activities like warfare or hunting. Third, these hazardous operations require *coordination* between men as they cannot be performed by isolated individuals. Fourth—here I am taking a leaf out of Michael Houseman's book—although initiates cannot justify the ordeals, they all agree that these episodes changed them, and the change is mostly about the *relationships* between the different actors in the ritual (Houseman 1993; Houseman 2002).

Warfare and collective hunting activate mental systems for *coalitional* behavior. Coalitions are a very special form of association. To have a common goal is not sufficient to build a coalition; you and I may wish our streets were cleaner, but that does not bring us into a coalition. It is not even sufficient that people are aware of having the same goal and cooperate to achieve that goal. For instance, factory workers need to coordinate their work to produce a manufactured good, but they do not usually construe this as a coalition. The latter presupposes an activity in which joining is (presumably) voluntary, defection is possible, benefits can be accrued by cooperation, and there is a notable cost in being a cooperator when others defect. Coalitional action will allow you to reap great benefits as long as everyone is in it together. But then in many situations it may be much more profitable for some individuals to withdraw cooperation at an awkward moment. There is just no ironclad guarantee that people will not blab or run away or, to put it more generally, *defect* to protect or enhance their immediate interest. This is why so few species actually have coalitions (chimpanzees and dolphins build alliances but not on the same scale and with the same stability as the human version) (Harcourt and de Waal 1992). Coalitions require complicated computation and therefore the mental capacities to run these computations in an intuitive, automatic way (Kurzban et al. 2001).

Although coalitional affiliation "comes naturally" to human beings, it is based on complex principles. It also requires constant monitoring of one's own and other agents' cost-benefit matrices in pursuing each of a set of possible courses of actions (Kurzban 2001). This is why members of coalitions are always extremely interested, indeed emotionally involved, in tracking other members' loyalties. This is manifested in several different ways. One feels a desire to punish those people who have defected from the coalition; one may also want to punish those who failed to punish the defectors.

One difference between ordinary groups and coalitions is that the latter can launch extremely risky operations if certain conditions of interaction are met. Each member of a coalition must signal that he will cooperate, regardless of the cost. Even if there is a high probability that the coalition will suffer losses, it must be intuitively obvious that the likelihood is equal between members. More importantly, coalitions for dangerous operations often have this specific property, that it is crucial to establish other members' reliability *before* engaging in the operation. By the time your partners defect, it is too late to recruit others. Whoever mistakenly assumed they could be trusted has to pay a heavy price.

Violent initiation rituals are typically found in cultural environments where males will be recruited for dangerous and cooperative operations, be they warfare (tribal, terrorist, or guerrilla) or large-scale hunting. These are all situations where success depends on cooperative interaction, where it is difficult in advance to assess people's dispositions to cooperate, where defection might be very tempting and would endanger all nondefectors, and where it would be difficult to punish a defector after the fact. Note that the dilemma is not just on the side of the present members of the group. Newcomers too have the symmetrical problem, that they should demonstrate their reliability, but the only way to do that is by being reliable, which means being accepted as a member of the coalition, which requires that one's reliability is demonstrated. In other words, coalitions create what economists would call "commitment problems" (Frank 1988).

There is one possible way out of this "initiation dilemma." The best way to assess whether young men are prepared *potentially* to pay a heavy cost *after* joining the coalition and for its benefit, is to invite them *actually* to pay a heavy price *before* joining. A necessary requirement for all successful cooperation in the form of coalitions is not just that people accept to pay a price for membership, but also that they trust others to cooperate too. Initiation does not seem to confer much benefit on the young participants, and in fact it costs them a great deal. But it also confirms (or makes more plausible) to each of them and their elders that they are indeed loyal members. Naturally, despite all this talk of strategies and utilities, people do not consciously follow rational-choice algorithms when they behave in this way. All we need is that the *results* of such computations are available to participants in the form of intuitions (e.g., that this fellow who balked at the idea of having his toes broken does not have the "stuff" it takes) or that the man who refused to obey obviously paradoxical orders cannot be trusted. Again, the organizers of initiation rituals did not deliberately fashion this clever way of overriding commitment problems. The invisible hand of cultural selection just makes initiation rites more convincing and emotionally compelling when they include this commitment logic.

This only explains part of the complex interaction found in such rituals (see Houseman 1993 for more detail), but it explains those features that would otherwise remain puzzling: that the rituals are a male affair, in situations of risky cooperative operations outside religion; that their conceptual content is generally vacuous; and above all that they create a *relational* change between participants. The explanation seems parsimonious in the sense that it is based on independently established behavioral traits and underlying psychological dispositions.

DOCTRINAL RELIGION: REVELATION OR SOCIAL NICHE?

The "doctrinal" mode too should be considered, in my view, as a candidate for reduction to external causes and principles. Whitehouse notes that, in contrast to traditional and tribal religions (and most spontaneous outbursts of prophetism), most organized religion is centred on repeated rituals with explicitly taught religious meaning, taught in the form of tightly argued propositional sermons. These rituals are usually not ethnically or locally based, they could potentially recruit members far from their point of origin, they maintain a high degree of uniformity, and they generally involve specialized personnel with a centralized organization.

Whitehouse's model provides an excellent account of the psychological and social dynamics that "bundle" the features of doctrinal religion. Because there are frequently repeated rituals, there is an opportunity to transmit verbal, argumentative content rather than salient images. Because the contents can be argued for and derived from a set of basic propositions, there seems to be greater scope for uniformity. This in turn makes the spread of such doctrines more likely.

All this, I would argue, makes sense as a description of features that fit together. But it could be completed with a simple set of hypotheses that explain why some of these features are copresent, in terms of external causes. To do this, it may be of help to add a few additional traits to the above description of the "doctrinal" mode. First, in about every single instance described by anthropologists, the doctrinal mode occurs in the context of large polities with a fair measure of social stratification, such as kingdoms or city-states. Second, in almost every instance reported, the content of the ritual lessons and in many cases the ritual sequences themselves are derived from written sources. Third, doctrinal institutions are rarely the only source of religious services, as Whitehouse has extensively demonstrated. There is always some informal source of religious services, usually of the imagistic type. Doctrinal religion may be limited in space (it does not monopolize religion; priests have to share with shamans) or time (it faces periodic outbursts of inspirational, prophetic contestation). Fourth, doctrinal institutions are generally hostile to the informal religion provided by shamans, seers, healers, and possessed people, which is all the more striking as this opposition is asymmetrical. Doctrinal religion, unlike imagistic and other informal modes, seems to be oppositional in nature.

These features may be better understood if we see doctrinal religion as only one of the many manifestations of social and cognitive dynamics that appear with the development of large-scale polities with social stratification. Such polities, kingdoms and city-states, gradually evolved out of the tribes and chiefdoms that were more typical of incipient agricultural societies (Maryanski and Turner 1992). They provided specific economic niches for individuals, and groups specialized in the provision of specific services, such as lineages or castes of specialized craftsmen, servants, functionaries, and scribes. Many of these groups were organized in ways that optimized each member's potential share of a limited market. This is why we find that the development of large polities with tradesmen and craftsmen also heralds the development of guilds and other such professional groups. Now we know a lot about the way these groups are organized, and some of their features seem to be present in doctrinal religious institutions, too. So it may be a sound strategy to see to what extent what seem to be purely "religious" features may in fact stem from the fact that this particular form of religion was and is put forward by such organized groups of professionals.

RELIGIOUS GUILDS

A religious guild is a group that derives its livelihood, influence, and power from the fact that it provides particular services, in particular the performance of rituals. In this way it can be compared to other specialized groups, like craftsmen. In a city-state or even an empire, craftsmen can afford to spend most of their time away from subsistence activities, such as tending herds and growing food, because they provide goods and services and receive some payment for these.

Such groups often try to control the market for their services. Throughout history, guilds and other groups of craftsmen and specialists have tried to establish common prices and common standards and to stop non–guild members from delivering comparable services. By establishing a quasimonopoly, they make sure that all custom comes their way. By having common prices and common standards, they make it difficult for a particularly skilled or efficient member to undersell the others. So most people pay a small price for being members of a group that guarantees a minimal share of the market to each of its members.

One might think that the services provided by religious scholars, like ritual performance and scriptural knowledge, are essentially different from making shoes or tanning leather. But this precisely makes the general tensions associated with imperfect markets even more relevant. For religious goods and services are indeed different but in a way that makes the providers' position more fragile than that of other specialists. Craftsmen often have no difficulty maintaining exclusive supply, either because other people are reluctant to perform their dangerous and polluting tasks (gathering garbage, burying the dead, butchering animals, etc.), or because these tasks require technical knowledge and a long apprenticeship (most crafts). By contrast, religious specialists supply something—rituals, a guarantee that they are efficient in dealing with supernatural agents—that could be provided easily by competitors. Indeed, in most places with such castes of religious specialists, there *are* other providers: local witch doctors, healers, shamans, holy men, and knowledgeable elders who can always claim that they too offer some interaction with supernatural agents or protection against misfortune.

This may be one of the reasons why religious castes or guilds very often try to gain maximal political influence. Not all religious guilds achieved control over the whole political process as the Christian church did for a large part of European history. For instance, the Indian groups of scholarly Brahmans did to some extent impose a specific form of religious practice, but they did not displace the political supremacy of kings. The Chinese "schools" (Taoism, Confucianism, Buddhism) never imposed themselves as paramount political forces. However, all these groups in these different circumstances did wield considerable political influence. Priests and other religious specialists are not necessarily central to large-scale political organization. But the ones that do not manage to gain any political leverage fall by the wayside.

Given the elusive nature of the services they provide, literate groups of religious specialists always remain in a precarious position. The difficult training and special knowledge make sense and can subsist only if there is some guarantee that people will actually need the special services. At the same time, the services in question are very easily replaced, or so it would seem. In all such groups, people have a precise though intuitive grasp of their group's position in the market. Perceiving all this and reacting to it appropriately does not mean that you have expert knowledge of political economy. It does not require much sophistication to realize that your position as a priest or religious scholar is potentially threatened by the alternatives offered by shamans and local healers.

One solution is to turn the guild's ministration into a *brand*, that is, a service that is (1) clearly distinct from what others could provide, (2) similar regardless of which member of the guild provides it, and (3) exclusively provided by one organization. A Catholic priest offers rituals that are quite different from the ancestor-based rituals his African congregation were used to; but Catholic rituals are also quite stable from one priest to another; some observable features make it easy for most observers to distinguish between say a Catholic mass and what is offered by rival guilds. There is nothing intrinsically demeaning in saying that some services are offered in the form of a particular brand. This is likely to occur whenever an organized group of producers is in competition with both local, independent producers and rival organizations. The creation of recognizable brands of religious services has important consequences for the kinds of concept put forward by religious institutions.

WHY ARE DOCTRINAL GUILDS AGAINST IMAGISTIC PRACTICES?

The kinds of religious concepts offered in the context of organized guilds are very different from those of local specialists, shamans, and healers. First, literate guilds tend to downplay intuition, divination, personal inspiration, and orally transmitted lore because all these naturally fall outside the guild's control. True descriptions of supernatural agents are said to come in the form of a stable and general doctrine, rather than on-the-hoof, contextual solutions to specific problems. A typical question in local religious activities is, "Will the ancestors be satisfied with this pig and help this child recover?" A typical one in a literate religion would be, "What animals must be sacrificed for what types of illnesses?" and the answer to that is a *general* answer.

Also, the use of texts tends to make religious doctrines more coherent, in the sense that all the elements that constitute the description of supernatural agents can be brought together for consideration much more efficiently than when they are stored in individual people's memories, in the form of particular episodes.

All human groups have some rituals to deal with corpses and some notion of how the "soul" or presence of dead people must set off on a journey, to be separated from the living. In many places, this is associated with concepts of particular ancestors, local heroes who settled the group, founders of the dead person's clan, gods of particular places, and spirits connected to particular families, which means that these gods and ancestors are specific to each group, or even to a village. This local god demands incense and flowers, that one requires sacrificed chickens, and the divinities of each particular mountain or river are likely to be the object of different ritual procedures.

As a guild claims to offer similar services throughout a large polity, it cannot claim to have a particular connection to *local* supernatural agents, such as ancestors and local spirits. The agents that the institution claims to interact with must be such that any member of the guild, wherever they are, could be said to be in contact with them. This is one of the main reasons why such "small" gods and spirits are usually demoted in the doctrines of religious institutions and replaced with more general, cosmos-wide agents. The Fang have ancestors who, they say, interact with them and usually protect them; they are also plagued by evil spirits. Both the benevolent and the malicious spirits are members of the same social groups as the living people they interact with. Christianity attempts to replace all this with a unique supernatural agent that *anyone* can interact with, provided they resort to the church's offices.

This is why organized literate guilds tend to promote a very specific understanding of death and the destiny of various components of the person. What happens to the soul is presented as a consequence of *general* processes that apply to all humans. Religious guilds replace the intrinsically local notions of "establishing" the ancestors, turning them into mountains or pillars of a house, with a general and abstract notion of salvation conditioned by moral behavior. Such a notion is found in most written religious doctrines, with important differences in how salvation is defined and what kind of morality is attached to such definitions. The Jewish and Christian versions imply proximity to God as well as a very vaguely defined (especially in the Jewish case) afterlife, while the Indian (Hindu or Buddhist) versions imply an exit from the cycle of reincarnations and the elimination of the soul as a self. These are among the variations on a theme found in many literate traditions. Death should not be construed only as a passage to the status of ancestor but also as a radical leave-taking from society. This makes sense, as the doctrine is offered by specialists who have no particular service to offer in terms of local cults to local characters, or in any case nothing that could be seemingly better than the services of local shamans and other religious specialists.

This may help solve what remains a mystery in Whitehouse's account. Although each mode sometimes borrows some superficial features from the other, it still remains, as Whitehouse rightly points out, that they mix no more

than oil and water; they really are *divergent* modes of religiosity. The practices organized around salient sensory arousal do not usually blend with
those that require organized argumentation and explication of a stable
dogma. Why is that? Each follows a specific route to memory consolidation,
making use of specific cognitive-emotional processes, with different consequences on people's memories. This would explain why you cannot use
both at the same time in the transmission of the same concepts. But why
could you not use them in different circumstances in a particular religious
tradition?

Whitehouse's own explanation is that each mode conveys a revelation and
that the latter is the basis of religious identity. All religious practices bind together members of the group; but doctrinal and imagistic practices do it differently (as noted above). The latter tie each participant to particular persons
who happened to take part in the same salient events; by contrast, doctrinal
practices foster a sense of generalized membership; you are there primarily,
and you associate with others principally, as a Christian or a Pomio-Kivung
member, not as so-and-so of this or that particular family and village. But
again, why cannot some traditions have it both ways, fostering a sense of
personalized membership through salient events as well as a sense of larger
community through doctrine? According to Whitehouse's own cognitive assumptions, such combined traditions would be conceptually heterogeneous
but probably very successful as well.

The main reason, I would argue, is a matter of marketing, that is, of politics. Doctrines are promoted by professional guilds, and guilds depend on
the stable and decontextualized provision of similar services. Guilds are cartels. Groups of craftsmen the world over try to make prices and services uniform and repress attempts to individualize the offer. In the same way, we
know that members of religious guilds intuitively perceive that charismatic
specialists dangerously threaten their group's overall grip on the market. The
conflict is a political and economic one between individuals located in different niches of the religious market. This would also explain why the opposition is always asymmetrical. The potential conflict between following
the guild and following more local specialists is invariably highlighted by the
guild's attempt to repress, suppress, or downgrade the local specialists, *not
the other way around*. In other words, shamans are much more dangerous
to priests than priests are to shamans. The survival of a religious guild requires that some limits be set on what local specialists can provide.

RELIGIOUS GUILDS AND LITERACY

Guilds offer an account of gods and spirits that is generally integrated (most
elements hang together and cross-reference each other), apparently deduc-

tive (you can infer the guild's position on a whole variety of situations by considering the doctrine's general principles), and stable (you get the same message from all members of the guild). This last feature is particularly important for diffusion. Even complex concepts can gradually become more and more familiar to the illiterate masses through consistent sermons and recitations. How do the guilds manage to keep their message stable and uniform?

There is an extraordinarily high correlation between doctrinal religion and the presence of literacy. It would be difficult to find a literate polity without a doctrinal system, or a doctrinal practice outside literate cultures. This may not be too surprising if we consider the general cognitive effects of literacy (Goody 1977; Goody 1986). Given that religious guilds only appeared in complex polities and that these very often had some writing system to begin with, it is not surprising that the guilds also used writing. A great advantage of writing is that it facilitates the uniformity of service and practice that is the main selling point of such professional groups. So religious guilds that set great store by literate sources, written transmission, and the kind of systematic argument made easier by writing are more likely to subsist than groups that ignored the technology of writing. Conversely, given that uniformity and substitutability are important assets of the guild, any appeal to personal charismatic features or shamanistic revelation is actively discouraged. This is not to suggest that literacy inevitably or mechanistically results in the kind of organized religious doctrines that Whitehouse describes. But it is a crucial causal factor, just like the accumulation of food surpluses is a crucial factor in the creation of large polities with social stratification.

In recent comments on the nature of doctrinal religion, Whitehouse played down the connection with literacy and large states for two distinct reasons. The first one is that there are *some* exceptions, such as the Pomio Kivung cult (Whitehouse 1995) or the Inca empire. But that is not compelling. In any empirical discipline, anyone who observes a .95 correlation between two features will try to explain their association rather than basing conclusions on the .05 exceptions (and I am sure the correlation in this case is even greater than a "mere" .95 here, given that some of these exceptions are clearly derivative; Pomio Kivung was after all built on the basis of the missionaries' religion). The second reason is that literacy "comprises an extremely heterogeneous set of practices" with different consequences (pp. 174–75) on religion and social organization. True, but the important question is whether these differences are relevant to the issue at hand. Whitehouse argues that "the principal characteristics [. . .] associated with literacy are *in fact* [my emphasis] features of the doctrinal mode of religiosity, whether or not a tradition operating in this mode happens to utilize a system of writing" (175). Given that practically *all* doctrinal specialists actually use some writing, the last clause is slightly misleading. Whitehouse's argument is that the choice of a "mode" that promotes semantic encoding via repeated lessons is the *original cause*, a prime mover, and the constitution of a clerisy, the constant use of literate sources, the insistence on literal renditions of these sources, the complex explicit arguments, all these are its *effects*.

There is, however, no good reason to decide that a mode of religiosity is a prime mover in social evolution. On the contrary, history and archaeology provide us with a wealth of information about social evolution that provides a broader causal context in which we can understand how a particular "mode of religiosity" might flourish. The similarities are striking, between the behavior of religious specialists (insisting on exclusive provision, recognizable services, uniformity of services, absence of competition inside the priesthood) and that of other craftsmen (excluding outside competition, maintaining identity and standards, constituting cartels). It seems difficult to ignore the similarities and parsimonious to understand them as rooted in the same economic and social conditions. .

MODES AND THE STANDARD MODEL

The arguments sketched here would suggest that it is indeed possible to progress toward a more historically specific version of cognitive understandings of religious practices and concepts. Although this has to remain programmatic, the standard model described above can be supplemented with a series of causal hypotheses derived from independent evidence concerning transmission processes and social dynamics.

As a first step, we should consider one major variable that intervenes to make *some* versions of this cognitively optimal religiosity more successful than others, namely a set of *frequency-related biases* (Boyd and Richerson 1995). Assuming that a variety of conceptual associations are equally salient and inferentially productive (which can be measured by experimental tests), their relative distribution at $t + n$ is certainly influenced by which one was present at t and the extent to which this frequency was perceived by members of the group. This is not just because acquisition of ready-made associations is more economical, as it were, but also because conformism carries its own individual benefits and may be an advantageous evolved disposition (Henrich and Boyd 1998). Moreover, perceiving distinctions (e.g., in terms of social status) between bearers of different versions of a religious notion may trigger prestige-based transmission bias. Unfortunately, the empirical study of such biases is still in its infancy, due to the paucity of empirical data on actual distributions of concepts and norms in groups (Aunger 1992).

In terms of the contents of religious concepts and norms, such an enriched standard model should take Whitehouse's distinctions between "modes" with their bundled features as an indispensable starting point. Religious concepts do seem to be transmitted in two different ways, imagistic and doctrinal, each of which comes with a bundle of associated features. There may be many discussions about the extent to which institutions or religious systems in fact mix these two modes. But such discussions seem mostly based on a misunderstanding of what the "modes" really are, namely a cognitive description of kinds of *situations* rather than whole religious systems. This is why a given religious community may well have both imagistic and doctrinal practices. It remains that the kinds of concepts and norms evoked by these two different types of situations differ in predictable ways, because of the memory dynamics described by Whitehouse.

So we can understand the distinctive modes of religiosity as two additions to the general description contained in the standard model. The model predicted higher likelihood for certain types of concepts and norms, but it did not specify the actual situations in which these would be acquired. The modes account allows us to go further. Religion as described in the standard model is minimally specified, so that the features described are true (if true) of many different types of religiosity. But we can now add several crucial specifications:

(1) Certain ("imagistic") situations include coalitional devices (what I called "commitment gadgets"), also found in other social contexts, which result in highly salient practices such as violent initiation rites. This is by no means necessarily religious, but such situations provide a highly salient context in which whatever cognitively optimal religious concepts are used will be particularly memorable.

(2) In many situations the urgency of repetition for rituals is provided by activation of cognitive systems such as the contagion-avoidance system. This explains why conceptually vacuous rituals may also be considered important and compelling.

(3) In situations of large-scale polities (usually accompanied by literacy) we will find a development of specialized guilds, including religious ones, the circumstances of which explain (a) what kind of services they provide, described as "doctrinal" religion, as well as (b) their attitudes toward other providers.

In several places, Whitehouse has cast doubt on this picture of (a) a general standard model that applies across the board, (b) specific reductionistic explanations for some imagistic rituals, and (c) specific reductionistic explanations for some features of doctrinal religion (Whitehouse 2000; Whitehouse 2004). One argument is that some tribal cultures, too, can produce subtle doctrines that go beyond cognitively optimal religion of the kind described in the "standard model." But that, it would seem, is not disputed. That some inspired illiterate individuals can create brilliant philosophies is

26 _Pascal Boyer_

quite clear. That religious systems based on such nonoptimal thoughts could spread without literacy and organized guilds is the issue. The examples cited by Whitehouse (Dogon, Tukano) are cases of sophisticated native philosophers (or of rich anthropological interpretation) but certainly not of belief systems widespread in a whole population. Inasmuch as we have _empirical_ evidence for possession of particular concepts (that is, through experimental means rather than highly interpretive reports), we find important and stable deviations from "cognitively optimal" systems in nonliterate cultures. Whitehouse also argues that, far from literacy creating religious guilds, religious guilds may well have created literacy for their own purposes. That is perfectly possible (although literacy, as the full transcription of speech, seems to have been often "created" for humble bookkeeping purposes rather than religious speculation [DeFrancis 1989]). This only strengthens the point, that literacy is a very useful tool for a religious guild that needs to "brand" its services, so much so that in history very few "doctrinal" systems were ever observed with no use of or influence from literacy.

Terms such as "revelation" (in the same way as "belief" and "worldview") are prime candidates for scientific reduction or elimination in a cognitively informed anthropology of religion. We can preserve the essential features of Whitehouse's rich psychological model without assuming that any religious practice ever delivers "revelation." Perhaps some do, some of the time, for some people, but that is neither necessary nor sufficient for transmission. What is necessary for transmission is that people identify some ways of doing things as appropriate (in contrast with possible alternatives) and that they perceive some ill-defined danger or some potential cost in not reproducing these occurrences to the best of their memory capacities. Imagistic practices do that because the events themselves are salient enough to remain engraved as unique episodes, together with all their irrelevant features. Doctrinal practices do it by offering a logical construction that multiple repetition and argumentation render more and more plausible, and by offering a guaranteed, similar, often monopolistic service throughout a complex society.

REFERENCES

Adler, C. M., P. McDonough-Ryan, K. W. Sax, S. K. Holland, S. Arndt, and S. M. Strakowski. 2000. fMRI of Neuronal Activation with Symptom Provocation in Unmedicated Patients with Obsessive Compulsive Disorder. _Journal of Psychiatric Research_ 34: 317–24.
Atran, S. A. 2002. _In Gods We Trust: The Evolutionary Landscape of Religion._ Oxford: Oxford University Press.
Aunger, R. 1992. The Nutritional Consequences of Rejecting Food in the Ituri Forest of Zaire. _Human Ecology_ 30: 1–29.

Bacharach, M., and D. Gambetta. 2001. Trust in Signs. In *Trust in Society*, ed. K. S. Cook, 148–84. Russell Sage Foundation Series on Trust, vol. 2. New York.

Barrett, J. L. 1996. Anthropomorphism, Intentional Agents, and Conceptualizing God. PhD diss., Cornell University.

———. 2000. Exploring the Natural Foundations of Religion. *Trends in Cognitive Sciences* 4: 29–34.

Barrett, J. L., and F. C. Keil. 1996. Conceptualizing a Non-natural Entity: Anthropomorphism in God Concepts. *Cognitive Psychology* 31: 219–47.

Barrett, J. L., and E. T. Lawson. 2001. Ritual Intuitions: Cognitive Contributions to Judgments of Ritual Efficacy. *Journal of Cognition and Culture* 1: 183–201.

Barrett, J. L., and M. Nyhof. 2001. Spreading Non-natural Concepts: The Role of Intuitive Conceptual Structures in Memory and Transmission of Cultural Materials. *Journal of Cognition and Culture* 1: 69–100.

Barth, F. 1975. *Ritual and Knowledge among the Baktaman of New Guinea*. Oslo: Universitetsforlaget; New Haven, CT: Yale University Press.

Boyd, R., and P. J. Richerson. 1985. *Culture and the Evolutionary Process*. Chicago: University of Chicago Press.

———. 1995. Why Does Culture Increase Adaptability? *Ethology & Sociobiology* 16: 125–43.

Boyer, P. 1990. *Tradition as Truth and Communication: A Cognitive Description of Traditional Discourse*. Cambridge: Cambridge University Press.

———. 1992. Explaining Religious Ideas: Outline of a Cognitive Approach. *Numen* 39: 27–57.

———. 1994a. Cognitive Constraints on Cultural Representations: Natural Ontologies and Religious Ideas. In *Mapping the Mind: Domain-Specificity in Culture and Cognition*, ed. L. A. Hirschfeld and S. Gelman. New York: Cambridge University Press.

———. 1994b. *The Naturalness of Religious Ideas: A Cognitive Theory of Religion*. Berkeley, CA: University of California Press.

———. 2000. Functional Origins of Religious Concepts: Conceptual and Strategic Selection in Evolved Minds [Malinowski Lecture 1999]. *Journal of the Royal Anthropological Institute* 6: 195–214.

———. 2001. *Religion Explained. Evolutionary Origins of Religious Thought*. New York: Basic Books.

———. 2003. Religious Thought and Behaviour as By-products of Brain Function. *Trends in Cognitive Sciences* 7(3): 119–24.

Boyer, P., and C. Ramble. 2001. Cognitive Templates for Religious Concepts: Cross-cultural Evidence for Recall of Counter-Intuitive Representations. *Cognitive Science* 25: 535–64.

Cosmides, L., and J. Tooby. 1994. Origins of Domain Specificity: The Evolution of Functional Organization. In *Mapping the Mind: Domain Specificity in Cognition and Culture*, ed. L. A. Hirschfeld, S. A. Gelman et al., 85–116. New York: Cambridge University Press.

———. 1999. Toward an Evolutionary Taxonomy of Treatable Conditions. *Journal of Abnormal Psychology* 108(3): 453–64.

DeFrancis, J. 1989. *Visible Speech. The Diverse Oneness of Writing Systems*. Honolulu: University of Hawaii Press.

Dulaney, S., and A. P. Fiske. 1994. Cultural Rituals and Obsessive-Compulsive Disorder: Is There a Common Psychological Mechanism? *Ethos* 22: 243–83.

Ekman, P. 1999. Facial Expressions. In *Handbook of Cognition and Emotion*, ed. T. Dalgleish and M. J. Power, 301–20. New York: John Wiley & Sons.

Fernandez, J. 1982. *Bwiti: An Ethnography of the Religious Imagination in Africa.* Princeton, NJ: Princeton University Press.

Fiske, A. P., and N. Haslam. 1997. Is Obsessive-Compulsive Disorder a Pathology of the Human Disposition to Perform Socially Meaningful Rituals? Evidence of Similar Content. *Journal of Nervous & Mental Disease* 185: 211–22.

Frank, R. 1988. *Passions within Reason. The Strategic Role of the Emotions.* New York: Norton.

Freud, S. 1922. *Totem und Tabu: Einige Übereinstimmungen im Seelenleben der Wilden und der Neurotiker* (Dritte, unveranderte Aufl. ed.). Leipzig: Internationaler Psychoanalytischer Verlag.

———. 1928. *Die Zukunft einer Illusion* (2.Aufl. [6.-16. Tsd.]. ed.). Leipzig: Internationaler Psychoanalytischer Verlag.

Goody, J. R. 1977. *The Domestication of the Savage Mind.* Cambridge: Cambridge University Press.

———. 1986. *The Logic of Writing and the Organization of Society.* Cambridge: Cambridge University Press.

Harcourt, A. H., and F. B. de Waal, eds. 1992. *Coalitions and Alliances in Humans and Other Animals.* Oxford: Oxford University Press.

Henrich, J., and R. Boyd. 1998. The Evolution of Conformist Transmission and the Emergence of Between-Group Differences. *Evolution & Human Behavior* 19(4): 215–41.

Houseman, M. 1993. The Interactive Basis of Ritual Effectiveness in Male Initiation Rite. In *Cognitive Aspects of Religious Symbolism*, ed. P. Boyer. Cambridge: Cambridge University Press.

———. 2002. Dissimulation and Simulation as Forms of Religious Reflexivity. *Social Anthropology* 10: 77–89.

Kurzban, R. 2001. The Social Psychophysics of Cooperation: Nonverbal Communication in a Public Goods Game. In *Journal of Nonverbal Behavior* 25: 241–59.

Kurzban, R., J. Tooby, and J. Cosmides. 2001. Can Race Be Erased? Coalitional Computation and Social Categorization. *Proceedings of the National Academy of Sciences of the United States of America* 98(26): 15387–92.

Lawson, E. T., and R. N. McCauley. 1990. *Rethinking Religion: Connecting Cognition and Culture.* Cambridge: Cambridge University Press.

Maryanski, A., and J. H. Turner. 1992. *The Social Cage. Human Nature and the Evolution of Society.* Stanford: Stanford University Press.

McCauley, R. N., and E. T. Lawson. 2002. *Bringing Ritual to Mind: Psychological Foundations of Cultural Forms.* Cambridge: Cambridge University Press.

Nemeroff, C. J. 1995. Magical Thinking about Illness Virulence: Conceptions of Germs from "Safe" versus "Dangerous" others. *Health Psychology* 14: 147–51.

Pyysiäinen, I. 2001. *How Religion Works. Towards a New Cognitive Science of Religion.* Leiden: Brill.

Rauch, S. L., P. J. Whalen, T. Curran, L. M. Shin, and Coffey. 2001. "Probing Striato-Thalamic Function in Obsessive-Compulsive Disorder and Tourette Syndrome Using Neuroimaging Methods. *Advances in Neurology* 85: 207–24.

Rozin, P., J. Haidt, and C. R. McCauley. 1993. Disgust. In *Handbook of Emotions*, ed. M. Lewis and J. M. Haviland. New York: The Guildford Press.

Sacchetti, B., C. Ambrogi Lorenzini, E. Baldi, G. Tassoni, and C. Bucherelli. 1999. Auditory Thalamus, Dorsal Hippocampus, Basolateral Amygdala, and Perirhinal Cortex Role in the Consolidation of Conditioned Freezing to Context and to Acoustic Conditioned Stimulus in the Rat. *Journal of Neuroscience* 19(21): 9570–78.

Slone, D. J. 2004. *Theological Incorrectness: Why Religious People Believe What They Shouldn't*. New York: Oxford University Press.

Sperber, D. 1996. *Explaining Culture: A Naturalistic Approach*. Oxford: Blackwell.

Whitehouse, H. 1995. *Inside the Cult: Religious Innovation and Transmission in Papua New Guinea*. Oxford: Oxford University Press.

———. 2000. *Arguments and Icons. Divergent Modes of Religiosity*. Oxford: Oxford University Press.

———. 2004. *Modes of Religiosity: A Cognitive Theory of Religious Transmission*. Walnut Creek, CA: AltaMira Press.

2

Modes Theory:
Some Theoretical Considerations

Robert A. Hinde

This contribution examines certain issues in current discussions about the nature of religion. They arise primarily from Whitehouse's (2000) theory of religious modes, with its implications for the political/social structure of the society; McCauley and Lawson's (2002) narrower theory of religious ritual; and Boyer's (1994, 2002) detailed examination of the elements of religious systems.[1] The perspectives of these writers involve a marriage between anthropological and cognitive psychological perspectives. My own background has been in biology and psychology, though I have attempted a broader synthesis in writing about the bases of religious systems and of moral codes (Hinde 1999, 2002). My aim here is to raise some issues that arise from my orientation, not to evaluate or compare these approaches. But in doing so I inevitably focus on matters where a biological background might have led to a somewhat different perspective: on no account should this be taken as a criticism of the originality or constructive nature of the approaches of the above authors.

DESCRIPTION AND CLASSIFICATION

Biologists and ethnographers share the view that the first stage in the study of either structure or behavior should be descriptive. This has certain consequences in the present context.

Scope of the Phenomenon of Interest

Whereas Boyer and Whitehouse take a broad view of religion, that of McCauley and Lawson is more restricted. Their focus is more strictly on ritual, and ritual defined in a somewhat idiosyncratic way. By their criteria, prayer, which does not fit their scheme, is excluded as a religious ritual on the grounds that an outsider cannot know whether an individual is "really" praying or only going through the motions; that you do not have to be an insider to the religion to pray as is the case, for instance, for taking Catholic Communion; and that prayer is not connected to other rituals. Nevertheless they include as (hypothetical) rituals actions by deities that form part of the structural description of the religious system's rituals—for instance, Jesus' statement that Peter was the rock on which he would build his church. The inclusion of nonrepeated hypothetical events and the exclusion of prayer is certainly contrary to common understanding of the meaning of ritual, but it is of course open to theorists to specify the limits of their theories, and they argue that their approach enables them to account for a wider range of ritual practices. But this difference seems not always to be borne in mind when they compare their approach with that of Whitehouse.

Analysis and Resynthesis

The understanding of any aspect of behavior depends first on its adequate description. Description without analysis of a complex system such as religion, even if possible, would be likely to lack form and to involve excessive emphasis on one aspect to the neglect of others. Description therefore requires an element of analysis into components and specification of the relations between the components. Thus an anatomist might describe first skeleton, muscles, and nerves and then attempt to specify the functional and causal relations between them. One could carve up religious systems in a variety of different ways, but in keeping with common usage it is convenient first to consider six components that differ in descriptive and functional characteristics:

1. structural beliefs, which are outside time and concerned with such concepts as the Trinity
2. narratives that usually expand the structural beliefs and place them in comprehensible contexts
3. ritual
4. moral code
5. religious experience
6. relations between the participants (Hinde 1999; Malinowski 1954).

All of these components need not be present, or be equally emphasized, in every religion. I will assume that, to be considered as part of a "religion," each must have some reference to an influence on human life that is in some way counterintuitive. Counterintuitive entities that do not affect individuals, like most concepts of fairies, are not part of the religious system, but devils are. This reference to a counterintuitive entity may be indirect: for instance, the relations between the participants may be due in part to their shared belief in the deity (see below). But some limitation on the meaning of religion is necessary if distinctions are to be made between religious narratives and history, or between religious and military rituals.

As we shall see later, these components are interrelated, each affecting and being affected by others. Thus, in discussing a religion one is discussing a system: separate consideration of the components is a convenient tool with which to gain understanding, but must be followed by examination of the relations between the components. Too great a focus on one component may impoverish understanding of the whole.

Description is not Explanation

Whitehouse's theory involves two contrasting (later three, Whitehouse 2004a and 2004b; see below) "modes" of religious dynamics, each of which has characteristic features that tend to "coalesce" and are not shared by the other. The "doctrinal" mode involves a tendency toward a system that depends on routinized worship and teaching, through which is transmitted a body of fairly complex doctrine, which is incorporated into the individuals' general knowledge. The "imagistic" mode consists of a tendency toward an emphasis on transmission through infrequent but intensely arousing collective rituals. The distinction is based primarily on his studies in Melanesia.

Whitehouse suggested that a comparison could profitably be made between the doctrinal and imagistic modes as shown by his studies in Melanesia, and the attempted changes in the European Reformation. The latter involved the imposition of a doctrinal approach to Christianity on the worship of the laity, which had involved worship of the Virgin and of saints and many celebratory feasts and festivals. It seems clear from his argument that the comparison he had in mind was primarily descriptive, its interest stemming from the doctrinal approach of the Christian missionaries in Melanesia.

McCauley and Lawson were dubious about the comparison, though they appear to read more into it than Whitehouse intended. Thus they interpret him as claiming that the "patterns are not confined to recent Melanesian movements but appear just as clearly in Christianity worldwide" (201). This Whitehouse did not do. However, McCauley and Lawson rightly stress that, when it comes to the causation of the changes, these were quite different in the two cases. Whitehouse had emphasized the role of tedium in the decrease in the appeal of doctrine, leading to the adoption of the imagistic mode by some participants. McCauley and Lawson, however, argue that splintering is always likely to be multicausal, and suggest factors unlikely to have been important in the changes involved in the Reformation. Thus whether changes in Melanesia are comparable with those in the Reformation depends on whether one is concerned with description or with the mechanisms involved.

Integration of the Components of a Religious System

Here we are concerned with the relations between the components of religious systems. This is a central issue for Whitehouse, but less so for McCauley and Lawson, who, in focusing on ritual, concentrate more on the relation between ritual form, ritual frequency, and the accompanying "sensory pageantry." The following considerations indicate that the mutual influences between components aid understanding of the differences between the two modes.

Whitehouse contrasts the doctrinal and imagistic modes primarily by the repetitive nature of worship in the doctrinal mode and the rare but striking nature of ritual in the imagistic mode. McCauley and Lawson emphasize the form rather than the frequency of ritual, differentiating between those in which a "culturally-postulated superhuman agent" (CPS agent) participates most immediately as an agent (as in a marriage ceremony where the deity acts through the priest), and those in which the CPS agent is involved in the ritual as a recipient (as in sacrifice) or intermediary (as in many divinations). These are referred to as special agent, special patient, and special instrument rituals respectively. Special agent rituals tend to involve more "sensory pageantry" and to be performed less frequently than the others.

Though not claiming that ritual is basic, both Whitehouse and McCauley and Lawson focus primarily on ritual, not only because of the problem posed by its stability over time in nonliterate societies, but also because (at least in the view of McCauley and Lawson, 83) rituals are integral to situating individuals within the community and to sustaining that community. This raises the question of the place of ritual in the system as a whole.

Considering first the doctrinal mode, Whitehouse initially described the several characteristics of the religious system as "coalescing" or causation as being bidirectional. In a later paper (Whitehouse 2002) he gave priority to ritual frequency as the defining characteristic of the doctrinal mode, only insofar as he wrote, "a great advantage of frequent repetition is that it allows the establishment of a great deal of explicit verbal knowledge" (297). However, his exposition clearly indicates that he sees the components as interrelated, and any emphasis on ritual comes primarily from the need to explain the transmission of rituals that are performed only rarely. However, McCauley and Lawson interpret Whitehouse's scheme as indicating that ritual frequency is the initiating influence in determining patterns of cognitive processing (110 and fig. 3.2).

If either doctrine or ritual is to be seen as causally primary in the doctrinal mode, it must surely be the former. In terms of the six components of religious systems (see above), the doctrinal mode aims at full acceptance by the participants of a body of doctrine, with frequency of repetition and ritual a means to that end. The doctrine has qualities, involving perhaps belief in salvation, that compensate up to a point for the boredom involved in repetitive worship. In other words, the message in the beliefs that the missionaries or priests try to convey makes up for the relative inadequacy of the ritual in gaining the hearts and minds of the participants. The beliefs integrate cosmology and morality, are illustrated and extended by the narratives, and provide a rationale for the ritual and an interpretation for religious experience. While the ritual contributes to group integration, and the transmission of the beliefs is in part ritualized (in a broad sense), the beliefs affect the form of the ritual to a greater extent than vice versa. In addition, group integration is made possible by shared beliefs by a mechanism less available in the imagistic mode: it can be facilitated by the (probably pancultural) tendency of individuals to be attracted to others who hold similar attitudes and beliefs, an attraction that is especially potent if the similarity involves beliefs that are unverifiable except through mutual confirmation (Byrne, Nelson, and Reeves 1966). This central role of unverifiable beliefs means that the attraction can be extended to anonymous others who never share a ritual performance. Thus a focus on doctrine provides understanding of more aspects of the religious system than does a primary focus on ritual frequency, and would cover also some of the sociopolitical aspects of interest to Whitehouse.

Perhaps because of the more limited scope of McCauley and Lawson's theory, they seem to be unwilling to ascribe any importance to religious meaning (9)[2] and (rather surprisingly) appear to claim that variability in meaning typically has no effect on the stability of the ritual actions' underlying forms (that is, I presume, the properties of special agent, patient, and instrument rituals). However, the fact that they differentiate between rituals by the role played by the deity implies that meaning in a loose sense is in fact rather basic. Indeed they argue that "how CPS-agents are implicated in their religious rituals, ultimately, determines whether or not religious rituals are repeatable as well as the mnemonic dynamics that those rituals enlist" (43). Of course, in many rituals the meanings ascribed differ between the participants (Hinde 1999), but a relation to improbable entities is necessarily present for at least some if the rituals are to be described as religious.

Turning to the imagistic mode, its most conspicuous elements are the rituals that are rarely repeated but often traumatic for the participants. Given the crucial role of the fear induced by ritual and/or the revelation of secrets that can never again be repeated with the same subjects, such rituals would lose their effectiveness if often repeated. The ritual may utilize references to ancestors or cultural myths, but otherwise appears to be largely unrelated to doctrine. The experience of the ritual is therefore open to idiosyncratic interpretation. Even if the "spontaneous exegetical reflection" postulated by

Whitehouse (an issue discussed in the next section) does bring some sort of cognitive coherence, the often traumatic nature of the ritual implies that such coherence can hardly be comforting and, being largely idiosyncratic, must have little social support. In the imagistic case, social integration depends largely on different mechanisms from those in the doctrinal mode—namely the consequences of shared trauma with other participants and a respect for the authority of the ritual experts based on their knowledge and control— together with, perhaps, understandings with their tormentors similar to those that develop between kidnappers and their victims.

Surprisingly, neither Whitehouse nor McCauley and Lawson give much attention to rules of behavior or ethics. In societies with little or no distinction between sacred and secular, the moral code presumably depends largely on conformity to shared understandings enforced by threat of revenge (Hinde 2002).

It can be argued, therefore, that focusing on ritual without assessing its relations with other aspects of the religious system is potentially misleading. It would seem that the relations between the doctrinal and imagistic modes can be understood as well, and perhaps better, in terms of the differing influence of doctrine, rather than ritual form or frequency. The relations between the components of religious systems must not be neglected.

THE QUESTION OF REVELATION

A question that arises here concerns the extent to which "revelation" as a consequence of exposure to the doctrine or ritual could facilitate either retention or the motivation to transmit the religious system. McCauley and Lawson pay little attention to the occurrence of revelation as a consequence of involvement in ritual, except insofar as heightened arousal facilitates episodic memory and religious motivation. For Whitehouse, revelation is more important.

In Whitehouse's view, "revelation" has different bases in the two modes— through the *word* in the doctrinal mode, and by "iconicity, multivocality and multivalence" in the imagistic mode. In the doctrinal mode, revelation comes primarily through meaning, perhaps through the perception of the relevance of the doctrine to everyday life. In later publications (Whitehouse 2004a, 2004b), attempting to get at the psychological processes involved, he points to the difficulty of attributing authorship to frequently repeated formulae (cf. Bloch 1992). Is it the priest, or the generations of priests, who have influenced him? When messages acquired in this way are triggered in everyday life, they are not exactly one's own thoughts. Thus, Whitehouse suggests, a common solution is to ascribe the messages and their activation to a higher source, as suggested by the priests. This, of course, is a speculation about the interpretation of the experience, not about the experience itself. As such, another possibility could be considered. It has been suggested that mystical experience or revelation is comparable to that experienced in other (e.g., aesthetic) contexts, and is distinguished as religious only by the interpretation put upon it (Hinde 1999). The meaning in any doctrinal religious practice has already been hammered home by the repetitive practice and could serve as a basis for interpretation and even a stimulus for both experience and revelation.

Whitehouse suggests that meaning is extracted from imagistic rituals by a process of "spontaneous exegetical reflection." The means by which this occurs are difficult to discern. Verbal commentary or discussion on the rituals is often ruled out. Schwartz (cited in Whitehouse, 132) "was struck by the absence of verbal allusions to the meanings and images elicited by the ritual" and was forced to focus "on the range of associations that these practices were likely to have evoked." McCauley and Lawson (9) remark, "Rituals often occasion an astonishingly wide range of interpretations" from both observers and participants, and in the Baktaman there is a low level of uniformity in the individual interpretations of symbols. In any case, any interpretations offered may be constructed "on the hoof" to satisfy the ethnographer.

Interpretations are possible in some cases (see Whitehouse, 132–33) even though they are often "not amenable to expression in words" (69), but to the outsider certain questions remain. Where there is no discussion or speculation about the meaning of ritual, and the emphasis is on the unknowable, what is the evidence for "spontaneous exegetical reflection" leading to "revelation"? For those rituals where esoteric mythology has at most a minor role and there is no verbal commentary, how can one be certain that "revelation" occurs at all? If ritual experience is concerned with the intense experience of mortal danger and pain (105), what else can it transmit? Do the terrifying initiation rituals communicate anything beyond fear and relief? Of course the initiated may ponder on the experience they have been through, and reflect on their new status, but should this qualify as a "revelation"? How do we know that the participants' interpretations concern transcendental influence at all? One wonders whether such rituals are assumed to carry "revelations" just because they are regarded by anthropologists as part of a religious system. Could it be that imagistic ritual is, like secular Christmas dinner, just something that people do, and even enjoy doing, without any deep meaning? It could be retained in memory through associations other than "revelationary understandings" (Whitehouse, 91).

And there are other points here. What does it mean for "theology to belong to the realm of the unspoken" (Juillerat 1992, cited in Whitehouse, 97)? What sort of thing is a "secret ritually transmitted"? (Whitehouse, 98): is it anything more than a Mason's handshake? Where exegetical accounts seem not to be available, is it presumed that exegesis is limited to an elite? And, if the ritual images are not capable of logical integration (Whitehouse, 96), if each iconic image "evokes a discrete set of mysterious, half-understood connotations" (Barth, cited in Whitehouse, 89), if individual participants reach different interpretations (though see below), can one describe the situation as involving *a* religion? At best, one is dealing with a religion that fails to bring commonly shared intellectual order—though it may promote group solidarity in other ways.

It is, I think, improper for a nonanthropologist to make suggestions about how complex and traumatic rituals should be understood, but perhaps it might be worth considering the parallels with techniques of "thought reform." Although this uses techniques and pressures that may be more cognitive and less physical than those described for initiation rituals, there are certain similarities. For instance, what was formerly called "brainwashing," as well as the more sophisticated and less physical techniques used in certain cults, include environmental control and restriction of communication with non–group members, mystical manipulation including convincing the subject of the higher purpose of the group and that the perspective of the reformers is true, insistence that dedication is essential for long-term change, reinterpretation of earlier experience, and threat of the consequences of failure to conform (e.g., Lifton 1961/1989). Of course there are differences, especially in the relative absence of physical hardship in sophisticated methods of thought reform, but both produce long-term changes. In thought reform, those involve attitudes, while with initiation rituals attention has been focused on the memory for the ritual procedure. But more detailed comparison between the two might guide speculation about the psychological processes involved in initiations.

THE FOUR WHYS

Discussions of the bases of religion sometimes fail to distinguish adequately between, and recognize the relations between, the four meanings of the question "Why?" (Tinbergen 1963). These meanings are as follows:

1. Causal why, asking, "What were the causal factors that caused the organism to show the behavior?"
2. Developmental why, asking the question, "How did the mechanisms underlying this behavior develop in the individual?"
3. Functional why, asking the question, "What use is this behavior?" This can lead to two types of answer, one concerning its immediate benefit to the individual, and the other concerning the consequences through which natural (or cultural) selection acted to maintain it in the organ-

ism's repertoire (i.e., functions, in a more biological sense). As Whitehouse implies, not all consequences are functions.
4. Evolutionary why, asking the question, "What were the stages in the evolution (biological or cultural/historical) of the behavior?"

These questions are all valid questions, and answers to all contribute to an understanding of the behavior. Thus, to take a structural example, in answering the question, "Why does the human thumb move differently from the other fingers?" the answer might be in terms of the differences in skeletal arrangements and muscle attachments (a causal answer); in terms of the embryology of the hand, and how the finger rudiments grew out (developmental); in terms of the utility of an opposable thumb for holding things (functional); or in terms of our descent from monkey-like ancestors that had opposable thumbs (evolutionary). These answers are all correct, but together they provide fuller understanding.

Of course it is not quite so simple as that. For one thing, actions usually depend on a nexus of causes, and causal explanations, if pursued backward in time, become developmental ones. Thus the existence of propensities to respond to some stimuli rather than others (e.g., faces) plays a part in answering both developmental and causal questions (though it requires further developmental analysis itself). But explanations of our responsiveness to facial configurations, or of movement, in terms of the consequences of this susceptibility through which natural selection acted earlier in our evolutionary history (i.e., social interaction; alerting to possible predators), is a functional answer. As another type of complication, the evolution of a religious system is a question of biological function if one is considering such elements, but largely a cultural/historical one when one is considering the diversity of religious systems. Indeed, evolutionary, functional, developmental, and causal questions are inevitably interrelated for this reason: any given character has many origins, D, C, B, or A, depending on how far one traces it back, and the progression from A to D depends on its functional properties at each stage. However, these complications do not detract from the importance of maintaining a clear conceptual distinction between the four whys.

Receptivity and Consequences

The distinction between the different meanings of the question "Why?" is important for cognitive science approaches to religion. Attempts to understand religion in terms of biology and/or psychology that focus on only one of these questions may reach incomplete answers.

For example, explanation in terms of the receptivity of the mind or basic psychological characteristics refers to only part of the causal nexus leading to acceptance of the religious system or to the behavior in question. One needs to know why some of the things to which the mind is receptive are interesting in a religious context and others are not. What are the criteria by which (cultural) selection takes place? There are some stimulus configurations, such as circles (Koffka 1935), and some concepts, such as obscene words, to which we are particularly responsive but that do not generally provide building blocks for religious systems. There is no disagreement that religious concepts are made more likely by certain pancultural cognitive processes (Boyer 2002, chap. 3, p. 343; Hinde, 1999, e.g., 81–96), but Boyer goes beyond this and dismisses discussion of the origins of the components of religious systems in terms of their beneficial consequences, arguing that such explanations are insufficient and misleading (17–38, 343–46; see appendix to this chapter). But the sensitivities of the mind to which he refers are relevant to both secular and religious contexts: what one needs to know in addition is the nature of the *consequences* of each component that make them attractive to human minds in the context of the religious system.

Scores of characters in fairy stories, myths, cartoons, and films have counterintuitive properties, but we do not treat them in the same way as deities or saints. To amplify a point made earlier, one issue, though perhaps not the only issue, important here is that most deities are presented to us as having done or being able to do something for (or to) us. For instance, anthropomorphic deities can satisfy certain human needs—they provide causal explanations for otherwise inexplicable events that affect or might affect individuals; individuals can feel some indirect control over their lives through appeals to the deity; deities can alleviate anxieties and render mortality somewhat more acceptable; and they can provide a sense of relationship for the lonely. To many, belief in a deity provides meaning for life (Hinde 1999, chap. 5). By contrast, fairies are not (generally) perceived as dangerous or helpful to us, and are not seen as part of the religious system. The devil can be nasty and at times has been included in the religious system. If witches and the like are seen as affecting our lives, belief in their existence leads them to be associated with the religious system. A vision or dream about Batman or Mickey Mouse is just a vision or dream; one about Christ is interpreted as something special. Our attitudes to the other components of a religious system depend on how we interpret them. The narratives, rituals, and moral codes are presented to us as in some way connected to the deity, and we perceive them as such. Religious believers even see cobelievers as special.

It must be added that this explanation of why some counterintuitive entities are not treated as part of the religious system may not be the whole story. For instance, it does not tell us why stories about fairies originated in the first place. One possibility is that the characteristics that fairies are perceived to have today are a remnant of times when they had greater powers and played a part in the religious system. In Ireland, fairies were formerly perceived as messengers from the underworld, and European fairies were apparently descended from the Roman *Parcae*, themselves versions of the Greek Fates. According to an ancient Breton tradition, when a baby is born, a table is set out with a lavish meal to placate the fairies (Chevalier and Gheerbrant 1982). As another example, in most Anglo-Saxon countries Santa Claus has some counterintuitive properties, but is not generally seen as a religious figure. But "Santa Claus" is a corruption of the Dutch dialect "Sante Klaas" (St. Nicholas), the patron saint of Dutch and German children, whose feast was celebrated on December sixth. A clue to the origin of the English "Father Christmas" is provided by the fact that Christmas is a corruption of Christ's Mass.

There are in addition figures that are part of religious mythology but are not (generally) worshipped and do not affect human beings. Examples from Christian mythology are the seraphim, members of one of the choirs of angels, and the cherubim, who not only formed one of the choirs of angels but have also been seen as guardians of paradise and bearers of Yahweh's/God's throne. Their more remote origins appear to be unknown, but they are likely to be the product of syncretism with earlier religions, where they may have had power over humans.

If it is correct that sacred beings have or have had power to influence human life, a further question is, of course, how did some of them come to lose some of their powers? No doubt this requires specific answers in specific cases.

PANCULTURAL PSYCHOLOGICAL CHARACTERISTICS

Much of our recently increased understanding of the nature of religious concepts has come from the realization that they "fit" certain basic psychological characteristics. Thus we have seen that anthropomorphic concepts of deities are acceptable (a) because their anthropomorphism provides the property of agency, (b) their counterintuitive characteristics make them interesting and memorable (Boyer 1994, 2002), and (c) because their anthropomorphism is accompanied by the ability to satisfy a number of human needs. Similar considerations apply to other aspects of religious systems.

Formulation in terms of "pancultural psychological characteristics" avoids the sterile debate over the relative importance of nature and nurture, for the near universality of any character may depend on commonalities in the environments of development as well as genes. Such characteristics include (a) greater responsiveness to some stimulus configurations than to others; (b) predispositions to learn some things, including cultural representations, more readily than others, and to learn more easily in some contexts than others; and (c) motivational concepts such as propensity, as well as (d) cognitive propensities such as those used by Boyer (lc.), McCauley and Lawson (lc.), and Whitehouse (lc.) The early work in this field, a reaction to the view that organisms were born as "blank slates" on which experience might write according to the vicissitudes experienced, was by students of animal behavior (Hinde and Stevenson-Hinde (review) 1973; Lorenz 1935; Seligman and Hager (review) 1972; Tinbergen 1963). It was then possible in many cases to rule out the role of certain types of experience experimentally by rearing animals under restricted conditions. For instance, Thorpe (1969), by rearing chaffinches in auditory isolation from chaffinch song from about six days of age was able to show that the development of normal chaffinch song depends on hearing chaffinch song during a certain sensitive period, and that the chaffinches would learn only songs having certain features in common with chaffinch song. It is important to note that these experiments did not show that experience before six days, or other types of auditory input, were unimportant. Thus they show that the song pattern is not "innate," that certain types of input to which the bird is responsive are necessary for song development, but many other types of input may also be relevant. With human cognition, experimental deprivation of experience would be unethical, and more indirect lines of evidence must be used (see below). However, certain dangers in the use of such concepts must be borne in mind.

Development

First, their development in the individual is rarely understood. The paucity of our knowledge about the details of ontogeny is insufficiently appreciated. For instance, the perception that the sun moves across the sky (Whitehouse 2004a) may depend on previous experience of the sun's apparent movement. We do not know, and an experimental approach would be impracticable as well as almost certainly immoral. But data may be available adventitiously. For instance, there may be circumstances where children never get a chance to see the sun's movement across the sky. That a characteristic is pancultural does not necessarily imply that it is "innate" or in the genes. Postulating that such a characteristic is part of human nature is only one stage along the road to explanation—though it can legitimately be said that the remainder of the route is not the province of the anthropologist.

The Instinct Fallacy

Second, there is always the possibility of falling into the "instinct fallacy." The term "instinct" lost its respectability when it was recognized that it was often used in circular explanations: Q. "Why does the organism do X?" A. Because it has an X instinct." Q. "How do you know it has an X instinct?" A. "Because it does X." The label "pancultural psychological characteristic," used as an intervening variable (MacCorquodale and Meehl 1954), could run into a similar difficulty unless additional support is adduced. For instance, the "faces in the clouds" concept, used to explain the acceptability of anthropo-morphic deities, is supported by the knowledge that it occurs in nonreligious contexts, that "good" representations are better than poor ones (leaving aside the question of the abstraction of features in caricatures), and that it is (probably) a pancultural characteristic (Guthrie 1993). But is comparable support available for the "moral feeling system" postulated by Boyer (359)?[3] Is an "intentionality seeking device" (Bloch, cited in Whitehouse 2004b) an entity in the brain?

The Elaboration of Cognitively Optimal Concepts

Whitehouse (2004a, 2004b) designates concepts that correspond closely with basic psychological characteristics as "cognitively optimal." Many as-pects of religious systems are much more complex than any basic psycho-logical characteristics that can reasonably be postulated—for instance the doctrines of redemption and transsubstantiation. How do they arise? White-house (2004b) has suggested that "modes dynamics" can transform simple concepts into far more complex ones by virtue of their "mnemonic infra-structure." He suggests that, with rountinization and repetition, people are susceptible to learning elaborate exegetical concepts that "migrate" or "drift away" from a cognitively optimal position. In this way, both religious rou-tinization and the spontaneous exegetical reflection resulting from imagistic practices (but see above) can result in revelation. He further suggests that such more complex religious concepts, having been acquired with consid-erable difficulty, carry considerable "motivational force." While a role of rou-tinization and repetition in *learning* complex concepts is readily acceptable, the manner in which modal dynamics can lead to the *elaboration* of simple concepts into complex doctrine awaits full explication.

Whitehouse also suggests that apparent exceptions to the two-modes the-ory can be accounted for on the assumption that there is a third mode in-volving a tendency to move toward a cognitively optimal position that, in certain circumstances, can be even stronger than those to move toward the purely doctrinal or imagistic positions. This suggestion, replacing the two-modes theory by a three-modes theory with tension between the modes, seems likely to be highly fertile.

LEVELS OF COMPLEXITY

The application of concepts from cognitive psychology has led to greatly in-creased understanding of the nature of religious concepts. It must, however, be integrated with other approaches. Understanding of practically any aspect of human behavior requires a wide perspective.

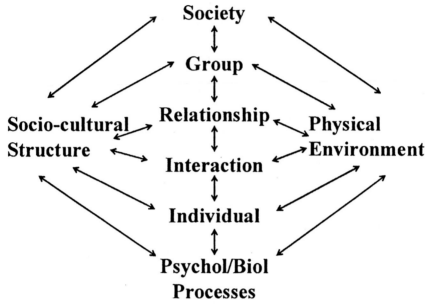

Figure 2.1 A simplified view of levels of social complexity. Each level continually in-fluences, and is influenced by, others and by the socio-cultural structure, with its beliefs, values, conventions, and institutions. The influences involve behavioral, affective, and cognitive processes in the individuals concerned, mediated by the meanings ascribed to events and situations. Each level, including that of the individual, is thus to be seen not as an entity but as involving processes of creation, maintenance, and degradation through the dialectical relations within and between levels. The diachronic aspect is not shown in the figure.

Human activities involve a number of levels of complexity—intraindividual (e.g., cognitive) processes, individual actions, short-term interactions be-tween individuals, relationships between individuals, groups, and societies (see figure 1). Each of these affects, and is affected by, others. For instance, cognitive processes affect individual behavior, and how an individual be-haves affects how he thinks; what goes on in an interaction influences, and is influenced by, the relationship in which it is embedded; and so on. Further-more, each of these levels affects and is affected by the physical environment and by the sociocultural structure, including the morals and beliefs shared with others in the group. Such effects can be immediate, as when a single in-teraction changes the whole course of a relationship, or may occur over time, as when a relationship is changed slowly by a series of less-than-satisfactory interactions. Indeed, such dialectical effects may involve quite long time spans. For instance, before World War II, divorce was both rare and disrep-utable in the UK. After the war, for a variety of reasons, it became more fre-quent; as it became more frequent, it became more respectable; as it became more respectable, it became more frequent; and so on. Thus the dialectical relations between what people do and what they are supposed to do resulted in a change in moral values. In a similar way, reduction in involvement in ritual could result in an increase in sensory pageantry, and boredom with doctrinal practices may lead to a reduction in the demands made by the religious authorities, or to the intrusion of imagistic rituals. *Each level, including that of the individual, is not to be seen as an entity but as involving processes of creation, maintenance, and degradation through the dialectical relations within and between levels.* The mutual influences between individuals and culture are termed here "dialectical" because they have the characteristic of a disputation involving continuous change on both sides.

The diachronic interchange is influenced by constraints and predispositions on both sides, and its complexity is not to be underestimated. (Of course, to talk of "two sides" in itself simplifies what one is trying to explain). Pancultural characteristics of individuals will be influenced to a greater or lesser extent by individual experience, both in the family of origin and subsequently. Common experience suggests that susceptibilities acquired in the earlier years become more deeply engrained so that cultural innovations become more difficult to digest. This effect of experience may itself be the product of selection, it being better to follow the practices that one knows than to acquire new tricks. And differences in experience may lead to differing interpretations of new material, or of material from a foreign culture (Bartlett 1932).

Experience may stem immediately from interactions with other individuals, in which case they may involve group effects, or from the values and beliefs of the culture. Changes, including changes from doctrinal to imagistic mode, are likely to be preceded by discrepancies between what people do and what they are supposed to do in a proportion of the individuals. The charismatic leader or priest capitalizes on such discrepancies and is much less likely to be successful in their absence. Tension is ubiquitous (e.g., Whitehouse 2002, 301).

On the sociocultural side, change may be facilitated by the charisma of innovators or retarded by the value placed on conservativism in the society. Conservativism will itself have been affected by dialectical exchanges with individuals, perhaps especially with the more influential ones. Literacy is also likely to enhance conservativism. The more influential may propagate practices or values that further their own interests; the less powerful may be influenced to accept them by the value they place on humility and obedience, these in turn having been instilled in the culture by the influential. Such influences have been facilitated by the fact that, in many societies, the religious and the secular have been indistinguishable, so that leaders could claim divine guidance. Even early in the second millenium BCE, Hammurabi claimed that his judgments had divine authority (Bottéro 1992). Another example is the manipulation of marriage laws in Europe by the church in such a manner that the church was likely to receive more bequests (Goody 2000).

A further complication stems from divisions within society. The beliefs, rituals, and/or ethical standards may come to differ between the sections of society. For instance, certain ideas or practices may be more acceptable to an elite, or to the "popular culture"; or an intellectual elite may hold a different view of their god from those less sophisticated, with the religious specialists tolerating a wide range of beliefs if doing so would keep individuals in the fold.

These mutual influences between levels indicate that too great a focus on the cognitive characteristics (narrowly defined) of individuals can lead to insufficient emphasis on other issues affecting religious systems. We have already seen how deities can satisfy certain human needs, as well as fitting cognitive susceptibilities. In addition, a variety of social influences are important—for instance tendencies toward conformism, and to emulate or follow charismatic figures, that in turn affect other individuals. Other social issues are mentioned in these accounts of religion—for instance the role of religious specialists and the intrusion of a government inspector. As Whitehouse stresses, the sociopolitical arrangements may be affected by the religious system, and vice versa. The imagistic mode cannot support large communities, because its effects on group integrity are limited to a relatively few individuals (see above), but equally the social arrangements may affect the religious system, as when leaders manipulate moral precepts for their own benefit.

CHANGES BETWEEN MODES

What is clear from the modes theory is that both doctrinal and imagistic modes have a limited degree of stability. Whitehouse has shown that, in at least some societies, a phase when imagistic ritual is prominent tends to follow a doctrinal one, and vice versa. The bases of these changes pose a major problem. Whitehouse points out that repetition in the doctrinal mode can lead to "boredom" unless this is prevented in some way. That is an entirely reasonable suggestion, backed up by some experimental support. But if the problem were the opposite, and it was the unexpected persistence of certain rituals that was to be explained, the concept of "functional autonomy" (Woodworth 1918; Bindra 1959) might well be called upon. This concept has been used to embrace cases in which the performance of a response increases the probability that it will be repeated. Both boredom and functional autonomy are psychological descriptive concepts ("intervening variables," in the sense of MacCorquodale and Meehl [1954]) whose strength lies in the range of phenomena that they cover: they are explanatory in only a superficial sense. Each *implies* a particular set of physiological processes but is not to be seen as a "hypothetical construct" with a specific neural mechanism only waiting to be discovered. What is needed is description of the circumstances in which either boredom or functional autonomy takes precedence.

On that issue, Whitehouse argued that boredom can be relieved by realization of the doctrinal meaning and its relevance to everyday life, or by the intrusion of an imagistic period: either of these may augment the motivation to continue. McCauley and Lawson also take the view that participation in arousing rituals, especially those in which deities have an agentic role, will increase motivation for religious participation. Even that may lead to habituation, though only if the rituals are repeated frequently, which probably rarely happens. Only then would habituation occur, though it could in theory be prevented by continuous elevation of the level of arousal, and that, of course has a limit. On their view, changes between modes are always likely to be multicausal (see above).

Other factors also may be involved. A limit to the performance of doctrinal observance may be set by the time taken, and to imagistic practices also by the energy consumed. An increasing number of studies are showing that energy consumption can be a crucial factor in controlling time budgets in animals. In humans, time constraints may even influence the moral/legal system. For instance, at one stage in the kibbutz movement, when life was hard and labor at a premium, the punishment meted out to offenders for a given indiscretion depended on their previous contribution to the community (Saltman 1985).

TRANSMISSION

The doctrinal and imagistic modes differ in the way in which they are transmitted across individuals and communities. A central problem is how ritual forms are transmitted in nonliterate societies when they are performed only at rare intervals. McCauley and Lawson rightly phrase this not as the "achievement of perfect accuracy" but rather as a "communal sense of continuity in the transmission of cultural materials."

Both Whitehouse and McCauley and Lawson point to the importance of memory, semantic memory in the case of the doctrinal mode and episodic and flashbulb memory for imagistic practices. (Whitehouse [2004] sees the role of episodic memory as stimulating "spontaneous exegetical reflection" and thus the motivational systems necessary for transmission). McCauley and Lawson (85) suggest that religious systems have evolved to exploit variables that enhance memory—or that those systems that were not conducive to memory died out.

But both Whitehouse and McCauley and Lawson stress that memories neither are lost nor persist unchanged. McCauley and Lawson suggest that memories tend to be more stable for rituals that are in one of the "attractor" positions (i.e., involve a deity as agent and are rarely repeated, or involve a deity as recipient or mediator and are frequently repeated). The evidence for the nature and potency of "attractor" positions requires further explication. Are they called "attractors" simply because rituals with the specified characteristics tend to be stable? "Attractor" implies movement toward these positions. Is this movement gradual or sudden? What are the forces that influence it? Whitehouse suggests that the subjective experience of the validity of the understandings gained may be an important issue, and evidence from a different context indicates that he is on the right track. While memories of their early relationship remained fairly constant over a two-year period for couples who had remained stable in their marital well-being, such memories changed and became more negative in couples who experienced a drop in marital well-being over that period (Holmberg and Veroff 1996). Thus memories that came to appear invalid were changed. That, however, concerns the more subjective interpretation put on the occasion rather than the ritual procedure.

Any insecurity in memory exacerbates the problem of accounting for the reproduction of rarely performed rituals. In discussing memories of imagistic rituals, Whitehouse and McCauley and Lawson rely on Barth's (1975) speculations about the "underlying thematic connections among concrete symbols in different contexts that constitute the knowledge" (67) in initiation ceremonies, and on the role of the seniors in recalling past performances and shaping the next, with social influences playing an important part. Whitehouse suggests that transmission depends on nonlinguistic symbols, the mental imagery being able to organize subsequent ritual performances. When all is said and done, however, it remains that the transmission of imagistic rituals without apparent overt discussion remains somewhat of a mystery.

Two other issues may help here. First, doctrine and rituals may be more likely to be remembered if they are presented to minds susceptible to them (Boyer, 38–43; McCauley and Lawson, 39–41). On this issue, they discuss, and reject, Dawkins's (1976) concept of "memes" as ideational analogues of genes and as possible elements in cultural transmission. This approach supposes that cultures are collections of transmissible units ("memes") that are copied by individuals and thus come to be shared by groups of individuals. The meme concept has been effectively criticized already (e.g., recently by Midgley 2003). Cultural transmission is not merely a matter of passing on items of information, but involves both selection by individuals (some items are more easily transmitted than others; some appeal to some minds and not to others) and change in the items in the process. In addition, there is a real difficulty in supposing that "culture" can be divided into isolatable chunks. That minds not only select in assimilating items from others, but also manipulate those items in the process, must be borne in mind when considering religious transmission. In addition, the concept of "susceptibility" lends itself to circular argument (see discussion of the instinct fallacy above); and, while "susceptibility" may contribute to memory, some well-remembered items were totally unexpected.

Second, developmental factors facilitating intergenerational transmission have been inadequately considered. Studies of western Christianity have shown the importance of processes of enculturation by example, "through the skin" as it were, as well as by doctrinal instruction. In our own culture, children of practicing Christians are taken to church long before they have any comprehension of what it means. When there, they do what other people do (with some parental guidance aided by social referencing in this situation of social uncertainty [Emde 1984]). Best clothes and the church atmosphere mark the situation as special, and the procedures are simply accepted. The religious system is reconstructed into the self-system as part of life (Granqvist, in press; Hood et al. 1996). It seems reasonable to suppose that the same would be true at least of second-generation converts to missionary Christianity in Melanesia. And it is difficult to believe that something similar does not occur even in the imagistic mode. During development, naturally occurring fears and anxieties are likely to be associated with cultural ideas of the supernatural as portrayed in myths and thus provide a basis from which interpretations, perhaps idiosyncratic, of traumatic rituals could be built. Children who have a view of the world as stable find the supernatural exciting just because anything might happen (Harris 1994, 1997). The rituals are certainly out of the ordinary, but, if cosmological issues are not discussed, they alone could hardly transmit the religious tradition as a whole.

MISCELLANEOUS ISSUES

In this section I raise some other issues that arise from considering this material.

Precision in the Use of Terms

At an early stage in research, it is often necessary to use descriptive terms and explanatory concepts rather loosely. As research progresses, however, it is necessary to sharpen them up. One example is "sensory pageantry," defined by McCauley and Lawson (103) as "the stimulation of participants' various sensory modes in order to arouse their emotions." What exactly does that include? Traumatic experiences in ritual? Apparently having a ritual bath is not included (McCauley and Lawson, 151), but yet nudity is? Not the sacrifice of ritual participants (190)? But both food deprivation and gluttony (188)?

As another example, is the characteristic of "cognitively optimal" applied to an anthropomorphic representation of a deity the same as when it is applied to a narrative (Whitehouse 2004b)? But it is easy to press this point too far: perhaps some will object to the use of the word "mind" in this chapter.

DIRECTION OF CAUSATION

There are dangers in specifying the direction of causation when dealing with what are essentially observational and correlational data. McCauley and Lawson often specify the direction of causation. For instance, they argue that an increase in sensory pageantry may occur "in order not only to" augment recall but also to increase motivation, and that rituals involving high arousal "will inevitably" take the form of a ritual in which the deity is the actor (188). Is it plausible to suggest that rituals develop high levels of "sensory pageantry" in order to overcome tedium, and *then* take the form of special agent rituals (190)? And how can a system invent rituals (McCauley and Lawson, 189)?

Whitehouse is generally more cautious, describing the different characteristics as "coalescing" or causation as being bidirectional. Later (2004a, 2004b) he was more specific, stating for instance that certain features of the doctrinal mode (e.g., diffuse cohesion, dynamic leadership, large-scale membership) will invariably be associated with high-frequency, low-arousal rituals. It seems likely that changes are often transactional and diachronic (see above). Precision in specifying the direction of effects must be a constant goal, but speculations about the direction of causation based on data that are essentially correlational must be treated with caution.

CONCLUSION

The issues raised in this chapter are heterogenous, but concern primarily the following:

1. The importance of description and resynthesis as a preliminary to analysis. This is as much part of the ethnographical approach as the biological. But it is easy to forget that there are dangers in considering the components in isolation.
2. The primary focus on ritual is questioned. The role of doctrine may be more important in distinguishing modes.
3. The occurrence and nature of revelation, especially in the imagistic mode, requires elucidation.
4. There is need to distinguish causal, developmental, functional, and evolutionary questions and to consider their interrelations. For instance, explanations of religiosity in terms of the receptivity of the mind

are incomplete: one needs also to understand why some hypothetical entities to which the mind is receptive are treated as sacred and others are not.

5. Caution is necessary in postulating basic psychological characteristics or special cognitive mechanisms. Circular reasoning can easily lead to the "instinct fallacy."

6. The multiplicity of causation and the ubiquitous influence of a variety of social processes, including dialectical influences between what people do or believe and what they are supposed to do or believe, must always be borne in mind in considering complex human activities.

7. Changes between modes are at least likely to be due to multiple causes.

8. The efficiency of memory mechanisms must not be overrated. Cosmological ideas acquired early in life may facilitate the transmission of religious systems.

ACKNOWLEDGMENTS

I am deeply indebted to Harvey Whitehouse for extended discussions about the issues raised in this paper. His willingness to discuss differences and criticisms objectively has been to me both a stimulus and an example. I hope that it will be apparent that this picking around the periphery of his ideas involves no doubts about the fertility of the whole. The theoretical ideas advanced both by Harvey Whitehouse and by Bob McCauley and Tom Lawson have led to important advances in the understanding of religious systems. I am grateful to both Harvey and to Bob McCauley for painstaking and helpfully penetrating comments on an earlier version of this chapter.

APPENDIX

Boyer has provided an important and stimulating account of religion from the perspective of a cognitive psychologist. In it he goes to some lengths to criticize the view that the needs satisfied by religious involvement are an important issue for its understanding. Since this is contrary to a view that I have advocated elsewhere, I feel entitled to defend it, but in doing so I would like to reaffirm my admiration for the magnitude of his achievement.

Boyer cites a number of popular views of the origin of religions in terms of the beneficial consequences that they provide. He rejects such arguments in general because the beneficial consequences of religious systems differ between societies. Thus no one of them can serve as the origin of all religions. With that there is no dispute, but there can be no doubt that some are important to many people in many cultures. It is important here not to think in terms of single factors. The appeal of a religious system may depend on different things for different people. A given consequence may be ineffective in one context, but important in another. Boyer dismisses the consequences of religious systems (I to IV below) for the reasons given at A, B, and so on, as indicated below. But his arguments are not all equally valid, for reasons given in italics.

I. Religion satisfies the mind's demands for explanations of natural or mental phenomena, the origins of things, or the existence of evil and suffering.
    A. The urge to explain the universe is not the origin of religion. *But it is a consequence of belief that makes religion attractive to some people.*
    B. General explanations are not universally desired, but explanations of specific phenomena. *Agreed. Religious explanations are used for many specific phenomena by many people.*
    C. Religious explanations differ from the explanations that we normally use in that they invoke complex and far-fetched scenarios. *Agreed, but they are used primarily for phenomena where ordinary explanations are not available.*
II. Religion allays anxieties and makes mortality more acceptable.
    A. Religious concepts do not always provide reassurance or comfort. *Agreed, but often they do, and whether they instill comfort or fear depends in part on how the system is manipulated by religious specialists.*
    B. Facts are awe inspiring only in places where a local theory provides a solution or cure. Therefore rituals might create the need, or each reinforces the other. *But (a) this does not apply to mortality, (b) evil witches and the like are only personifications of real fears of death or misfortune, (c) belief in witches and other evil influences may be exacerbated by the religious specialists whose position depends on dealing with them.*
    C. Anxieties are ubiquitous, so religious comforts are not doing a very good job. *But if anxieties did not prevail, individuals would take no precautions against mishaps. (Boyer makes a related point on p. 25).*
    D. Deliverance from mortality is not universally desired. *Agreed, but it is pretty potent for many people.*
    E. Reassuring religion is not found in places where life is dangerous. *But in such places it is essential that anxieties should prevail or individuals would not be able to cope with them.*
    F. People do not worry so much about mortality in general, but about their own death. *Boyer does not deny that religion provides comfort in the face of death. (There are, of course, also other ways of coming to terms with one's own death—see Lifton 1979; Hood and Morris 1983).*

III. Religion is a good thing for society.
  A. Religion holds society together. *Boyer denies this, on the grounds that the needs to keep society together or maintain morality cannot create an institution. But social integration is a beneficial consequence of many (all?) religious systems, and charismatic figures like Moses may deliberately inculcate religion and ethics with that goal in mind (e.g., Whitehouse 2000). However Boyer argues, and I agree, that the connection between religion and the social order may not be as simple as that. Elsewhere I have argued that some basic principles affecting social behavior are common to all societies, and are ultimately the product of natural selection acting through the beneficial consequences of group living. These basic principles give rise to moral precepts that are more or less culture specific through dialectical and diachronic transactions between what individuals do and what they are supposed to do over prehistorical and historical time. And religion has been used to purvey the moral code, although along the way it may have been manipulated by priests or rulers in their own interests (Hinde 2002). Thus religion facilitates group living and morality in part by providing a framework and sanctions.*

IV. Religion is an illusion. *That this is inadequate as an explanation for the origin of religion needs no comment.*

Boyer argues further that we must search not for one cause for the diversity of religions, but for the ways in which fewer variants of religious systems have been selected from the many potential ones. Agreed, and the consequences are just what cultural selection acts upon.

NOTES

1. All page references are to these books unless otherwise stated.

2. Later they refer to the conceptual schemes of rituals, and this presumably implies the importance of meaning in relation to belief (17).

3. An alternative model for the moral sense is based on the concept of the self-system or self-concept. We all have a view of the sort of person that we are, and that includes our values (e.g., one sees oneself as honest). Individuals strive to maintain congruency between how they see themselves, how they see themselves behaving, and how they perceive others to perceive them. Thus if P considers himself to be intelligent, but O implies he is not or P finds himself unable to solve a simple problem, P experiences emotion. He may try to prove O wrong, or find a reason to discount his testimony, or try to convince himself of his intelligence (Backman 1988). This can be extended to the moral sphere. If P considers himself to be honest, but finds he has behaved dishonestly, he experiences emotion in the form of guilt and may endeavor

to correct his behavior (Hinde 2002). Thus morality does not require the postulation of a special system.

REFERENCES

Backman, C. W. 1988. The Self: A Dialectical Approach. *Advances in Experimental Social Behavior* 21: 229–60.

Barth, F. 1975. *Ritual and Knowledge among the Baktaman of New Guinea.* New Haven: Yale University Press.

———. 1987. *Cosmologies in the Making: A Generative Approach to Cultural Variation in Inner New Guinea.* Cambridge: Cambridge University Press.

Bartlett, F. 1932. *Remembering: A Study in Experimental and Social Psychology.* Cambridge: Cambridge University Press.

Bindra, D. 1959. *Motivation: A Systematic Reinterpretation.* New York: Ronald.

Bloch, M. 1992. *Prey into Hunter: The Politics of Religious Experience.* Cambridge: Cambridge University Press.

Bottéro, J. 1992. *Mesopotamia: Writing, Reasoning, and the Gods.* Chicago, IL: University of Chicago Press.

Boyer, P. 1994. *The Naturalness of Religious Ideas.* Berkeley, CA: University of California Press.

———. 2002. *Religion Explained: The Evolutionary Origins of Religious Thought.* London: Vintage.

Byrne, D., D. Nelson, and K. Reeves. 1966. Effects of Consensual Validation and Invalidation on Attraction as a Function of Verifiability. *Journal of Experimental Social Psychology* 2: 98–107.

Chevalier, J., and A. Gheerbrandt. 1982. *Dictionary of Symbols.* London: Penguin.

Dawkins, R. 1976. *The Selfish Gene.* Oxford: Oxford University Press.

Emde, R. 1984. The Affective Self. In *Frontiers of Infant Psychiatry*, vol. 2, ed. J. D. Call, E. Galenson, and R. L. Tyson. New York: Basic Books.

Goody, J. 2000. *The European Family.* Oxford: Blackwell.

Granqvist, P. In press. Attachment Theory and Religious Conversions: A Review, and a Resolution of the Classic and Contemporary Paradigm Chasm. *Review of Religious Research.*

Guthrie, S. 1993. *Faces in the Clouds.* New York: Oxford University Press.

Harris, P. L. 1994. Unexpected, Impossible and Magical Events: Children's Reactions to Violations. *British Journal of Developmental Psychology* 12: 1–7.

———. 1997. The Last of the Magicians? Children, Scientists, and the Invocation of Hidden Causal Powers. *Child Development* 68: 1018–20.

Hinde, R. A. 1999. *Why Gods Persist.* London: Routledge.

———. 2002. *Why Good is Good.* London: Routledge.

Hinde, R.A., and J. Stevenson-Hinde, eds. 1973. *Constraints on Learning: Limitations and Predispositions.* London: Academic Press.

Holmberg, D., and J. Veroff. 1996. Rewriting Relationship Memories. In *Knowledge Structures in Close Relationships*, ed. G. J. O. Fletcher and J. Fitness, 345–68. Hillsdale, NJ: Erlbaum.

Hood, R. W., and R. J. Morris. 1983. Towards a Theory of Death Transcendence. *Journal for the Scientific Study of Religion* 22: 353–65.

Hood, R. W., M. Spilka, B. Hunsberger, and R. Gorsuch. 1996. *The Psychology of Religion*. New York: Guilford.

Juillerat, B. 1992. *Shooting the Sun: Ritual and Meaning in West Sepik*. Washington, DC: Smithsonian Institution Press.

Koffka, K. 1935. *Principles of Gestalt Psychology*. New York: Harcourt, Brace.

Lifton, R. J. 1961/1989. *Thought Reform and the Psychology of Totalism*. Chapel Hill, NC: University of North Carolina Press.

———. 1979. *The Broken Connection*. New York: Simon and Schuster.

Lorenz, K. 1935. Der Kumpan in des Umwelt des Vogels. *Journal für Ornothologie* 83: 137–213, 289–413.

McCauley, R. N., and E. T. Lawson. 2002. *Bringing Ritual to Mind: Psychological Foundations of Cultural Forms*. Cambridge: Cambridge University Press.

MacCorquodale, K., and P. E. Meehl. 1954. In *Modern Learning Theory*, ed. Estes et al. New York: Appleton Century Crofts.

Malinowski, B. 1954. *A Scientific Theory of Culture*. Chapel Hill, NC: University of North Carolina Press.

Midgley, M. 2003. *The Myths We Live By*. London: Routledge.

Saltman, M. 1985. The Law is an Ass: An Anthropological Appraisal. In *Reason and Morality*, ed. J. Overing, 226–39. London: Tavistock.

Schwartz, T. 1962. The Paliau Movement in the Admiralty Islands, 1946–1954. *Anthropological Papers of the American Museum of Natural History* 49: 210–421.

Seligman, M. E. P., and J. L. Hager, eds. 1972. *Biological Boundaries of Learning*. New York: Appleton Century Crofts.

Singer, M. T., and R. Ofshe. 1990. *Psychiatric Annals* 20: 4. (Not consulted in the original.)

Thorpe, W. H. 1969. *Bird Song*. Cambridge: Cambridge University Press.

Tinbergen, N. 1951. *The Study of Instinct*. Oxford: Clarendon.

———. 1963. On the Aims and Methods of Ethology. *Zeitschrift für Tierpsychologie* 20: 410–33.

Whitehouse, H. 2000. *Arguments and Icons: Divergent Modes of Religiosity*. Oxford: Oxford University Press.

———. 2002. Modes of Religiosity: Towards a Cognitive Explanation of the Sociopolitical Dynamics of Religion. *Method and Theory in the Study of Religion* 14: 293–315.

———. 2004a. *Modes of Religiosity: A Cognitive Theory of Cultural Transmission*. London: AltaMira.

———. 2004b. Toward a Comparative Anthropology of Religion. In H. Whitehouse.

———. 2004c. and J. Laidlaw, eds. *Ritual and Memory: Toward a Comparative Anthropology of Religion*. Walnut Creek, CA: AltaMira.

Woodworth, R. S. 1918. *Dynamic Psychology*. New York: Columbia University Press.

3

Ritual Form and Ritual Frequency: From Ethnographic Reports to Experimental Findings

E. Thomas Lawson

One of the crucial issues we face in theorizing about the relationships between cognitive processes and cultural forms involves the dynamics of cultural transmission. Cultural forms come in many guises: the tip of the hat, the scarification of the face, the sacrifice of a lamb, the rituals leading to the enthronement of a king, and the secret whisperings in subterranean caverns are just a handful of examples of an indefinitely large number of cultural forms that human minds generate, transmit, and acquire. Of particular interest to those of us pursuing theoretical developments in the cognitive science of religion is one kind of cultural form: religious rituals. These cultural forms intrigue us because, despite their lack of apparent utility and their expense in terms of time and energy, they are nevertheless both widespread and recurrent features of cultural systems both geographically and historically. Though the contents of these cultural forms vary from situation to situation, their cultural shapes, when viewed from a sufficiently abstract level, reveal certain general properties that invite investigation and explanatory theorizing. What we would like to understand and explain is what is involved in making it likely that such cultural forms will be transmitted despite their problematic status from a common-sense point of view.

One way of dealing with this transmission problem is to analyze the ways in which ritual knowledge informs religious ritual practices either intuitively or explicitly. What variables can account for successful transmission? On the face of it, the transmission of any cultural form is not particularly problematic if we focus on those forms that are repeated frequently. In a bygone era, for example, the cultural act of a gentleman tipping his hat when passing a lady on the street was transmitted effortlessly from father to son and from generation to generation—until hats began to go out of fashion. Every boy during the Victorian era knew that the rules of politeness required such an action both because he was told in no uncertain terms that this was the right thing to do, but also because he observed it so frequently. Any cultural action performed frequently enough is likely to be remembered, and any action remembered has a good chance of being transmitted. As every anthropologist has discovered, when the people they are studying are asked why they do certain things, they are frequently told, "Because we have always done it that way." Sometimes, of course, the person being interviewed is willing to speculate about the reasons why, and occasionally one even finds someone who is willing to act as an expert interpreter, but much of the time the reasons for actions performed are simply referred to the "tradition." While there might be an interesting story to tell about the transmission of any cultural form from an epidemiological point of view, in this chapter I shall focus on issues involving the transmission of ritual knowledge and argue that *ritual form* is the principal variable that determines a ritual's performance frequency and, therefore, the probability of its successful cultural transmission.

Harvey Whitehouse, in a number of important and admirable works (1992, 1995, 2000, 2004), has advanced a set of intriguing cognitive proposals about religious modes that are directly relevant to issues concerning cultural transmission. What I wish to suggest in this chapter is that the outcome of these proposals by Whitehouse can be enhanced by paying attention to the ritual form hypothesis that McCauley and I have put forward (McCauley and Lawson 2002). We think that ritual form provides a solid cognitive foundation for Whitehouse's theory of religious modes. My aim is, therefore, constructive in that it suggests a missing element in an otherwise elegant theory. What motivates this suggestion is an interest that both Whitehouse and McCauley and I have in the connections between religious ritual and the dynamics of both human memory and motivation as well as the relevance of these connections for a deeper understanding of the processes of cultural transmission. Whitehouse and McCauley and I together insist that any theory about social and cultural forces that does not refer to the micromechanisms of cognition and cultural communication will fail to account for some of the most significant and interesting features of religious ritual behavior as these take shape in the processes of cultural transmission (Whitehouse 1995, 220; McCauley and Lawson 2002).

Whitehouse has argued that the frequency of ritual performance is the critical variable that determines how much emotional stimulation any ritual will require in order to make its transmission likely. Stated most succinctly, Whitehouse claims that the amount of sensory pageantry and, therefore, the amount of emotional stimulation any religious ritual involves are inversely proportional to the frequency with which that ritual is performed. This is an interesting and fruitful claim. McCauley and I agree with Whitehouse that processes of cultural transmission have rendered mnemonic considerations crucial for understanding why some religious rituals incorporate more emotionally arousing features than others do. In fact, as McCauley and I have argued in *Bringing Ritual to Mind*, we share *three* assumptions with Whitehouse: (1) that participants find rituals that are loaded with sensory pageantry emotionally provocative, (2) that, whatever the mechanisms, this emotional provocation tends to increase the probabilities that at least some features of these rituals will prove more memorable than they would otherwise be, and (3) that such emotional provocation also increases the probabilities that participants will be motivated to transmit their religious representations to others, thus increasing the probability of their cultural success (McCauley and Lawson 2002, 103).

Our major difference with Whitehouse lies in identifying *which* rituals include such emotionally arousing features. In other words, McCauley and I are concerned to specify the conditions under which rituals will typically include not only instances but also varying degrees of emotional arousal. I should add that it is primarily because of the excellent fieldwork that Whitehouse has engaged in, and his fine-grained description of particular ritual actions in Melanesia, that we now possess the information that makes possible an appeal to a set of ethnographic facts capable of providing evidence for fueling both our agreements and disagreements. Ideally, of course, it would greatly enhance the plausibility of both the ritual form and the ritual frequency hypotheses if we could go beyond ethnographic data by adding the kind of confirming or disconfirming evidence that experimental work could provide. When relevant, I shall refer to experiments that have in fact been performed as well as others that are now in the making.

As is clear from Whitehouse's ethnographic reports, in the life of a participant in the religious ritual systems that he has studied, some rituals are performed with greater frequency than others. Furthermore, given an obvious variation from one religious ritual system to another, most one-off rituals are replete with sensory pageantry in relation to other rituals in the same system, while most repeated rituals lack the attendant emotional stimulation. The infrequently performed rituals are typically magnificent, boisterous, loud, attention-grabbing events that stand out in relation to other rituals in that same system in often vivid contrast. These rituals may also be traumatic, painful, and even humiliating in their effects on the patients undergoing the ritual acts. But whether joyous or painful, such one-off rituals are capable of capturing the attention of the ritual participants because of the sensory pageantry that attends them. In contrast, the frequently performed rituals are typically restrained, quiet, run-of-the-mill, even boring, repetitive actions that border on being habitual practices requiring little energy to perform. Most scholars who study religious ritual systems seem to recognize the difference between these kinds of rituals. They recognize, for example, the difference between a simple act of anointing oneself with oil and acting as the patient of a set of life-altering acts that permanently change one's status in a rite of passage.

On the face of it, it would seem that both kinds of rituals stand a significant chance of being transmitted across the generations because, in the case of rituals loaded with sensory pageantry and provocative stimulation, these very features almost guarantee their memorability and, therefore, their transmittability. Whether producing experiences of ecstasy or suffering, their memorability is substantially increased by their appeal to, and occasionally their assault on, the senses. Moreover, in the case of the run-of-the mill ritual acts, their very frequency would seem to be sufficient to ensure their successful transmission. Anything rehearsed repeatedly stands an excellent chance of being remembered. So far, so good. McCauley and I think, however, that there is a deeper story to tell because *not all religious rituals are created equal.* Rituals vary not only in their frequency but also in their form. We need, therefore, to pay very close attention to the form of the ritual if we are to develop an explanatory understanding of just how the dynamics of memory and emotional arousal play a role in cultural transmission.

With respect to the form of a ritual, while *all* rituals involve an agent acting upon a patient, typically by means of some instrument, some rituals focus on the quality of the *agent* performing the ritual, some on the qualities of the *instrument,* and some on the qualities of the *patient,* the recipient of the ritual acts. *Special agent rituals* are those types of ritual in which the most direct connection with the gods is through the role of the current ritual's agent, for example a priest, by the power of the gods, initiating an uninitiated person into a group of initiands. *Special instrument rituals* and *special patient rituals* are ones in which the most direct connection to the gods is either through the patient (rather than the agent) or through the act itself and whatever instruments may be employed in the performing of the act. However, the surface features of a ritual's form do not indicate everything that is important for understanding their structure because any particular ritual action frequently presupposes prior ritual actions that have a logical and temporal connection to them. For example, in order for a ritual agent to be able to perform a ritual such as the initiation of a ritual participant into a cohort, the agent performing the ritual of initiation would already have had to be a participant in a previously performed ritual that qualified him to perform the initiation. This means that some rituals enable other rituals. A full structural description of a ritual, therefore, will disclose hidden features not obvious to a surface examination. It is as if the prior rituals are embedded in the overall structure of the ritual. This means that a complete description of a ritual will often disclose a great deal of complexity, because the ritual act under observation will presuppose hidden levels that are not at all obvious simply by paying attention to the immediate acts.

Given this structural complexity and given the specific ways in which the special qualities differentiate agents, instruments, and patients, the question becomes, *which* rituals will incorporate varying levels of sensory pageantry? This is where we differ most significantly from the approach that Whitehouse has adopted. Our view is that in any particular religious ritual system, *the special agent rituals will typically incorporate higher levels of sensory pageantry in relationship to all of the other rituals endemic to that system.* We also claim that the *participants in the ritual performance will have strong intuitions leading to judgments about their structure*, intuitions that can be teased out by carefully designed experiments. On the basis of very limited experimental evidence, it seems that such intuitions do, in fact, play a significant role in making the ritual memorable and transmissible (Barrett and Lawson 2001; Malley and Barrett, forthcoming).

There are a number of considerations that need to be clarified in this claim. The most important of these is that judging what level of sensory pageantry is actually involved in a ritual system will be a *comparative* matter. So, the level of sensory pageantry in religious ritual system A, where the ritual involved is a special agent ritual, will not necessarily be equivalent to the ritual with the same form in system B or C. But in system A, B, and C, or any other religious ritual system for that matter, the level of sensory pageantry will typically be higher in special agent than in special instrument and special patient rituals, even though these levels might not be equivalent across systems. Obviously this claim is subject to empirical confirmation by appealing to ethnographic reports and the intuitive judgments made by subjects in experiments designed to test the claims involved. Whitehouse's ethnography about the evolution of the Dadul Maranagi splinter group's ritual innovations has provided especially telling examples capable of supporting his claims about the levels of sensory pageantry and our claims about the role of ritual form in the types of ritual that occur.[1]

In the creation of new religious ritual systems or the reinvigorating of old ones, one of the intriguing puzzles is how the individuals responsible for establishing novel ritual systems or breathing new life into existing ones know what to do to increase the probability of either their short-term or occasionally their long-term success. (Of course the ones who are not successful in this endeavor do not get the chance to make history.) The two basic problems facing individuals in the process of either creating religious ritual innovations or reinvigorating extant ones involve (1) the difficulty of motivating people to follow their lead and (2) the challenge of ensuring the memorability of the rituals they are creating or reinvigorating. The obstacles the ritual systems face that innovators have brought about and inspired are tedium and habituation, the latter often leading to the danger of sensory overload. Tedium is the consequence of doing the same thing again and again and again. Habituation opens the door to sensory overload. It is the consequence of having too much of a good thing. It is like having ice cream five times a day every day. Surfeit sets in. Religious ritual innovation is no easy road to travel. The moral is that good things come in small doses, but if you have to do some things repeatedly, you had better have an outlet to balance the repetition with occasional surprises that either delight or terrify.

When religious ritual innovation appears, especially in a system burdened with the same old same old, it seems obvious that special agent rituals will have to bear the motivational burden because their very infrequency marks them as being something very special in the life trajectory of an individual. After all, if we only go through this once, it had better be a powerful experience that sets it aside from the daily grind. Because these special agent rituals are typically one-off events, they will need to be suitably marked off from the rest of the ritual actions to ensure that they are remembered. Only if they are remembered will they be transmitted to the next generation. Thus individuals designing a new religious ritual tradition would have to take such matters into consideration. However, there is little evidence that these innovators explicitly make such plans or think such matters through dispassionately. It seems to be the case that some innovators just have the right intuitions about what will work and what won't. It is equally important to insist, therefore, that the successful transmission story must be at least partially a selectionist one. Novel ritual systems just happen to be successful to the extent that the innovators possess the appropriate intuitions and recognize the advantage of incorporating the ritual features that will motivate the followers and ensure that some of the rituals contain a sufficient amount of sensory pageantry to increase the probability of their transmission. Such success will also be enhanced to the extent that obstacles such as tedium and habituation leading to sensory overload are either avoided or held to a minimum. It is worthwhile emphasizing that environmental conditions play a significant selective role in the possibility and likelihood of transmission. After all, you might have a powerful new idea that even persuades a number of people to adopt your insights and perform the rituals associated with them, but if you are all wiped out in a sandstorm in the desert, the unrecorded insights will have been discovered in vain.

In the light of these considerations, analyzing the religions of humankind and the ritual behavior they typically include seems to disclose a number of patterns. We do find, for example, some religious systems that have rituals that have only special patient rituals with little sensory pageantry. Such systems are always in danger of falling prey to the tedium effect. Unless they are energized by the infusion of special agent rituals by prophetic individuals intent on shaking up the system and even breaking away from it, they tend to tread dangerous territory where they face the threat of fading away or going into precipitous decline. It is also possible for such breakaway groups to run into trouble because they might have special agent rituals but overdo them.

This is the "too much of a good thing syndrome." Whitehouse's ethnography has provided a wonderful example of the Pomio Kivung religious system that initially contains only special patient rituals leading to the tedium effect and having to be cyclically energized by the introduction of special agent rituals inspired by breakaway prophets. Whitehouse has provided compelling evidence for a kind of oscillating from boredom to excitement to boredom. This oscillation points to a highly unstable and unbalanced system that seems to survive only in virtue of its oscillation.

What then would a balanced system be like? It would clearly have to incorporate both special agent and special patient (and special instrument) rituals in order to ensure the appropriate motivational and mnemonic effects and in order to avoid the obstacles associated with tedium and habituation. Even then, however, such systems are not home free. Splinter movements can and do occur in such systems as well. The reasons appear to be that such splintering occurs for conceptual reasons. What happens in such cases is that the groups that break off from the primary system either become extinct or become independent religions with their own form of balance incorporating special agent rituals as well as special instrument and special patient rituals. However, conceptual control can become excessive, and in such situations there is the danger of diminishing sensory pageantry. Excessive conceptual control, which can emerge in what Whitehouse has referred to as doctrinal systems, involves a preoccupation with the development of ever more sophisticated theological pursuits that lead to more and more fine-grained distinctions more and more removed from what Barrett and Keil (1996) have called online religious reasoning. This tends to produce the requirement that religious ritual participants pay undue attention to being "theologically correct" (Slone 2004).

While excessive attention to theological nuance makes it probable that a strong intellectual tradition within a religious tradition can be maintained over a significant period of time among an elite group of intellectuals, it can have a profoundly dampening effect on a vital religious system in which ritual participants live with the knowledge that when the gods do things, their actions (via the mediators who represent them) are worth celebrating in very special ways on very special occasions. Such participants also know that these gods need to be attended to on a regular basis. As recipients of the ritual gifts of the gods that serve to mark, for example, the important transitions of life, the religious ritual participants are secure in the knowledge that only what the gods do can they undo. They also know that the knowledge of these gifts is worth perpetuating, and therefore they will be motivated to transmit this information and these practices. The gods may only act when they please, and when they do so, the effects will be important enough to celebrate or to endure with suffering depending upon what they require of the participants. However, they will require close attention by small and frequent, even insignificant, acts. These two factors seem to be worth transmitting to those who follow.

The cognitive science of religion, as the above discussion shows, is clearly entering a period of intense examination of various proposals aiming to account for the complex ways in which our rapidly developing knowledge of cognition is beginning to provide a deeper explanatory understanding of cultural transmission. What is called for is not only more penetrating empirical work of the kind practiced by Harvey Whitehouse in his ethnographic studies, but also a wide range of experimental investigation into the ways in which microprocesses of transmission lead to a better understanding of culture. As I have already hinted at above, such experimental investigation is beginning to happen with greater frequency and with intriguing results. I am happy to report that those aspects of the ritual frequency hypothesis involving emotional arousal have begun to be subjected to experimental tests, for example, Whitehouse's claim that one-off rituals that are emotionally arousing will lead to spontaneous exegetical reflection with a consequence for issues involving transmission. If such low-frequency, high-arousal rituals did not contain such features, they would prove incapable of instilling the kinds of memories and stimulating the kinds of motivations that would increase their chances of transmission. In chapter 7 of this volume, Richert, Whitehouse, and Stewart report on a set of experiments designed to test the hypothesis that levels of arousal during ritual performances will correlate directly with levels of spontaneity, connectivity, and structural depth. The specific aim of the experiments focused on whether participants taking part in a ritual that possessed highly arousing features were more likely to employ analogical reasoning leading to spontaneous exegetical reflection than were participants performing in rituals with low arousing qualities. Subjects in these experiments consisted of two groups, one of which participated in a ritual in which the accompanying features involved low emotional arousal, and the other, high emotional arousal. In one experimental condition, each subject individually and alone engaged in a series of prescribed ritual acts in a controlled environment involving low emotional arousal, for example by hearing quietly performed music at specific junctures, whereas in the other condition, each subject was surrounded by very loud music as they were performing certain prescribed acts. The subjects in both groups were not only given initial exit interviews but also were interviewed again one month later. The investigators hoped that, having been exposed to a one-off, unknown ritual, and taking into consideration the different level of emotional arousal in each condition, the subjects would not only engage in analogical reasoning about what these novel acts they had been asked to perform might mean, but that there would be a differential response on the part of subjects in the high-arousal condition. Would participants in the high-arousal condition engage in deeper reflection on the possible meaning of the acts they had been asked to perform than those in the low-arousal condition? While I will leave it to the investigators to state and discuss what they think these experiments demonstrate, I would like to discuss what I take to be some significant features of the data from the experiments that they have kindly shared with me.

First, these experiments confirm that there is a difference in response on the part of subjects in low-arousal and high-arousal conditions. This is good news for both the ritual frequency and the ritual form hypotheses, because, as I pointed out earlier, all of us engaged in this discussion of the relative merits of the two hypotheses expect emotional arousal to play a significant role in memory dynamics. Of course the issue of the accuracy of memory has exercised a number of investigators, but there are good reasons to believe (1) that accuracy, while not irrelevant, is not a necessary condition for transmission and (2) even if it were, there are certain conditions in which the cognitive alarm hypothesis plays a key role in making accuracy of transmission likely (McCauley and Lawson 2002, 77). The cognitive alarm hypothesis involves the claim that sudden, substantial emotional arousal acts as a warning or attention-grabbing device. It demands that what is happening to us require our attention. In the high-arousal condition of the experiments under discussion, the subjects certainly do respond differentially to the introduction of sudden onslaughts of sound not only by their reports but also by their objectively monitored galvanic skin responses. A significant number of the subjects reported the emotion of fright.

Second, both initially and in the longer term, the subjects did seem to engage in the type of reflection about the possible meanings of the acts they had been asked to perform. Obviously part of this tendency toward exegesis is the natural result of human curiosity. When you have been paid to perform strange acts that you have never performed before, you would naturally wonder what these acts could mean, especially when you have been told ahead of time that these were rituals from other societies, the meanings of which the investigators were attempting to reconstruct. But whether this tendency toward curiosity, natural or not, is sufficiently motivating in high-arousal contexts to play a significant role in transmission is still up for grabs. While the results do seem to provide some support for claims about the likelihood of spontaneous exegetical reflection in the high-arousal condition, they do not yet support claims about the relationship between spontaneous exegetical reflection and transmission. Further experiments are called for. It is important for the investigators to show that this type of reflection is an important motivating, causal factor in transmission.

Third, what intrigued and pleased me most in examining the data provided to me by the investigators was the evidence hinting at the possible relevance of the results for the ritual form hypothesis. Remember that McCauley and I have claimed that people have intuitions about ritual form, which means they are sensitive to the differences between the underlying cognitive structures (intuitions) that contribute to the judgments ritual participants are likely to make based upon their implicit understanding of the difference between special agent and special patient rituals. I saw this when I read the subjects' responses to suggestions about their commenting on what they had undergone in these rituals. Some of the subjects seemed to be searching not only for the meaning of what they had undergone, but also, significantly, for what their *role* in the series of acts they had performed might have been. It appeared that they were speculating not only about whether a particular act was, for example, a birthing ritual or an expiatory ritual, but also about whether they themselves were agents or patients in the ritual. One subject, for example, says, "I was like a priest, or maybe the other person who came in was the priest or a god-like being; but standing at the altar was more like a priest sort of thing, so the other person could have been more like a servant."

The Richert, Whitehouse, and Stewart experiments were not designed to test the ritual form hypothesis, and therefore we need to be cautious in drawing any conclusions about the significance of the data for this hypothesis; however the design of the ritual points to possible ways of testing McCauley and Lawson's claims about the role that ritual form plays in cultural transmission. It would be instructive, for example, to design an experiment in such a way that the participants would be required to make a judgment about the difference between a set of acts in which they are clearly the agents rather than the patients of a ritual. The rituals, which the investigators designed, are ambiguous about whether they are special agent or special patient rituals.

Finally, the set of experiments that Richert, Whitehouse, and Stewart have conducted do not meet the challenge posed by Pascal Boyer, who has queried the claim that low-frequency, high-arousal rituals stimulate spontaneous exegetical reflection such that they can motivate the transmission of the knowledge gained to others and to succeeding generations. Even though Richert, Whitehouse, and Stewart produce evidence that spontaneous exegetical reflection does occur in varying degrees in the exit interviews, and that the high-arousal condition is conducive to making analogical connections, the issue of the role that spontaneous exegetical reflection plays in cultural transmission remains a problem. McCauley and I have maintained that transmission can occur even without the participants in ritual assigning meaning to the acts that they perform. Clearly, as the Richert, Whitehouse, and Stewart experiments demonstrate, the meanings produced by the subjects vary from subject to subject. There is no good reason to suspect that this variability of the meanings attributed to the acts performed has an effect on the stability of the underlying forms of the ritual actions. There will still be a difference between a ritual action in which the participant is an agent rather than a patient. Participants will know when they are on the receiving rather than on the giving end of the actions that are taking place in the ritual. There are good reasons for these strong intuitions; our ordinary action representation systems are so structured. Not only do we intuitively know the difference between events and actions, but we also know the difference between the roles that agents and patients play in any set of actions. Such intuitive knowledge is simply our basic cognitive equipment with which we relate to the world.

What is genuinely encouraging about the experimental work that I have briefly commented on is that the cognitive science of religion is moving into that exciting world of inquiry in which the predictions that we make about religious behavior in general and religious ritual behavior in particular on the basis of historical and ethnographic evidence are now proving susceptible to experimental confirmation. This is the mark of a maturing science.

NOTES

1. For a full discussion of these issues see McCauley and Lawson (2002) and Whitehouse (2004).

REFERENCES

Barrett, J., and E. T. Lawson. 2001. Ritual Intuitions: Cognitive Contributions to Judgments of Ritual Efficacy. *Journal of Cognition and Culture* 1: 183–201.

Barrett, J. L., and F. C. Keil. 1996. Conseptionalizing a Nonnatural Entity: Anthropomorphism in God Concepts. *Cognitive Psychology* 31: 219–47.

Malley, B and J. Barrett. Forthcoming.

McCauley, R. N., and E. T. Lawson. 2002. *Bringing Ritual to Mind: Psychological Foundations of Cultural Forms.* Cambridge: Cambridge University Press.

Slone, D. J. 2004. *Theological Incorrectness: Why Religious People Believe What They Shouldn't.* Oxford: Oxford University Press.

Whitehouse, H. 1992. Memorable Religions: Transmission, Codification and Change in Divergent Melanesian Contexts. *Man*, n.s., 27: 777–97.

———. 1995. *Inside the Cult: Religious Innovation and Transmission in Papua New Guinea.* Oxford: Clarendon Press.

———. 2000. *Arguments and Icons: Divergent Modes of Religiosity.* Oxford: Oxford University Press.

———. 2004. *Modes of Religiosity: A Cognitive Theory of Religious Transmission.* Walnut Creek, CA: AltaMira Press.

4

Divergent Religion: A Dual-Process Model of Religious Thought, Behavior, and Morphology

Todd Tremlin

The scientific study of religion is a relatively recent affair. For hundreds of years in the Western world, religion—or more correctly, theology—was regarded as the "queen of the sciences," offering the framework in which all other knowledge was to be explained. Religion itself required no explanation. Divine revelation was accepted both as a sufficient condition for truth and as self-authenticating. Religion provided thought with its interpretive lens; few imagined that thought needed to explicate religion.

Today the study of cognition is not only revealing the processes of the human mind but also explaining many of its products, including religion. From a cognitive standpoint, religion is neither revelatory nor enigmatic nor inexplicable. Religion is simply one outcome of faculties of thought common to all normal brains. Beyond explaining the natural arising and persistence of religious ideas, investigation of cognitive mechanics can also offer explanations for certain behaviors of religious people and the morphology of their religions.

Introducing a dual-process model of cognition to the study of religion, this short chapter argues that a crucial influence on how religious people think and act is the way the human brain handles religious representations. Evidence drawn from social psychology, cognitive psychology, neuroscience, and comparative religion suggests that religious concepts proceed along two contrasting mental pathways to differing effect. This account provides a new way of explaining divergent forms of religious thought, of predicting puzzling divergent religious behaviors (e.g., doctrinal and ritual innovation, revivalism, syncretism, new religions, and conversion), and, ultimately, of mapping an important set of selective forces at work on the shape and stability of religious systems.

A DUAL-PROCESS MODEL OF RELIGIOUS THOUGHT

Take as a starting point some standard anthropological fare. Students of religion have long noted that *religious people* and their *religions* are not always harmonized. Often this disparity is captured in the literature as two contrasting modes of religiosity—one corresponding to an "official" set of beliefs and behaviors prescribed in texts, maintained by institutions, and communicated by specialists, the other a "popular" form of religion practiced by regular people in everyday life. The usual explanations for this phenomenon are sociopolitical in nature. Max Weber distinguishes between routinized and charismatic religious forms (1930, 1947). Ernest Gellner differentiates urban and rural religion (1969). Jack Goody dichotomizes literate and nonliterate religion (1968, 1986). Richard Werbner notes distinctions between regional cults and local cults (1977). Stephen Sharot outlines disparities between a religion of the elites and of the masses (2001). Most recently, Harvey Whitehouse has offered an account of divergent religiosity that suggests religious systems are structured in accord with two modalities—a "doctrinal" mode and an "imagistic" mode—with differing styles of codification, cognitive processing, transmission, and political organization (1995, 2000, 2004).

A truly cognitive explanation for divergent religion begins with individual minds, the source of cultural products. A telling piece of psychological research bearing on this puzzle is Justin Barrett's identification of "theological correctness," which cuts beneath the public appearance of religious knowledge to how such knowledge is privately represented and employed (1998, 1999; Barrett and Keil 1996). In experiments with subjects from diverse cultures and religions, Barrett shows that people hold in their minds two parallel, often incompatible representations of a religious concept like "god," one an explicit, "theological" representation learned through instruction, the other an implicit, "basic" representation rooted in intuitive expectations about intentional agents. Engagement of these representations is related to processing demand, with the theological-level representation used for reflective, "offline" thought, and the basic-level representation employed in real-time, "online" tasks.

Barrett's work is significant on several fronts. First, it highlights an important feature of cognition: in some domains at least, brains employ parallel conceptual/computational strategies. Second, it confirms that built-in cognitive biases operate on religious and nonreligious concepts alike, and that these biases render some religious concepts easier to use than others. Third, it distinguishes between people's professed religious knowledge and the form of religious knowledge they utilize in online thought. Together, these findings cast new light on a cause of divergent religion.

To begin to see how, it is helpful to take a closer look at the nature of the two levels of representation identified by Barrett's work (see figure 4.1).

	Theological Level	Basic Level
Representation	1. Explicit 2. Analytical 3. Abstract	1. Implicit 2. Intuitive 3. Inferentially rich
Computation	4. Slow 5. Reflective 6. Conscious	4. Fast 5. Reflexive 6. Unconscious/automatic

Figure 4.1   Barrett's parallel conceptual/computational strategies

Among the frequently encountered contrasting terms are these: theological representations are *explicit, analytical,* and *abstract,* while basic representations are *implicit, intuitive,* and *inferentially rich.* With respect to the computational process engaged by each level of representation, theological representations employ *slow, reflective* thinking, while basic representations provide for *fast, reflexive* thought. This is because theological representations require *conscious* activation, while basic ones are *unconscious* and automatic.

The coexistence of two fundamentally different conceptual/computational strategies leads one to wonder how both reside in the mind. One fruitful though neglected approach to this question is thinking of the brain using the dual-process models of information processing discussed in social psychology (see Chaiken and Trope 1999). While the available models and theories range broadly, they all connect the presence of two alternative processing modes (with discrete problem domains, rules of operation, brain systems, and affective links) to the way people think about and respond to information—often with great inconsistency. Connecting dual *representation* with dual *processing* may elucidate not only Barrett's discovery of theological correctness but also manifestations of layered thought in nonreligious domains, such as differences between "folk" explanations and scientific ones (McCauley 2000; Keil 2003).

Interestingly, dual-process theorists use precisely the kinds of terms listed in figure 1 when they speak of "two qualitatively different modes of information processing," one a "fast, associative information-processing mode based on low-effort heuristics," the other a "slow, rule-based information-processing mode based on high-effort systematic reasoning" (Chaiken and Trope 1999, ix). A promising example of dual-process-model building is the "cognitive experiential self-theory" (CEST) offered by Seymour Epstein and Rosemary Pacini (see figure 4.2). According to these researchers, the theological-level processing mode, which they would call the "rational system," is a "deliberative, analytical system that operates primarily in a medium of language and is relatively affect-free." It is "capable of high levels of abstraction" but is "inefficient for reacting to everyday events." It also has a "relatively brief evolutionary history." In contrast, the basic-level processing mode, what they would call

Rational System	Experiential System
1. Deliberative, analytical	1. Automatic, rapid, effortless
2. Medium of language	2. Holistic, nonverbal form
3. Relatively affect-free	3. Intimate affect / highly compelling
4. High-level abstractions	4. Crude, concrete conceptions
5. Brief evolutionary history	5. Long evolutionary history

Figure 4.2   Features of the CEST dual-process model

the "experiential system," is a "relatively crude, albeit efficient, system for automatically, rapidly, and effortlessly processing information." It "encodes information in a concrete, holistic, primarily nonverbal form; is intimately linked with affect; and is inherently highly compelling." This system has a "very long evolutionary history and is the same system through which nonhuman, higher-order animals adapt to their environments" (1999, 463).

Parsing the mind in terms of parallel or concurrent processes is neither new nor confined to social psychology. The brain has long been understood to be a complex of specialized processing systems evolved to solve specific computational problems. Research in cognitive psychology, neuroscience, and other related fields has ingeniously teased many of these systems apart, demonstrating some phenomena of mentation, such as vision, to involve analytic, concurrent processing (Van Essen and DeYoe 1995), and others, such as memory, to involve independent, parallel systems (Tulving and Schacter 1990). Crucial cognitive faculties such as attention and language also fit into dual-process frameworks. Indeed, a more gestalt perspective on the brain suggests distinctions between cognitive processes that are cortical and subcortical in nature, as well as between processes related to hemispheric specialization.

Most salient to the current discussion, though, is the brain's use of dual pathways for information processing. Extensive research in cognitive science has demonstrated that information proceeds along two discrete routes, one involving conscious reasoning and decision making, the other involving automatic, unconscious responses. Furthermore, it is clear that conscious reasoning is itself built on tacit inferences and internal calculations beyond phenomenal awareness and voluntary control: "The vast majority of mental processes that control and contribute to our conscious experience happen outside our conscious awareness; we are conscious only of the content of our mental life, not what generates the content" (Gazzaniga et al. 1998, 532).

The evolutionary development of a brain organized to process knowledge along conscious and unconscious pathways is explained in part by Steven Pinker's cost/benefit analysis of information processing. In designing brains best fitted to a "cognitive niche" (Tooby and DeVore 1987), natural selection had to take into account the cost of space, the cost of time, and the cost of resources—costs that necessarily limit access-consciousness. As a result, brains are comprised of specialized processors that achieve computations in the quickest, most efficient way possible. Time-consuming, cognitively expensive reflection is one available option, but real-time thought proceeds with access restrictions: "Only information *relevant* to the problem at hand" is allowed, or "routed," in (Pinker 1997, 138).

The language used to describe conscious versus unconscious processing varies in the literature. Rigorous models have distinguished between "automatic" and "controlled" processing (Schneider and Shiffrin 1977; Shiffrin and Schneider 1977), between "implicit" and "explicit" thought (Holyoak and Spellman 1993), between "reflexive" and "reflective" mental systems (Lieberman et al. 2002), between "intuitive" and "rational" cognition (Denes-Raj and Epstein 1994), and between "associative" and "rule-based" reasoning (Sloman 1996, 1999). One can also refer to the *contents* of these processing paths, as when distinctions are made between "declarative" and "procedural" knowledge, "implicit" and "explicit" memory, and "intuitive" and "reflective" beliefs. Recently, Illka Pyssiäinen has collated the many terms used to describe dual processing along with their affiliated functions, brain structures, computational characteristics, and psychological effects (2003, in press).

As summarized in figure 3, "explicit processing" (to settle on one of the available terms) is both accessible to and requires conscious control, is performed serially, and is slow in execution. The representations this processing system yields are explicit, analytical, abstract, and affect free. In contrast, "implicit processing" (to pick a contrasting term) takes place automatically and reflexively, demands no effort or attention, and performs fast, parallel operations. The products of this processing system are implicit, intuitive, inferentially rich, and highly affective. Three additional, though less technical, terms have been added here to further highlight the qualitative differences between these representations—differences that bear directly on links between cognition and culture. Explicit representations are "learned," their full content acquired through instruction, while implicit representations are "tacit," acquired through innate inference-based construction. Explicit representations are also "malleable," readily open to manipulation or revision, while implicit representations are "rigid," the result of incorrigible default assumptions. Lastly, explicit representations are stored as "propositional" data, while implicit representations are stored as personal, "experiential" data.

At a minimum, then, dual-process models can help make sense of layered thought, for instance in the realm of religion as identified by Barrett. The fact that brains employ parallel conceptual/computational strategies contributes to answers for long-standing questions in religious studies, such as how people simultaneously hold multiple, incongruent religious representations, why abstract theological reflection exists side by side with intuitive forms of religion,

	Explicit processing	*Implicit processing*
Computation	1. Slow	1. Fast
	2. Serial	2. Parallel
	3. Reflective	3. Reflexive
	4. Conscious	4. Unconscious
	5. Controlled	5. Automatic
Representation	1. Explicit	1. Implicit
	2. Analytical	2. Intuitive
	3. Abstract	3. Inferentially rich
	4. Affect-free	4. Highly affective
	5. Learned	5. Tacit
	6. Malleable	6. Rigid
	7. Propositional	7. Experiential

Figure 4.3   Summary of dual processing/representational modes

and why individuals with a firm grasp of their religion's theological concepts generally do not employ them in everyday thought. Theological-level representations and basic-level representations are the products of different processing systems, and are therefore naturally coextant in the same mind.

A second, broader application of a dual-process model of religious thought is its potential as an explanation for divergent religion. How people process religious representations may influence their behavior vis-à-vis their religions. It may be the case that common events of religious change, even the stability and durability of public religious systems themselves, are linked to the same cognitive constraints that govern private religious thought. In order to show how the preceding model might illuminate stability and change in religion, let me begin with Pascal Boyer's engaging conceit—"the tragedy of the theologian."

A DUAL-PROCESS MODEL OF RELIGIOUS BEHAVIOR

Boyer, too, has noted the common discrepancy between "official" and "popular" religion and given the situation a particularly interesting slant (2001). For Boyer, the problem of divergent religiosity is one-sided. Part of the business of religious leaders and literati is instilling in laypeople the utility and relevance of their theological representations. The "tragedy of the theologian" is that this task is doomed to failure. In spite of efforts by religious specialists to define what is theologically correct for their people, "there *always* seem to be some nonstandard beliefs and practices left sticking out" (2001, 281). More trying still, though theologians attempt to get people to *think* according to official concepts, "people always add to or distort the doctrine"

(2001, 281). "Theological *in*correctness," as D. Jason Slone dubs it, appears to be the norm in everyday religious thought (2004).

But why? Recognizing that minds handle information in at least two different ways is not yet to explain why one processing path is chosen over another. Furthermore, it would seem that a religious concept like "god" is a perfect example of a theological-level representation that requires coherent and constant instruction to stabilize and that, therefore, necessarily engages explicit processing. While the first assumption is partly right, the second is mostly wrong. Just what a particular god is like (purpose, powers, principalities, etc.) clearly is the result of deliberate, conscious reflection, but it is not the case that explicit processing is the most natural mental pathway for thinking about gods in general.

Foundational to any discussion of religious representations is the insight that gods are, first and foremost, *intentional agents.* For this reason, many cognitivists studying religion have focused their efforts on the role of agency in religious thought, whether explicating the naturalness and ubiquity of god concepts (Boyer 1994a), charting their place in the structure of religious rituals (Lawson and McCauley 1990; McCauley and Lawson 2002), or defining their "counterintuitive" features (Pyysiäinen 2001; Barrett 2004). Much of the headway made in the new cognitive science of religion is the result of demystifying its subject matter. That gods are intentional agents means that they should be treated not merely as imaginative fictions for hermeneutics but as computational facts of social cognition.

Herein lies the value of looking to cognitive models from social psychology. Though social psychologists are primarily interested in such topics as attribution theory, attitude formation, person perception, persuasion, and stereotyping, they largely agree that humans employ unconscious, spontaneous inferences and associative categories to help them construct and negotiate the social world (e.g., Fiske and Taylor 1991). God concepts also belong to the social world. In studying human perception of and response to agents—whether concrete and familiar or ethereal and counterintuitive—students of social psychology and students of religion are working with the same mental apparatus.

Boyer has been instrumental in delineating the cognitive foundations of god concepts, showing how they connect with intuitive knowledge bases and activate key features of the social mind (2000, 2003). In keeping with tacit assumptions about agents in general, god concepts are naturally represented as beings that are subjective, personal, interactive, and consequential. What is crucial here, however, is seeing that the contract for this mental work is held by the implicit processing system. Mentally building a "god" requires first building a "thinking agent"—a task that all minds carry out with alacrity. Regardless of the theological attributes applied to god concepts, they are continually underwritten by the intuitive ontology and inference connections that make agency detection and theory of mind the powerful, efficient adaptations that they are (Guthrie 1993; Barrett 2000).

Thus in addition to the qualitative differences between theological and basic representations already mentioned, there is also priority within the alternative processing modes. Not only are theological representations structurally parasitic on basic representations, but, given this consolidative relationship, the implicit processing system remains the default mode in online thought. Explicit processing, as a discrete system whose inputs are symbols, language, and logic, is not engaged without conscious effort. Both of these relationships—consolidation in content and priority in processing—are clearly exposed by Barrett's experiments, where cumbersome abstract concepts are shown to rest on first-level, first-use ontology. Yet this model suggests a slight nuance to the explanation for theological correctness. The assumption that online, implicit processing saves time and effort is correct, but where the representation of agents is involved, people default to basic concepts because, more fundamentally, the implicit processing system is the controlling system. As manifest in cases of stereotyping and of theological incorrectness, basic representations govern social thought unless care is taken to override them.

> People use intuitive expectations about how a mind works, which are available automatically since they are constantly activated to make sense of people's behavior at all times. When the task allows for conscious monitoring, we get the theological version; when the task requires fast access, we get the anthropomorphic version. This not only shows that the theological concept has not displaced the spontaneous one but also that it is not stored in the same way. Very likely the theological concept is stored in the form of explicit, sentence-like propositions. In contrast, the spontaneous concept is stored in the format of direct instructions to intuitive psychology, which would explain why it is accessed much faster. (Boyer 2001, 89)

But there is more to this story. While the representation of agents falls primarily to the implicit processing system, people clearly can and do think about agents using explicit reasoning. Indeed, this processing shift is responsible for constructing theological representations; it is the *modus operandi* of "official" religion. Nevertheless, such "cross-system" concepts exist in tension. While the differences between theological and basic representations are manifold, two examples—"computational utility" and "psychological relevance"—will suffice to illustrate the cognitive tension inherent to religious thought.

(1) *Computational utility*: One of the distinctions between the two types of representations is that the theological are *abstract* while the basic are *inferentially rich* (cf. figure 4.3). Against the backdrop of social

cognition, this is a distinction of significance. Because they connect directly with the natural ontological categories and intuitive knowledge bases underpinning implicit processing, basic representations are computationally robust. By contrast, abstract theological representations are not only slow and effortful, grounded as they are in explicit processing, but also offer less inference potential. Theological gods are learned propositions with little functional utility; they do not lead to further inferences. You cannot infer anything from the knowledge that god is impassible, for example, other than that god is impassible. Abstractions like this erode the web of inference connections that make agent concepts useful in the first place. From a processing standpoint, abstract agents make poor computational tools. Barrett seems to be saying much the same thing when he observes that a theological concept might not be "a full-blown concept" that can naturally generate predictions, explanations, and inferences (1998, 616). Rather, theological representations are stored simply as "a list of rehearsed, non-integrated attributes, and have no causal efficacy" (1998, 612).

(2) *Psychological relevance*: We should expect, then, that the computational utility of basic representations—what Sperber and Wilson describe as the relationship between inference potential and computational effort (1995)—lends them greater relevance in the marketplace of ideas. Equally significant to social cognition are the contrasts between theological representations as *propositional* and *affect free* and basic representations as *experiential* and *highly affective* (cf. figure 4.3). In addition to utilizing the ontological categories and intuitive expectations needed to represent agents as such, the implicit processing system also assigns intentional agents social meaning and personal relevance by connecting theory of mind with theory of self. Furthermore, implicit processing does not operate in an affect-free way but is tied with the brain's emotion systems. As Smith and DeCoster report, the implicit processing mode "generates what are experienced as affective responses to objects and events" (1999, 328). Representations produced via this processing system come complete with emotional coloring that makes them more evocative and relevant. It is this experiential characteristic of basic representations that leads researchers to attribute the mediation of motivation to the implicit processing system; many agree, for example, that in the realm of social cognition, "experiencing is believing."

As noted in figure 4.4, all of this is unlike the affect-free propositions of theological reasoning, whose abstract qualities both minimize their computational utility and reduce their psychological relevance. Abstractions not only make poor computational tools, but they also make poor agents. Mel Gibson's *Passion of Christ* will always be more compelling than Paul Tillich's

	Representation of Agents	
	Theological	*Basic*
Processing	Explicit (optional)	Implicit (default)
Computational utility	–	+
Psychological relevance	–	+

Figure 4.4   Variables of representational modes

"Ground of Being." Again, Barrett seems to be saying the same when he writes that with thinking about gods, "not just anything goes" (1998, 617); or Boyer, when he notes that the distortion of standard representations is inevitable since "they must produce inferences to make them coherent or relevant" (2001, 283); or Whitehouse, when he affirms that "a complex body of doctrine cannot 'live' in people's minds" (2000, 152).

Initially, then, computational utility and psychological relevance have to do with functionality, but ultimately they elucidate such crucial issues as belief and motivation. The processing disconnections just described not only make theological concepts less useful and salient but also less believable. As Boyer argues, what we call "belief" is the result of "aggregate relevance" (2001, 298). The combined activation of mental inference systems that makes the representation of religious agents *possible* also makes them *plausible*. But this phenomenon is dependent on implicit processing, which maximizes the suite of nonconscious mental tools used to produce quick, concrete inferences (Barrett 2004). Explicit processing decouples tacit connections, undermining aggregate relevance. In short, there is a direct correlation between the way the brain forms representations and the beliefs that we hold.

Dan Sperber offers a similar perspective when he distinguishes between two fundamental kinds of beliefs represented in the mind: "reflective beliefs" and "intuitive beliefs" (1996, 1997). Intuitive beliefs are the products of, and owe their rationality to, innate, spontaneous, and unconscious perceptual and inferential processes. Intuitive beliefs are concrete, descriptive, reliable, rigidly held, and ground a commonsense understanding of the world. Reflective beliefs, on the other hand, are "interpretations of representations embedded in the validating context of an intuitive belief" (1996, 89). Reflective beliefs owe their rationality to explicit reasoning or to an external source of authority, are more explanatory than descriptive, and are often not fully understood. Consequently, people's commitment to reflective beliefs varies widely, from loosely held opinions to dogmatic convictions.

So theological incorrectness is inevitable in part because in each person there is both an "official" concept and an "implicit" concept that they can use, but more completely because official, theological-level concepts—while

mentally manageable and publicly managed—are in fact conceptual over-
lays on tacit knowledge people bring to functional, coherent, and meaningful thought about agents, real or imagined. The truer "tragedy of the theologian" is that he or she is shopping second-rate wares. Given the dynamics of
dual processing and social cognition, basic representations provide for robust computational utility and psychological relevance. Abstract, theological
representations can be dispensed with, and often are. None of this, of
course, requires conscious intent: "Empirical evidence of preconscious and
subconscious precepts, memories, and thoughts reminds us that we are not
always aware of why we do what we do" (Kihlstrom 1999, 198).

If religious thought is guided in large part by tacit mental processes, then
a wide range of religious behaviors should also be grounded in them.
Clearly there are several ways a person can respond to the cognitive tension
inherent in religious representations. For instance, it may simply go unnoticed. Few religious people are theologians, and few theologians, like scientists off the job, are always theological. Indeed, an appreciable number of
religious adherents display little understanding of their tradition's formal
conceptual schemes and operate, for all intents and purposes, beneath
them. Those who do possess abstract theological representations appear to
naturally default to basic ones during online thought. Interestingly, there is
evidence that theological incorrectness surfaces even in reflective and not
just in spontaneous processing. Studies of Christian small groups by Robert
Wuthnow and colleagues, for example, discovered many individuals' representations of God to be decidedly different from the divine attributes
found in formal church doctrines, which the same individuals nevertheless
knew well (1994a, 1994b).

Cognitive tension may manifest itself more directly, however, as Boyer
points out, in people's willingness to add to, distort, or modify their religion.
There is reason to suspect that some common episodes of religious change—
phenomena such as doctrinal and ritual innovation, revivalism, syncretism,
new religions, and conversion—occur in response to overtly abstract or un-
satisfying religious ideas and related practices. As a working hypothesis, I
propose that when religious systems perpetuate ideas distanced from the
cognitive constraints imposed by implicit processing, divergent religious behaviors will result.

As both Pyysiäinen and I have pointed out elsewhere (Tremlin 2002;
Pyysiäinen, in press), this working hypothesis, which arises from a dual-
process model of religious thought, constitutes a new research program with
multiple lines of investigation. Case studies in comparative religion, for instance, should help confirm or disconfirm a range of claims and predictions regarding religious change at both the personal and systemic level. As an example, in his chapter in this volume, Pyysiäinen suggests a relationship between
psychological and social factors in religious conversion. Likewise, attention to

cognition might well cast new light on a wider range of religious change, from historic shifts in mainstream traditions, to the emergence of temporary revival movements, to the formation of more permanent movements like charismatic Christianity, to the genesis of entirely new religions, to the ubiquity of syncretistic practices like those coloring the supposedly austere tradition of Sri Lankan Buddhism (Tremlin, in preparation). This is not to say that all events of religious change are due to purely cognitive factors; there are, of course, a host of ecological reasons for such episodes. But much of the observable modulation in religious behavior is likely due to the constraining effects of dual processing outlined here.

IMPLICATIONS FOR THE
MORPHOLOGY OF RELIGIOUS SYSTEMS

A final implication of the dual-process model is what it possibly contributes to discussions of the morphology of religious systems. If, as Boyer points out, "the implicit assumption behind the notion of cognitive constraint is that cultural transmission is an inherently *selective* process" (1994b, 392), then the shape and stability of public religious systems ought to be linked to the same cognitive constraints that govern private religious thought.

Given the sociopolitical demands of public religion and the constraints of private cognition, religious systems will necessarily display features of both "official" and "popular" religiosity. On the one hand, organizing and transmitting religion as a stable cultural system requires that it assume a theological form, employing generalized, abstract, logical doctrines that require literal memory and activate effortful, analytical, explicit processing. On the other hand, the process of religious acquisition and representation is largely an implicit exercise that employs the affect-laden, experiential system of cognition. If religions are to remain cognitively coherent and psychologically relevant to participants, then they must allow for personalistic practices that engage implicit processing. Pyysiäinen, who also emphasizes that theological traditions are an epiphenomenal overlay on natural religiosity (2001, 2004), adequately summarizes this position when he writes (borrowing from Whitehouse's "modes" terminology) that "imagistic-like phenomena provide individual motivation while doctrinal-type phenomena offer systems-level tools for the preservation of stable traditions" (this volume, 160).

This chapter began by noting the internal disharmony that characterizes all religious systems, yet some religious systems are clearly more stable and durable than others, and a relatively small number of religions have become widespread cultural fixtures. The dual-process model offered above suggests that *successful* religious systems will gravitate toward a balance of explicit and implicit forms of religiosity.

What I am describing, then, is a kind of "cognitive optimum" operative at the level of cultural systems. Religious belief and practice are motivated and sustained by computational utility and psychological relevance. If public religion is to continue to be acquired and transmitted, it must conform to and foster these same functional requirements. Religious systems that fail to maintain this balance are likely to be revised or abandoned.

REFERENCES

Barrett, J. L. 1998. Cognitive Constraints on Hindu Concepts of the Divine. *Journal for the Scientific Study of Religion* 37: 608–19.

———. 1999. Theological Correctness: Cognitive Constraint and the Study of Religion. *Method & Theory in the Study of Religion* 11: 325–39.

———. 2000. Exploring the Natural Foundations of Religion. *Trends in Cognitive Sciences* 4: 29–34.

———. 2004. *Why Would Anyone Believe in God?* Walnut Creek, CA: AltaMira.

Barrett, J. L., and F. C. Keil. 1996. Conceptualizing a Nonnatural Entity: Anthropomorphism in God Concepts. *Cognitive Psychology* 31: 219–47.

Boyer, P. 1994a. Berkeley: University of California Press.

———. 1994b. Cognitive Constraints on Cultural Representations: Natural Ontologies and Religious Ideas. In *Mapping the Mind: Domain Specificity in Cognition and Culture*, ed. L. A. Hirschfeld and S. A. Gelman. Cambridge: Cambridge University Press.

———. 2000. Functional Origins of Religious Concepts: Ontological and Strategic Selection in Evolved Minds. *Journal of the Royal Anthropological Institute* 6: 195–215.

———. 2001. *Religion Explained: The Evolutionary Origins of Religious Thought.* New York: Basic Books.

———. 2003. Religious Thought and Behavior as By-Products of Brain Function. *Trends in the Cognitive Sciences* 7: 119–24.

Chaiken, S., and Y. Trope. 1999. Preface to *Dual-Process Theories in Social Psychology.* New York: Guilford Press.

Chaiken, S., and Y. Trope, eds. 1999. *Dual-Process Theories in Social Psychology.* New York: Guilford Press.

Denes-Raj, V., and S. Epstein. 1994. Conflict between Intuitive and Rational Processing: When People Behave against Their Better Judgment. *Journal of Personality and Social Psychology* 66: 819–29.

Epstein, S., and R. Pacini. 1999. Some Basic Issues Regarding Dual-Process Theories from the Perspective of Cognitive-Experiential Self-Theory. In *Dual-Process Theories in Social Psychology*, ed. S. Chaiken and Y. Trope. New York: Guilford Press.

Fiske, S. T., and S. E. Taylor. 1991. *Social Cognition.* New York: McGraw Hill.

Gazzaniga, M. S., R. B. Ivry, and G. R. Mangun. 1998. *Cognitive Neuroscience: The Biology of the Mind.* New York: W. W. Norton.

Gellner, E. 1969. A Pendulum Swing Theory of Islam. In *Sociology of Religion: Selected Readings*, ed. R. Robertson. Harmondsworth: Penguin Education.

Goody, J. 1968. Introd. to *Literacy in Traditional Societies.* Cambridge: Cambridge University Press.

———. 1986. *The Logic of Writing and the Organization of Society*. Cambridge: Cambridge University Press.

Guthrie, S. E. 1993. *Faces in the Clouds: A New Theory of Religion*. Oxford: Oxford University Press.

Holyoak, K. J., and B. A. Spellman. 1993. Thinking. *Annual Review of Psychology* 44: 265–315.

Keil, F. C. 2003. Folkscience: Coarse Interpretations of a Complex Reality. *Trends in Cognitive Sciences* 7: 368–73.

Kihlstrom, J. F. 1999. Conscious Versus Unconscious Cognition. In *The Nature of Cognition*, ed. R. J. Sternberg. Cambridge, MA: MIT Press.

Lawson, E. T., and R. N. McCauley. 1990. *Rethinking Religion: Connecting Cognition and Culture*. Cambridge: Cambridge University Press.

Lieberman, M. D., R. Gaunt, D. T. Gilbert, and Y. Trope. 2002. Reflexion and Reflection: A Social Cognitive Neuroscience Approach to Attributional Inference. *Advances in Experimental Social Psychology* 34: 200–50.

McCauley, R. N. 2000. The Naturalness of Religion and the Unnaturalness of Science. In *Explanation and Cognition*, ed. F. C. Keil and R. A. Wilson. Cambridge, MA: MIT Press.

McCauley, R. N., and E. T. Lawson. 2002. *Bringing Ritual to Mind: Psychological Foundations of Cultural Forms*. Cambridge: Cambridge University Press.

Pinker, S. 1997. *How the Mind Works*. New York: W. W. Norton.

Pyysiäinen, I. 2001. *How Religion Works: Towards a New Cognitive Science of Religion*. Leiden: Brill.

———. 2003. Dual-Process Theories and Hybrid Systems: A Commentary on Anderson and Lebiere. *Behavioral and Brain Sciences* 25: 617–18.

———. 2004. Corrupt Doctrine and Doctrinal Revival: On the Nature and Limits of the Modes Theory. In *Theorizing Religions Past: Archaeology, History, and Cognition*, ed. H. Whitehouse and L. H. Martin. Walnut Creek, CA: AltaMira.

———. In press. Intuitive and Explicit in Religious Thought. *Journal of Cognition and Culture*.

Schneider, W., and R. M. Shiffrin. 1977. Controlled and Automatic Human Information Processing. *Psychological Review* 84: 1–66.

Sharot, S. 2001. *A Comparative Sociology of World Religions: Virtuosi, Priests, and Popular Religion*. New York: New York University Press.

Shiffrin, R. M., and W. Schneider. 1977. Controlled and Automatic Human Information Processing, II: Perceptual Learning, Automatic Attending, and a General Theory. *Psychological Review* 84: 127–90.

Sloman, S. A. 1996. The Empirical Case for Two Systems of Reasoning. *Psychological Bulletin* 119: 3–22.

———. 1999. Rational versus Arational Models of Thought. In *The Nature of Cognition*, ed. R. J. Sternberg. Cambridge, MA: MIT Press.

Slone, D. J. 2004. *Theological Incorrectness: Why Religious People Believe What They Shouldn't*. Cambridge: Cambridge University Press.

Smith E. R., and J. DeCoster. 1999. Associative and Rule-Based Processing: A Connectionist Interpretation of Dual-Process Models. In *Dual-Process Theories in Social Psychology*, ed. S. Chaiken and Y. Trope. New York: Guilford Press.

Sperber, D. 1996. *Explaining Culture: A Naturalistic Approach*. Oxford: Blackwell.

————. 1997. Intuitive and Reflective Beliefs. *Mind and Language* 12: 67–83.

Sperber, D., and D. Wilson. 1995. *Relevance: Communication and Cognition*. Oxford: Blackwell.

Sternberg, R. J., ed. 1999. *The Nature of Cognition*. Cambridge, MA: MIT Press.

Tooby, J., and I. DeVore. 1987. The Reconstruction of Hominid Evolution through Strategic Modeling. In *The Evolution of Human Behavior: Primate Models*, ed. W. G. Kinzey. Albany, NY: SUNY Press.

Tremlin, T. 2002. A Theory of Religious Modulation: Reconciling Religious Modes and Ritual Arrangements. *Journal of Cognition and Culture* 2: 309–48.

————. In preparation. *Divine Minds: The Cognitive Foundations of God and Religion*. Book manuscript.

Tulving, E., and D. L. Schacter. 1990. Priming and Human Memory Systems. *Science* 247: 301–6.

Van Essen, D. C., and E. A. DeYoe. 1995. Concurrent Processing in the Primate Visual Cortex. In *The Cognitive Neurosciences*, ed. M. S. Gazzaniga. Cambridge, MA: MIT Press.

Weber, M. 1930. *The Protestant Ethic and the Spirit of Capitalism*. London: George Allen and Unwin.

————. 1947. *The Theory of Social and Economic Organization*. Oxford: Oxford University Press.

Werbner, R. P., ed. 1977. *Regional Cults*. London: Academic Press.

Whitehouse, H. 1995. *Inside the Cult: Religious Innovation and Transmission in Papua New Guinea*. Oxford: Clarendon Press.

————. 2000. *Arguments and Icons: Divergent Modes of Religiosity*. Oxford: Oxford University Press.

————. 2004. *Modes of Religiosity: A Cognitive Theory of Religious Transmission*. Walnut Creek, CA: AltaMira.

Wuthnow, R., ed. 1994a. *"I Come Away Stronger": How Small Groups Are Shaping American Religion*. Grand Rapids: Eerdmans.

————. 1994b. *Sharing the Journey: Support Groups and America's New Quest for Community*. New York: Free Press.

5

Rethinking Naturalness: Modes of Religiosity and Religion in the Round

Matthew Day

If the goal of science is to carve the world at its joints, the final rung of the Linnaean ladder would appear to be an unqualified success. The bifurcation of nature into the plant and animal kingdoms not only captures the profound differences between, say, roses and cheetahs. By virtue of how effortlessly this partition seems to fall out of our experience, it also represents the kind of natural division that Plato originally had in mind when he suggested that our understanding must not treat the world "as a bad carver might." Although the clear and distinct boundaries that Linnaeus drew around plants and animals are forever smudged by Darwinian descent with modification, his taxonomic intuition can nevertheless be preserved and recast in orthodox evolutionary terms. Adopting the lexicon of contemporary game theory, for example, we can speak of two relatively distinct and evolutionarily stable strategies for survival (Maynard Smith 1974). On the one hand, plants usually take on the strategy of evolutionary squatters—organisms that claim a corner of the earth as their own, hunker down, and then hope for the best. Animals, on the other hand, typically assume the strategy of evolutionary dodgers—organisms that are free to move around in their environment but as a result must be capable of identifying food, friends, or foes in real time and acting accordingly. At this soaring level of theoretical abstraction, one might say that, ceteris paribus, the history of life on earth has blindly gravitated toward two "modes" of survivability.[1]

Drawing on the same broadly Darwinian theoretical framework, Harvey Whitehouse contends that he has isolated a natural division that allows us to carve the world of religion at its joints. The modes of religiosity theory claims that, ceteris paribus, religious systems (or at least the components of such systems) are naturally drawn toward two centers of gravity. Around one focal point—the imagistic mode of religiosity—we find an array of low-frequency, high-arousal, and doctrinally elusive practices that are typically associated with small, cohesive communities and decentralized structures of sociopolitical authority. A paradigmatic example of what Whitehouse has in mind here would be something like the annual "peyote hunt" of the Huichol Indians (Meyerhoff 1974). Around the other hub of attraction—the doctrinal mode of religiosity—we discover a collection of high-frequency, low-arousal, and doctrinally explicit practices that are strongly correlated with geographically scattered communities and centralized forms of authority. A helpful illustration for modeling the salient features of these practices would be the weekly observation of the Eucharist in Roman Catholic parishes. While much of this suggests a Weberian interest in ideal types, structures of authority, and the social dynamics of religious communities, part of what distinguishes the modes of religiosity theory is its explicit appeal to the mechanism of natural selection to explain these ethnographic patterns. That is to say, Whitehouse adopts a "selectionist" stance toward cultural representations and treats the two modalities of religion as evolutionarily stable strategies for the inter- and intragenerational transmission of religious concepts, norms, and practices. The barebones argument is that the long-term stability of these two strategies—that is, their ability to resist the continuous threat of distortion and erosion through transmission—ultimately rests on the ways in which they exploit the biases of human episodic and semantic memory. While the imagistic mode invokes our capacity to recall the details of shocking or poignant events, the doctrinal mode calls upon our ability to accumulate massive stores of information through explicit training. The working hypothesis is that the features of religious traditions that activate either episodic or semantic memory will tend to be the most robust because they fit the native computational profile of human cognition.

As the chapters in this volume and others attest, the modes theory is currently being put through its academic paces. How much of the core conceptual structure can withstand such withering inspection, and the degree to which the surviving remnant will be applicable across the anthropological and historical boards, remains to be seen. Rather than adding my voice to this critical chorus, however, I want to draw attention to what I take to be a programmatic strength of Whitehouse's project.

One of the distinctive features of the mainstream cognitive approach is the claim that religious belief and behavior is far less dependent upon cultural input and social arrangements than previously assumed. In fact, many cognitive theorists argue that religion should been seen as a phenotypic analogue to the linguistic capacity that is our evolutionary birthright. Rephrased with an eye for controversy, this means that religious activity is no more "cultural" than stereopsis or bipedalism. Religion is a predictable side effect of the human cognitive engine's performance, just as heat is a predictable side effect of the combustion engine's performance. The theoretical hunch that the study of religion is more akin to an inquiry about human biology than human culture has produced an exciting new field of inquiry that sets out to identify how apparently universal properties of human cognitive architecture shape and constrain religious systems.

Yet, my experience in the hallways and seminar rooms of university life suggests that much of the academic community remains suspicious of the project as a whole. The temptation for those of us who are advocates of the cognitive approach is to discount this resistance as a charmingly old-fashioned allegiance to the antireductionism of the sui generis agenda or an even more sinister rejection of neo-Darwinian thought. This undoubtedly accounts for certain pockets of opposition, but as an all-purpose explanation, I don't think it works. One criticism that I hear quite often is that, in view of its interest in the universal psychological mechanisms that make religious activity in general possible, the cognitive science of religion fails to explain anything in particular. The fact that religious rituals trigger intuitive contagion-avoidance systems, for example, doesn't help these scholars make sense of why this group at this time calls upon this practice to achieve this goal. When we consider this sort of disagreement over the value of the cognitive approach against the full history of scholarship on religion, something peculiar happens: the counsel of the field's "dinosaurs" begins to sound surprisingly up-to-date (Malley 2002). As a case in point, I'm willing to bet that Durkheim continues to speak for a number of academics when he writes in *Rules of Sociological Method* that

> it has been held that a certain religiosity is innate in man, as is a certain minimum of sexual jealousy, filial piety or fatherly affection, etc., and it is in these that explanations have been sought for religion, marriage, and the family. But history shows that these inclinations, far from being inherent in human nature, are either completely absent under certain social conditions or vary so much from one society to another that the residue left after eliminating all these differences—which alone can be considered of psychological origin—is reduced to something vague and schematic, infinitely removed from the facts which have to be explained. (Durkheim 1982, 131–32)

Given the temptation to write the cognitive critics off as antiscientific Luddites, I think it is important to recognize that Durkheim's hard line against the idea of a substantive human nature is logically independent of his criticism regarding the explanatory value of general "inclinations" embedded in our human nature that fail to explain particular phenomena.[2] There is no contradiction between adopting a vigorously Darwinian theoretical stance when it comes to the origins of biological complexity and simultaneously rejecting the evolutionary psychological case for massive, domain-specific modularity (Kitcher 2003). Likewise, there is no contradiction between accepting the findings of cognitive psychology and concurrently deciding that these results aren't terribly relevant for unraveling this subset of human thought and behavior. Thus, what the critics' reservations suggest to me is that the fault here may lie not in our stars but in our selves. Despite its remarkable growth over the last decade, I'm not sure the cognitive community has done a good enough job demonstrating how talk of computational architectures or psychological subroutines is anything more than another vague and schematic toolbox infinitely removed from the facts that most scholars of religion want to understand.

So far, the theoretical scope of the cognitive platform has been to describe in probabilistic terms the mental states and processes found in most people, most of the time, in most religious contexts. Deliberate oversimplification is a common tactic in scientific practice, and the decision to remain at this wide-ranging level of analysis makes good sense for a project just trying to get off the ground. If nothing else, the strategy of assembling a very general theoretical framework that is appropriate for many purposes has allowed the field to avoid the awful predicament of being all limbs and no body (Ryle 1990, 258). However, at some point theoretical stage setting and methodological throat clearing must give way to work at a much finer grain of analysis. There is clearly room for progressively more refined accounts of the cognitive devices and implicit conceptual knowledge that make religion in general possible. Nevertheless, my gut tells me that unless we are able to demonstrate how the design of our evolved control systems engages particular sociocultural conditions to generate particular religious systems, the cognitive science of religion will never reach beyond a relatively small "coalition of the willing." This is where, for me, the true significance of the modes theory begins to emerge.

Recent work in anthropology (Hutchins 1995), cognitive science (Clark 1997), philosophy (Dennett 1996), psychology (Tomasello 2000), and theoretical biology (Goodwin 1995) gives us reason to think that human thought and behavior could depend on a much wider web of causal influences than some contemporary theorists seem to allow.[3] That is to say, by treating the cumulative effects of social structures, cultural practices, material artifacts, and historical trends as extraneous features of a biologically fixed cognitive system, we may actually end up with an abnormal portrait of what a normal human mind actually is. Paul Griffiths and Karola Stolz memorably observe that from the perspective of embodied and situated cognition, the bid to capture the contours of the human mind cut loose from such all-too-human scaffolding is "as misguided as seeking to investigate the true nature of an ant by removing the distorting influence of the nest" (Griffiths and Stolz 2000, 44–45). Whitehouse shares some version of this hunch and over the past decade has been trying to forge a theoretical trajectory that can account for the ways in which human religious actors are embedded in a sociocultural ecology of cognition. Reflecting on the ongoing debate between evolutionary psychology and ethnographic practice, for example, he has observed that "restricting the cognitive project to the identification of causes internal to organisms impoverishes the explanatory potential of psychological models" (Whitehouse 2001a, 207–8). In fact, the modes theory often reads like an attempt to negotiate the tensions that currently exist between the ethnographer's hard-won sensitivity to, and the cognitive theorist's studied indifference toward, the peculiarities of place.

I believe that there are few projects in the cognitive science of religion more important than overcoming this rift, and in what follows I want to call attention to the nascent portrait of ecologically embedded religious cognition that the modes theory promotes. Section one is dedicated to selectively reviewing the "standard model" of religious cognition as articulated by Pascal Boyer, and will emphasize how the lens of modest counterintuitiveness forces us to explain why one subset of religious concepts are more recurrent, and thus more probable, features of the world's religious systems. In general, my goal is to provide a summary of Boyer's contention that religious belief and behavior are natural for a mind like ours. With this theoretical background established, in section two I turn my attention to the modes theory and highlight the link it proposes between immodest counterintuitiveness and the kinds of sociocultural scaffolding that the two forms of religiosity are said to generate. Here my overarching ambition is to offer a synopsis of Whitehouse's twofold claim that the net of "natural" religion fails to capture the full range of relevant phenomena and that the two modalities of religion create the necessary conditions for unnatural religious activity. Since most of this essay will consist of reconstructing the work of others— albeit with a strong editorial hand—in section three I will try to punch things up a bit. Self-consciously adopting the role of an agitator, I will suggest that even if the modes theory is dead wrong about the universality of bifurcating religious modalities, or naively confuses the causal relationship between ritual form and ritual frequency, it may nevertheless force the cognitive science of religion to drop a favorite intuition pump.[4]

TAKE A LOAD OFF: PASCAL BOYER AND THE STANDARD MODEL OF RELIGIOUS COGNITION

No one has done a better job of showcasing how cognitive science has the theoretical power to vividly reconfigure our understanding of religion than Pascal Boyer. Step by step, he has carefully pieced together a compelling argument for viewing religion as a haphazard by-product of our evolved cognitive architecture. The backbone of Boyer's analysis—and of what has quickly become the "standard" cognitive model of religious thought—is that religious concepts are intrinsically counterintuitive. By this he does not mean to suggest that religion somehow belongs in the same category as Simpson's paradox, the puzzling statistical outcome where the losers in several distinct groups suddenly become the winners when those groups are combined into a single population (Sober 1984). Rather, his goal is to draw our attention to the manner in which religious concepts violate some of our implicit conceptual knowledge about the world and its furniture while preserving other bits of tacit folk wisdom. The easiest way to understand what this amounts to is to briefly focus on supernatural or extrahuman agents.

At the same time that these creatures cohere with our intuitive assumptions about what a person is, they concurrently breach other assumptions by displaying counterintuitive biological properties, physical powers, or psychological traits. So while a particular god may have beliefs, make decisions, and perceive current events just like everyone else in our neighborhood, he is noteworthy because unlike our neighbors he doesn't die, can walk on water, and knows everything. When we dissolve the concept of ghosts, gods, and spirits into the cognitive template it employs ("person") and observe the particular violation(s) of biological, physical, or psychological expectations involved, the seemingly infinite ethnographic cacophony of supernatural agents can be economically reduced to a surprisingly limited catalog of possibilities. As a demonstration of what he has in mind, Boyer suggests that a good anthropologist of human gastronomy ignores the transparent differences between enchiladas verdes, shrimp etouffee, and beef Wellington to uncover how a limited set of cooking techniques and a large but nevertheless bounded set of ingredients can give rise to the practically endless variety of human cuisine.[5] He similarly contends that a good anthropologist of religion should ignore the obvious differences between Jesus, Vishnu, and Buddhist yakshas to demonstrate how the never-ending register of these extrahuman agents is generated by a restricted set of cognitive techniques and materials. Like the absurdist café in the Monty Python sketch whose offerings all include Spam, from this vantage point the carte du jour of religious agents consists of little more than variations on a simple theme.

However, much as the inventory of actual recipes occupies a smallish corner in the evolutionary design space of all possible recipes, Boyer argues that the actual supernatural concepts that we find in the wild represent a small subset of all possible religious representations. Upon inspection, some religious concepts turn out to be far more recurrent, and therefore more probable, features of the world's religious systems than others. "It seems clear from the anthropological record," he writes, "that socially significant supernatural concepts are largely about agents spontaneously (and in large part tacitly) represented as having psychological processes (perception, belief, intention) that agree with our intuitive theory of mind" (Boyer 2000, 201). This means that regardless of whether a supernatural concept activates the person, animal, plant, or artifact template, the crucial feature that recurrent, socially significant supernatural agents or objects all share is that they fit our intuitive expectations about what it means to have a mind. Obviously, the ten-thousand-dollar question is "why?": Why does this subset of supernatural concepts appear to have a leg up on the others?

Rather than chalking up this pattern to a naive "anthropomorphizing" tendency, Boyer maintains that it is instead just the sort of thing we should expect from a mind cobbled together by Mother Nature to cope with the complexities of the social world. The Darwinian rationale for this claim is more or less the same that underwrites Leda Cosmides and John Tooby's prediction that "the mind should contain organized systems of inference that are specialized for solving various families of problems, such as social exchange, threat, coalitional relations and mate choice" (1992, 166). In broad outline, the story goes something like this. Our hominid ancestors were faced with two very different classes of adaptive hurdles. Not only did they have to survive the gauntlet of ecological threats that included avoiding predators, tracking prey, and identifying nonpoisonous foods. They also had to successfully navigate the obstacle course of group living such as selecting mates, forming friendships, and detecting cheaters in social contracts. Since the cognitive subroutines implicated in locating good food are discontinuous with those for detecting cheaters, the prediction is that functionally specialized mental systems and capacities were designed to generate appropriate behavioral responses to both ecological and social challenges. Thus, the theoretical gambit is that if we are serious about uncovering the cognitive origins of religion, we must appreciate how our evolved "faculty of social cognition" makes the representation of supernatural agents or objects with minds (1) computationally easy and (2) socially relevant.

As the ever-growing experimental literature on children's "theories of mind" clearly demonstrates, developmentally normal humans by the age of five have, for the most part, mastered the fine art of interpreting, predicting, and capitalizing on the behaviors of others by treating them as mindful, intentional agents who act on the basis of unobservable beliefs and desires. From an evolutionary perspective, this standard maturational program makes sense when we stop to consider how all social primates "must be able to calculate the consequences of their own behavior, to calculate the likely behavior of others, to calculate the balance of advantage and loss—and all this in a context where the evidence on which their calculations are based is ephemeral, ambiguous and likely to change" (Humphrey 1976, 309). The recognition that we are natural psychologists is significant in this context because whether we find ourselves in a community worried about the trees that hear our thoughts or the gods who control the weather, at the end of the day we are still dealing with agents who accommodate our intuitive belief-desire psychology. Trafficking with such mindful religious creatures is unbelievably easy for us because this is precisely what the vast array of domain-specific structures that constitute our faculty of social intelligence was designed to do! So when we set out to discern what the gods and spirits want from us and act accordingly, we are doing something that comes quite naturally. Nevertheless, Boyer believes there is something distinctive about the concept of a supernatural mind that sets these agents and objects apart.

One of the methodological virtues of game theory is that it highlights the strategic qualities of decision making. That is to say, rather than treating the agent "as if he is the isolated inhabitant of an unresponsive world," game theoretic models assume that players take into account the interactive relationship between their choices and the decisions of others when charting a course of action (Samuelson 1997, 2). These themes are nicely illustrated by the childhood (two-player) game "paper, rock, scissors." For each round, a player must choose one of the three available options, and the winner is determined according to the following payoff schedule: paper beats rock, rock beats scissors, and scissors beats paper. Since each player's success depends on what the other player picks, any knowledge about the tendencies of one's rival will be rewarded. Yet this creates an intriguing strategic dilemma:

> If you know what your competitor will pick, you will always win. But what the other kid picks is going to depend on what he thinks you will pick. So, you have to know what he thinks you will pick in order to pick the best strategy, and so on backwards ad infinitum. There is no end to the calculation problem, and therefore no optimal strategy in the Rock-Paper-Scissors game. Game theorists have labeled the problem of this sort of game with no finite solution—no best strategy for any player—"the problem of common knowledge." In principle, the problem of having to infinitely iterate calculations about what other players will do bedevils most strategic games. (Rosenberg 2000, 129)

The problem of complete knowledge extends far beyond such idealized game theoretic models as paper, rock, scissors or the prisoner's dilemma. The fragmentary nature of social information provides the foothold for tactical deception throughout the natural world and is often associated with a potential "theory of mind" in social primates (Povinelli 1996; Whiten 1996).

Closer to home, most of us are acutely aware that our knowledge of another actor's motives is far from complete. Daniel Dennett likes to say that we have been designed by evolution to be informavores: "epistemically hungry seekers of information, in an endless quest to improve our purchase on the world" (Dennett 2003, 93). This key Darwinian insight is even more telling if we emphasize how our evolutionary history of group living has turned us into social informavores, epistemically hungry seekers of strategically valuable information about our actual and potential social partners. As a consequence of this, we spend a great deal of time and energy trying to plug the gaps in our knowledge about the players, relationships, and intentions that constitute our social worlds. For example, Robin Dunbar estimates that nearly two-thirds of our conversations are concerned with such basic matters of social importance as who is doing what with whom. On this basis, he concludes that "Our much-vaunted capacity for language seems to be mainly used for exchanging information on social matters; we seem to be obsessed with gossiping about one another" (Dunbar 1996, 7). This is where the social relevance of mindful supernatural agents and objects breaks the surface.

Boyer submits that although gods, ghosts, and spirits resemble any other run-of-the-mill intentional creature, what is noteworthy about these agents is that they routinely have full access to the strategic social information that we limited-access actors so desperately want. Consider the feature of omniscience that so many supernatural agents possess. While this aptitude would necessarily include knowing such things as the contents of every vending machine or the weight of every farm animal, for most religious systems what really seems to matter is that these extrahuman actors know who is stealing my cattle or who is guilty of lying. That is to say, if we use the ethnographic record as our guide, it seems that it is not omniscience per se but social omniscience that distinguishes the minds of the gods. By virtue of having unique access to the kinds of information that our faculty of social intelligence craves, the gods are cognitively significant because they trigger the evolutionary arsenal of domain-specific cognitive machinery that guides our social reasoning. More to the point, what makes dealing with the gods easy and natural also makes them relevant. These agents invariably know more about the nitty-gritty details of social life than we do, and Boyer believes this explains a great deal about why the gods are both everywhere and everywhere important. In a passage worth quoting at length he writes,

> What is "important" to human beings, because of their evolutionary history, are the conditions of social interaction: who knows what, who is not aware of what, who did what with whom, when and what for. Imagining agents with that information is an illustration of mental processes driven by relevance. Such agents are not really necessary to explain anything, but they are so much easier to represent and so much richer in possible inferences that they enjoy a great advantage in cultural transmission. (Boyer 2001, 167)

For a mind like ours, stymied by the strategic problem of complete knowledge and perpetually hungry for any scrap of information that might improve our leverage in the social world, the promise of full-access supernatural agents is just too great to ignore.

RELIGION IN THE ROUND: HARVEY WHITEHOUSE AND
THE MODES OF RELIGIOSITY

Given that Boyer and Whitehouse are each attempting to harness the apparatus, techniques, and assumptions of cognitive science to make sense of religious activity, it should come as no surprise that there are huge areas of
agreement between them. Both theorists agree, for example, that the sieve
of inter- and intragenerational cultural transmission produces religious concepts that spontaneously drift toward a position of cognitive optimality
where the eye-catching qualities of counterintuitiveness are balanced out by
the inferentially rich potential of representations that preserve our intuitions.
In addition, both believe that the basic profile of human cognition shapes
and constrains religious systems in quite fundamental ways. Because he believes this profile makes the window of cultural success relatively narrow,
Boyer predicts that the constellation of beliefs and practices that occupy the
cognitive optimum position (COP) will essentially exhaust the range of
ethnographically relevant religious phenomena.[6] However, Whitehouse believes that this is where things begin to get interesting.

When he reviews the anthropological record, Whitehouse finds that religious systems are rarely the minimalist affairs of modestly counterintuitive,
easily acquired concepts that Boyer's cognitive optimum hypothesis fore-
casts. The fact that these traditions often make invidious distinctions between the beliefs and practices that gather around the COP and those that require more effort to acquire and transmit, for instance, suggests to him a
general "tendency for religious traditions to eschew certain cognitively optimal concepts and to peddle more complex bodies of knowledge in their
stead" (Whitehouse 2004, 46). From this perspective, religious systems are a
kind of parallelogram of forces where the inherent tendency of supernatural
concepts to gravitate toward the COP can be opposed and even reversed by
one interfering force or another. The modes theory predicts that the real-
world outcomes of these competing causal vectors are increasingly counterintuitive representations that are "pushed" toward either the imagistic or doctrinal forms of religious belief and behavior. To see how this framework
draws our attention to what might be called the unnaturalness of religion,
consider what Whitehouse has to say about supernatural actors.

It is a fool's errand to argue that the world's religions aren't populated with
the kinds of mindful extrahuman creatures that Boyer's project prepares us
to find. Whitehouse's own fieldwork among the Mali Baining of Papua, New
Guinea, convinces him that a great deal of religious activity is indeed tied up
with our interactions with such modestly counterintuitive religious agents.
Nonetheless, he insists that in addition to this restricted menu of gods,
ghosts, and spirits, we also find a catalog of computationally heavy, fluores-
cently counterintuitive concepts that are fiendishly difficult to acquire and

transmit—much less understand. So while it is undeniably true that the Mali Baining colonize the surrounding forests with the cognitively optimal *sega*, we only have half of the ethnographic story if we fail to scrutinize the flamboyantly counterintuitive "village government" of the Pomio Kivung. The trouble with only having half a story, of course, is that at the end of the day we probably only have half of an explanation.[7]

Cecilia Heyes has recently complained that the research agenda epitomized by Cosmides and Tooby's (1992) case for an innate cheater-detection module does not deserve the all-purpose label of "evolutionary psychology." Her objection isn't that this school of thought fails to absorb key lessons of neo-Darwinian theory, or that the current neuroscientific evidence appears to undermine their commitment to massive, domain-specific modularity. Rather, her criticism is that this enterprise—and the set of theoretical commitments that it typically embraces—is much too narrow for such a comprehensive-sounding title. The fact that evolutionary psychology "has come to refer exclusively to research on human mentality and behavior, motivated by a very specific nativist-adaptationist interpretation of how evolution operates," Heyes writes, "is a strange, anthropocentric usage, akin to identifying human biology with 'biology' generally" (Heyes 2000, 3). In response to this curious state of affairs, she issues a call for evolutionary psychology in the round, a broad field of inquiry that explores the evolution of cognition in general (i.e., in both nonhuman and human animals) without demanding allegiance to any given stance (Heyes 2003). I think something similar can be said on Whitehouse's behalf regarding cognitively optimal forms of religious activity. Although he sees nothing wrong in principle with taking religion to refer exclusively to the "natural" beliefs and behaviors that collect around the COP, he nevertheless seems to believe that for the cognitive science of religion to be worthy of its name the enterprise must take into account the "unnatural" religious activity found in the ethnographic wild (Whitehouse 2004, 45–46). On my reading, when the modes theory stretches to make sense of the costly activities coupled with the imagistic and doctrinal forms of religiosity, it is after something we might call religion in the round. That this is the larger issue at stake in his discussion of extranatural agency, for example, becomes clear when we are told that

> explaining the transmission of cognitively costly aspects of religion is a different kind of enterprise from explaining the transmission of language or minimally counterintuitive concepts. A comprehensive theory of the way the standard cognitive architecture operates in all known human environments would be sufficient to why humans learn to speak or entertain concepts of ghosts. But that is not sufficient to explain religion. (2004, 58)

In other words, the standard cognitive model has "explained" religion only by focusing the academic spotlight on the narrow range of phenomena that surrounds the COP and shoving everything else offstage.

According to the cognitive optimum hypothesis, religious concepts that are relatively effortless to acquire, generate, and transmit will also be the most recurrent ones because, "[b]eing easier to learn and memorize, they will have a greater 'survival value'" (Boyer 1994, 406). The flip side of this coin is that those religious concepts that carry a heavy computational burden should show up far less regularly in the anthropological record. As we have already seen, Whitehouse contends that these more difficult and more infrequent concepts must be a central concern for any cognitive enterprise worth its salt—if only because the "heavier concepts are often the more valued ones" within religious communities (2004, 46). One result of this commitment is that the most pressing question isn't why one subset of supernatural concepts has a selective advantage over others. In fact, it is quite the opposite. The issue now is how such demanding representations could ever reach these rarefied corners in the evolutionary design space of all possible religions in the first place.

The anthropologist in Whitehouse is convinced—and has been for years—that accounting for the heavy computational burdens of immodestly counterintuitive religious representations requires greater sensitivity to our sociocultural embeddedness (cf. 1996). In general, Whitehouse believes that the strategy of exclusively appealing to culturally invariant bundles of domain-specific conceptual knowledge to explain supernatural concepts leaves us powerless to explain the manifest ethnographic variations within and between religious systems. He judges that at the same time that Boyer's account demonstrates that the supernatural concept of an agent with counterintuitive properties "is capable of being represented by any normal person in normal developmental circumstances, regardless of cultural peculiarities, it does not set out to predict whether such concepts will be imported into particular cultural settings" (Whitehouse 2001b, 172). At various points, we are left with the impression that because the standard model ignores the context-dependent nature of religious systems, it not only does not but in fact cannot explain why some supernatural concepts appear in some cultural settings and not others. If he is right about this—and for now I'll leave this an open question—it could mean that the mainstream approach will never be able to assuage the intellectual anxieties of those critics who swear that the cognitive toolbox is useless when it comes to understanding why this group at this time believes and behaves as it does. The modes theory intends to cover this shortfall and proposes that the twin problems of unnatural religious cognition and ethnographic particularity can both be resolved once we acknowledge how our cultural embeddedness makes complex forms of religious belief and behavior possible.

Both Boyer and Whitehouse agree that the tendency of religious concepts to drift toward the COP is an effect of the constraints that the human cognitive engine imposes on the transmission of cultural knowledge: only those beliefs and practices that can withstand the constant danger of distortion and erosion through transmission survive to become components of religious systems. This fact, combined with a thorough grasp of our native computational strengths and weaknesses, leads Boyer and others to argue that the province of modestly counterintuitive supernatural concepts is a massive basin of attraction in the evolutionary landscape of religion. Although Whitehouse doesn't disagree with this conclusion, he believes that these cognitive constraints are considerably relaxed by the social practices and cultural scaffolding associated with either the imagistic or doctrinal modes of religiosity. I take it that the general theoretical point is that the amount and kind of nongenetic information that can be consistently exchanged between generations will shift in the direction of increasing complexity as more powerful techniques of transmission are discovered and fine-tuned. More specifically, however, the idea seems to be that the gravitational pull of the COP can be offset by the sociopolitical consequences of mode dynamics in such a way that religious traditions are free to construct increasingly complex and extravagantly counterintuitive supernatural concepts. Unnatural religious activity owes its existence to a religious system's strategic use of nonneural resources to shepherd natural modes of cognition into these hard-to-reach territories in the Space of Reason. A strong interpretation of this line of thought leads to the recognition that these hybrids of cultural scaffolding, institutional practices, and other minds create distributed sociotechnical systems that display cognitive properties that cannot be reduced to the cognitive properties of individual minds. Even if the modes theory prefers to shy away from this high-octane thesis, however, it is willing to bet that it is only through the processes and conditions established through the alternative modalities of religion "that intrinsically hard-to-acquire revelatory knowledge can be generated and culturally transmitted" (Whitehouse 2004, 76).

Another way of putting this is to say that in many anthropological contexts, Whitehouse thinks working out the macrodynamics of social infrastructure and local customs is no less important for a vigorous explanation of religion than understanding the microdynamics of human cognition. Without the nonneural resources that the modes of religiosity make available to the naked biological brain, some forms of religious activity are for all practical purposes impossible to sustain. For example, he points out that the high-frequency repetition, administrative supervision, and bureaucratic structures associated with the doctrinal mode hang together in such a way to produce a transmissive strategy that can reliably pass on a stable body of cognitively demanding religious doctrine. Anything less, we are told, and such computationally heavy cultural knowledge "will be garbled or simply forgotten" (2004, 75). The notion that in their own ways each mode of religiosity creates the necessary conditions for religious systems to preserve modifications in a way that generates greater complexity over time is, at bottom, another version of what Michael Tomasello and others have christened the "ratchet effect" in human cultural evolution (Tomasello, Kruger, and Ratner 1993; Tomasello 2000).

The only snag in the ratchet effect's ability to accumulate innovations is that while it makes progress possible, it does not make it inexorable. Even a small amount of "slippage" in the transmission process can quickly reduce the scope and precision of the effect, and erratic transmission is capable of canceling the effect out altogether (Boesch and Tomasello 1998). White-house is plainly aware of this threat and indicates that the gravitational tug of the COP can easily overwhelm the mode dynamics as soon as any element of the sociocultural scaffolding begins to give way. He writes, "In the ab-sence of pedagogic support and effective policing, we often find that lay ver-sions of world religions migrate away from both of our modal attractor posi-tions and settle around more easily acquired, intuitive concepts and practices (the cognitive optimum position) that consequently require neither rou-tinization nor high arousal to maintain" (Whitehouse 2004, 76). In both physics and religious cognition, it turns out, there can only be temporary vic-tories over gravity's relentless pull.

GODS, WORDS, AND NUMBERS:
ONE OF THESE THINGS IS NOT LIKE THE OTHERS

So, what do the differences between the standard model of "natural religion" and the modal theory of "unnatural religion" amount to? In the past, White-house has been content to view his work as no more than an "enriched" ver-sion or "slight refinement" of Boyer's project. On this reading, the standard model is perfectly adept at accounting for the origins and content of eco-nomical religious thought, but we are forced to shift gears whenever we are confronted with prodigal forms of religious cognition. However, in my self-appointed role as agent provocateur, I want to point out that a more ambi-tious interpretation may be in the cards. It is common for representatives of the mainstream cognitive approach to summarize the theoretical agenda by suggesting that acquiring a language and acquiring a religion should be viewed as roughly analogous. This move is under foot, for example, when Justin Barrett recaps the naturalness of religion thesis this way: "Much as lan-guage is naturally acquired as a result of cognitive preparedness plus expo-sure to a typical sociolinguistic environment, ordinary cognition plus expo-sure to an ordinary environment goes a long way towards explaining religion" (Barrett 2000, 29). However, the modes theory's bid to make the cognitive science of religion responsible for explaining religion in the round may seriously weaken the force and utility of this intuition pump.

Let's assume that Steven Pinker is largely correct about the acquisition of language being underwritten by a "language instinct" (see Tomasello 1995 and Cowie 1998 for dissenting opinions). One of the pieces of evidence used to construct this case is that every human community ever encountered speaks a strikingly complex natural language. Yet the recognition that a given anthropological pattern is universal doesn't mean that it is part of our biological makeup. To help justify the stronger biological claim, Pinker proposes that we need only contrast complex linguistic systems with undeniably cultural creations like the wheel or the Rubik's Cube. As we read near the beginning of *The Language Instinct*,

> The universality of complex language is a discovery that fills linguists with awe, and is the first reason to suspect that language is not just any cultural invention. Cultural inventions vary widely in their sophistication from society to society; within a society, the inventions are generally at the same level of sophistication. Some groups count by carving notches on bones and cook on fires ignited by spinning sticks in logs; others use computers and microwave ovens. Language, however, ruins this correlation. There are Stone Age societies, but there is no such thing as a Stone Age language. (1994, 15)

The point here isn't simply that the Victorian conceit about "civilized" and "uncivilized" languages is demonstrably false. Rather, it is that since linguistic systems are everywhere and always complex—and cultural products display divergent degrees of complexity depending on time and place—language should be viewed as a genetically secured element of our Darwinian biological inheritance. Compare this with the example that Pinker himself invokes in the previous passage: counting.

There is reason to think that the human mind comes preequipped with an innate mechanism for handling limited numerical quantities. As early as four months old, infants appear to have the cognitive equipment necessary to perform simple calculations dealing with sets of up to four objects. The early experimental data are just beginning to tell the fascinating story of our native mathematical talent (Wynn 1992; Starkey, Spelke, and Gelman 1990; Gallistel and Gelman 1992). At the same time, however, the ethnographic and historical data also force us to recognize that this innate sensitivity to number often leads to very different results. From the presence or lack of negative numbers to the tools for performing arithmetical functions beyond addition and subtraction, number systems have routinely displayed varying degrees of complexity in the manner that Pinker regards as a hallmark of cultural inventiveness. The anthropological tendency in the past was to adopt a muscular social constructivist stance and maintain that possessing abstract numerical concepts is strictly determined by the contours of the local numerical system. Proof positive of this inclination can be found in Tobias Dantzig's infamous claim that the "Bushmen of South Africa have no number words beyond one, two, and many, and these words are so inarticulate that it may be doubted whether the natives attach a clear meaning to them" (1954, 2). The idea was that if a linguistic community didn't provide the cultural input that a word for three provides, its members couldn't possibly have the concept of three. Thanks in part to the modern sciences of the mind, this strategy for dealing with the observable cross-cultural differences between number systems is no longer very convincing. Over the past decade, psychologists have begun to argue that for these sorts of differences to exist at all, there must first be an innate computational "skeleton" for numerical ability that is regulated by domain-specific organizing principles (Gelman and Brenneman 1994). In other words, the basic levels of numerosity that the concepts of oneness, twoness, and threeness exemplify—and which prelinguistic children consistently exhibit in discrimination tasks—do not depend on the cultural input of symbolic number systems.

Yet, the recognition that cross-cultural differences in the domain of numbers may ultimately rest on a computational substrate that all developmentally normal humans possess only seems to underscore the long-term significance of the cognitive scaffolding that a symbolic number system affords. Depending on the idiosyncrasies of a given numerical system, some mathematical problems are not only unsolvable; they are locally inconceivable. In a community where the numerical concepts consist of one, two, many, and a lot, for example, problems like $\sqrt{-1}$ or entities such as π are cognitively invisible. But in a richly structured sociocultural world stocked with the necessary mind tools, the same innate but limited mechanism for numerosity can be transformed into an arithmetical dynamo capable of solving $\sqrt{-1}$ or tracing π out to the millionth decimal point. Appreciating this dramatic transformation gives new life to Bo Dahlbom and Lars-Erik Janlert's aperçu that "Just as you cannot do much carpentry with your bare hands, there is not much thinking you can do with your bare brain" (quoted in Dennett 1996, 134). So, not only does the brain-plus-scaffolding present us with a profoundly different problem-solving profile than the bare biological brain, but, in addition, the ability to culturally reprogram ourselves in such a way that we create a powerful "virtual machine" of complex arithmetical competence begins to undermine the idea that mathematics can be accurately described as being either natural or unnatural.[8] Although human infants, rats, and chimpanzees all demonstrate a proficiency for discriminating between small sets of objects, much of what is recognizably human mathematical cognition is a hybrid—the outcome "of a complex and heterogeneous developmental matrix in which culture, technology, and biology are pretty well inextricably intermingled" (Clark 2003, 86).

Although I have only skimmed the surface, I hope the intended goal of this rudimentary contrast between languages and number systems is apparent. For a theoretical scalawag looking to make waves, the modes theory's double-barreled claim that (1) religious cognition is sensitive to the macrodynamics of sociocultural conditions and (2) religious systems as a whole exhibit varying degrees of cross-cultural complexity is more than enough. On this basis alone, one can arrive at the conclusion that if Whitehouse's project is on the right track, the process of acquiring a religion is much more like acquiring a number system than a language. Simply but luridly put, without the nonneural resources that richly structured environments make available to the naked biological brain, much of what passes for religious and mathematical cognitive activity could be practically impossible. It is undoubtedly the case that certain native talents are necessary for all three phenomena to exist. Nevertheless, it seems clear that neither religious nor number systems share language's conspicuous independence from the structures, practices, and techniques associated with externally supported and culturally scaffolded learning. The innate computational "skeleton" for numerical ability is a necessary prerequisite for wrestling with $\sqrt{-1}$ or π, but to actually grapple with these entities requires the resources made available to us through cumulative cultural evolution. So too, our intuitive belief-desire psychology might be nothing more than a crucial precondition for our commerce with the gods. But to figure out how we get from there to religion in the round— that is to say, to the beliefs and practices that really matter to people—we must understand how the ratchet effect's ability to generate increasing levels of complexity has worked in particular sociocultural conditions to generate particular religious systems—a move, our firebrand would point out, that depends on our willingness to stop thinking of religion as a feature of our lives that is as natural as language and finally come to terms with the peculiarities of place.

No doubt, many would consider this idea to go dangerously, perhaps even stupidly, out on a limb. However, there's a good chance that the limb in question is strong enough to support the weight. Kim Sterelny has recently argued on evolutionary grounds that the enthusiasm for adopting Chomsky's portrait of language as a basic model of human cognition is a mistake. When he considers the lay of the land, the distinctive features of language that make modular theories so compelling (e.g., poverty of the stimulus arguments) also tend to make language "an outlier, not a paradigm" of human cognition (2003, 184). I believe that the portrait of culturally embedded cognition that the modes theory assumes forces us to address a similar problem. If we look at the full range of religious belief and behavior through the lens of situated cognition, it seems to depend on cultural input and particular forms of external cognitive scaffolding in ways that language simply does not. This alone should make us pause and critically reflect on the idea that religion, like language, is a natural product of the human mind. Perhaps the time has come for us all to rethink naturalness (Elman et al. 1996). Does it make sense to distinguish between "natural" and "unnatural" forms of religious activity if it is the synthetic outcome of a developmental matrix in which the contributions of culture, technology, and biology are "inextricably intermingled"? I'm just not sure. But it is a virtue of Whitehouse's project and its theoretical ambitions that this question is now on the table.

NOTES

1. Yet, considering how descent with modification rarely—if ever—distributes phenotypic characteristics in a universal and exclusive fashion, one must be careful not to overstate the case. The strategic division between plants and animals that I have sketched is anything but immutable, as the countless examples of moving plants (e.g., cytoplankton) and anchored animals (e.g., barnacles) brilliantly demonstrate.

2. Moreover, the issue doesn't seem to be the move away from ethnographic specificity per se. Whether one prefers a deductive-nomological (Hempel 1965), causal mechanical (Salmon 1984), or unificationist (Kitcher 1989) treatment, nearly all parties agree *in principle* that a successful explanation expands our understanding of the world by appealing to a more general state of affairs to account for a particular phenomenon or empirical pattern. As a result, we shouldn't jump to the conclusion that our critics are objecting to the "subpersonal" strategy of cognitive explanation that dissolves the unified person into a cohesive organization of subsystems (Dennett 1978). The concern—or, at least the concern we should be addressing—is whether the cognitive approach generates sufficient explanatory and/or predictive leverage to warrant collective academic allegiance.

3. The recognition of *causal symmetry* does not mean, however, that we must reject *asymmetrical explanations* that pivot around privileged elements within the complex causal nexus as some proponents of ecologically-oriented models of cognition have argued. For example, Tim Ingold suggests that we must rethink all of neo-Darwinian evolutionary thought because it fails to capture the "interactionist" quality of ontogenetic development (2001). Yes, the portrait of embedded cognition forces us to take external, nonneural scaffolding seriously when we set out to explain how a particular outcome is produced. Nevertheless, as Michael Wheeler and Andy Clark forcefully argue, the general explanatory trajectory remains clear: "It is characterized by achievements that still rest fairly heavily on the use of internal information-bearing resources, but that rely on a variety of additional factors and forces that take up the substantial slack left by the information-based story" (1999, 131; see also Clark 2000).

4. Robert McCauley and Thomas Lawson (2002) take Whitehouse's project to be principally concerned with the variable of transmissive *frequency* and its inverse relationship with sensory stimulation. According to their analysis, the modes theory is fatally weakened by the recognition that (1) it cannot account for why we find variations in the frequency of ritual performance at all, and (2) their ritual form hypothesis not only covers the patterns that the modes theory describes but identifies the underlying causes of such divergent forms of ritual activity. They contend that Whitehouse either has the wrong target in mind or has part of the causal story back-

ward by putting transmissive frequency in the driver's seat. The conceptual mistake that worries them can be unearthed if we translate these issues into a simple biological example. Do we say that female gorillas reproduce relatively slowly, and thus invest heavily in their young (i.e., they invest in their young because they have nothing better to do)? Or do we say that female gorillas invest heavily in their young, and thus reproduce relatively slowly (i.e., the degree of investment constrains the rate at which they can reproduce)? The first option represents what could be called *the reproductive frequency hypothesis* of gorilla mating, while the second offers *the reproductive form hypothesis.* Just as it is a relatively obvious mistake to make "frequency" the engine driving the relevant features of gorilla reproduction rather than "form," it would seem to be a mistake to make ritual frequency rather than ritual form the fulcrum of causal leverage in religious systems.

Whitehouse protests that this interpretation fails to reckon with the multicausal theoretical structure of his approach. He insists that there "is no independent variable driving the rest, only a set of conditions that some patterns of human activity manage to satisfy, thus accounting for their cultural success" (2004, 75). For now, I want to take a firmly agnostic stand on whether the McCauley and Lawson criticism is on target and make a general observation about the dispute. Part of the problem seems to be that at the same time the modes theory clearly argues that the divergent forms of religiosity do not rest on a single variable, it is hard not to come away with the feeling that transmissive frequency is—if nothing else—clearly primus inter pares. As a case in point, Whitehouse argues that the riddle of why the concept of a *witch* is common in Zande populations but relatively rare in English populations may be solved "if we take into consideration variations in transmissive frequency" (2004, 24).

5. Although he strikes different notes, J. Z. Smith also suggests that *religion* may be fruitfully compared to *cuisine.* However, where Boyer begins with a strictly limited constellation of cognitive templates that allows for a vast number of possible arrangements, Smith begins with "an almost limitless horizon of possibilities" that particular cultures arbitrarily reduce to a set of basic elements. After this initial cultural choice has been made, he writes, "a most intense ingenuity is exercised to overcome the reduction . . . to introduce interest and variety. This ingenuity is usually accompanied by a complex set of rules" (Smith 1982, 40). The idea that specific cultural traditions (a) only exist by virtue of a restricted "menu" but (b) must then tackle the "gastronomic" boredom that is the predictable consequence of such restrictions, has obvious parallels with Whitehouse's interest in the gimmicks that highly routinized religious traditions must invent to overcome the "tedium effect."

6. More precisely, Boyer judges that more cognitively complex forms of religious cognition are a special case and should not be taken as a reliable guide to either the cognitive contents or causes of religious activity (Boyer 2003). Robert McCauley (2000) seconds this approach and argues that while second-order, theological reflection appears to require the same elaborate cultural scaffolding that scientific thought demands, everyday forms of religious activity do not.

7. In a similar vein, Whitehouse argues that the cognitive science of religion must overcome the standard model's deliberate neglect of explicit, first-person beliefs and motivations if we are to fully appreciate how the immodestly counterintuitive concepts of the doctrinal and imagistic modes are acquired, generated, and transmitted (2004, 24–26, 139–40).

8. Daniel Dennett has compared this transformation of a naked brain and its initial competences to the "virtual machines" that can be run on top of a computer's hard-wired architecture. Consider the familiar suite of games commonly installed on an IBM-compatible PC: Solitaire, Minesweeper, Hearts, and Freecell. Each game is a different virtual machine, a distinct pattern of rules imposed on and supported by the real machine's fixed hardware. While you are playing Solitaire, the computer looks just like a dedicated solitaire-playing machine, but if you close that game and open Minesweeper, the computer suddenly looks like a minesweeper-playing machine. Yet these games are only *virtual* machines because each one is "a temporary set of highly structured regularities imposed on the underlying hardware by a *program*: a structured recipe of hundreds of thousands of instructions that give the hardware a huge, interlocking set of habits or dispositions-to-react" (Dennett 1991, 216). According to Dennett, the human ability to culturally reprogram ourselves is more than another version of a virtual machine's structured computational regularities being imposed on a real machine's hardwired architecture; it is the sine qua non for transforming a naked brain into a full-fledged mind. A mind is a "chameleonic transformer . . . a virtual machine for making more virtual machines. And where are they, these virtual machines? Centered on a brain, to be sure, but not explicable without looking outside the brain into the world" (Dennett 2000). When seen in this light, one might say that brains are biologically given but minds are environmentally forged.

REFERENCES

Barrett, Justin. 2000. Exploring the Natural Foundations of Religion. *Trends in Cognitive Sciences* 4, no. 1: 29–34.

Boesch, Christophe and Michael Tomasello. 1998. Chimpanzee and Human Cultures. *Current Anthropology* 39: 591–614.

Boyer, Pascal. 1994. Cognitive Constraints on Cultural Representations: Natural Ontologies and Religious Ideas. In *Mapping the Mind: Domain Specificity in Cognition and Culture*, ed. L. A. Hirschfeld and S. A. Gelman. Cambridge: Cambridge University Press.

———. 2000. Functional Origins of Religious Concepts: Ontological and Strategic Selection in Evolved Minds. *Journal of the Royal Anthropological Institute* 6: 195–214.

———. 2001. *Religion Explained: The Evolutionary Origins of Religious Thought.* New York: Basic Books.

———. 2003. Religious Thought and Behavior as By-products of Brain Function. *Trends in Cognitive Sciences* 7: 119–24.

Cosmides, Leda and John Tooby. 1992. Cognitive Adaptations for Social Exchange. In *The Adapted Mind*, ed. Jerome Barkow, Leda Cosmides, and John Tooby. New York: Oxford University Press.

Cowie, Fiona. 1998. *What's Within? Nativism Reconsidered.* Oxford: Oxford University Press.

Clark, Andy. 1997. *Being There.* Cambridge, MA: MIT Press.

———. 2000. Twisted Tales: Causal Complexity and Cognitive Scientific Explanation. In *Explanation and Cognition*, ed. Frank Keil and Robert Wilson. Cambridge: MIT Press.

———. 2003. *Natural-Born Cyborgs*. Oxford: Oxford University Press.

Dantzig, Tobias. 1954. *Number: the Language of Science*, 4th ed. New York: Free Press.

Dennett, Daniel. 1978. *Brainstorms*. Cambridge, MA: MIT Press.

———. 1991. *Consciousness Explained*. Boston: Little, Brown and Co.

———. 1996. *Kinds of Minds*. New York: Basic Books.

———. 2000. Making Tools for Thinking. In *Metarepresentations*, ed. Dan Sperber. Oxford: Oxford University Press.

———. 2003. *Freedom Evolves*. New York: Viking.

Dunbar, Robin. 1996. *Grooming, Gossip and the Evolution of Language*. Cambridge, MA: Harvard University Press.

Durkheim, Emile. 1982. *Rules of Sociological Method*. New York: Free Press.

Elman, Jeffrey, Elizabeth Bates, Mark Johnson, Annette Karmiloff-Smith, Domenico Parisi, and Kim Plunkett. 1996. *Rethinking Innateness: A Connectionist Perspective on Development*. Cambridge, MA: MIT Press.

Gallistel, Randy, and Rochel Gelman. 1992. Preverbal and Verbal Counting and Computation. *Cognition* 44: 43–74.

Gelman, Rochel, and Kimberly Brenneman. 1994. Learning about Music and Number. In *Mapping the Mind: Domain Specificity in Cognition and Culture*, ed. A. Hirschfeld and S. A. Gelman. Cambridge: Cambridge University Press.

Goodwin, Brian. 1995. *How the Leopard Changed Its Spots*. Princeton: Princeton University Press.

Griffiths, Paul, and Karola Stolz. 2000. How the Mind Grows: A Developmental Perspective on the Biology of Cognition. *Synthese* 122: 29–51.

Hempel, Carl. 1965. *Aspects of Scientific Explanation and Other Essays in the Philosophy of Science*. New York: Free Press.

Heyes, Cecilia. 2000. Evolutionary Psychology in the Round. In *The Evolution of Cognition*, ed. Cecilia Heyes and Ludwig Huber. Cambridge, MA: MIT Press.

———. 2003. Four Routes of Cognitive Evolution. *Psychological Review* 110(4): 713–27.

Humphrey, Nicholas. 1976. The Social Function of Intellect. In *Growing Points in Ethology*, ed. P. Bateson and R. Hinde. Cambridge: Cambridge University Press.

Hutchins, Edwin. 1995. *Cognition in the Wild*. Cambridge, MA: MIT Press.

Ingold, Tim. 2001. From the Transmission of Representation to the Education of Attention. In *The Debated Mind: Evolutionary Psychology Versus Ethnography*, ed. Harvey Whitehouse. Oxford: Berg.

Kitcher, Philip. 1989. Explanatory Unification and the Causal Structure of the World. In *Scientific Explanation*, ed. Phillip Kitcher and Wesley Salmon. Minneapolis: University of Minnesota Press.

———. 2003. Giving Darwin His Due. In *Cambridge Companion to Darwin*, ed. Jonathan Hodge and Gregory Radick, 399–420. Cambridge: Cambridge University Press.

Malley, Brian. 2002. Review of "Arguments and Icons." *Journal of Ritual Studies* 16: 5–7.

Maynard Smith, John. 1974. The Theory of Games and the Evolution of Animal Conflict. *Journal of Theoretical Biology* 47: 209–21.

McCauley, Robert. 2000. The Naturalness of Religion and the Unnaturalness of Science. In *Explanation and Cognition*, ed. Frank Keil and Robert Wilson. Cambridge: MIT Press.

McCauley, Robert, and E. Thomas Lawson. 2002. *Bringing Ritual to Mind: Psychological Foundations of Cultural Forms*. New York: Cambridge University Press.
Meyerhoff, Barbara. 1974. *Peyote Hunt*. Ithaca: Cornell University Press.
Pinker, Steven. 1994. *The Language Instinct*. New York: Harper Collins.
Povinelli, Daniel. 1996. Chimpanzee Theory of Mind?: The Road to Strong Inference. In *Theories of Theories of Mind*, ed. Peter Carruthers and Peter Smith. Cambridge: Cambridge University Press.
Rosenberg, Alexander. 2000. *Darwinism in Philosophy, Social Science and Policy*. Cambridge: Cambridge University Press.
Ryle, Gilbert. 1990. *Collected Essays 1929–1968*, vol. 1. Bristol: Thoemmes.
Salmon, Wesley. 1984. *Scientific Explanation and the Causal Structure of the World*. Princeton: Princeton University Press.
Samuelson, Larry. 1997. *Evolutionary Games and Equilibrium Selection*. Cambridge, MA: MIT Press.
Smith, Jonathan. 1982. *Imagining Religion*. Chicago: University of Chicago Press.
Sober, Elliott. 1984. *The Nature of Selection: Evolutionary Theory in Philosophical Focus*. Cambridge, MA: MIT Press.
Starkey, Prentice, Elizabeth Spelke, and Rochel Gelman. 1990. Numerical Abstraction by Human Infants. *Cognition* 36: 97–127.
Sterelny, Kim. 2003. *Thought in a Hostile World: The Evolution of Human Cognition*. Oxford: Blackwell Publishing.
Tomasello, Michael. 1995. Language Is Not an Instinct. *Cognitive Development* 10: 131–56.
———. 2000. *The Cultural Origins of Human Cognition*. Cambridge, MA: Harvard University Press.
Tomasello, Michael, Ann Kruger, and Hilary Horn Ratner. 1993. Cultural Learning. *Behavioral and Brain Sciences* 16: 450–88.
Wheeler, Michael, and Andy Clark. 1999. Genic Representation: Reconciling Content and Causal Complexity. *British Journal of the Philosophy of Science* 50: 103–35.
Whitehouse, Harvey. 1996. Jungles and Computers: Neuronal Group Selection and the Epidemiology of Representations. *Journal of the Royal Anthropological Institute* 2: 99–116.
———. 2001a. Conclusion: Towards a Reconciliation. In *The Debated Mind*, ed. Harvey Whitehouse. Oxford: Berg.
———. 2001b. Transmissive Frequency, Ritual, and Exegesis. *Journal of Cognition and Culture* 1: 167–81.
———. 2004. *Modes of Religiosity: A Cognitive Theory of Religious Transmission*. Walnut Creek, CA: AltaMira Press.
Whiten, Andrew. 1996. Imitation, Pretense and Mindreading: Secondary Representation in Comparative Primatology and Developmental Psychology. In *Reaching Into Thought: The Minds of Great Apes*, ed. Anne Russon, Kim Bard, and Sue Taylor. Cambridge: Cambridge University Press.
Wynn, Karen. 1992. Addition and Subtraction in Human Infants. *Nature* 358: 749–50.

II

TESTING THE MODES THEORY

6

In the Empirical Mode: Evidence Needed for the Modes of Religiosity Theory

Justin Barrett

Whitehouse's modes of religiosity theory (2000, 2004), like other cognitive theories, draws upon insights regarding the normal functioning of human minds to make broader predictions about the sorts of religious ideas and practices that become cross-culturally recurrent. This appeal to both the functioning of individual minds and the features of distributed ideas and group behaviors requires methodological pluralism for garnering support. Some observers of the cognitive science of religion seem to regard experimentation as the silver bullet for empirical challenges, and on the other end of the spectrum, some favor the more ecologically sensitive methods of ethnography. The breadth of the modes theory's claims, however, requires both of these classes of empirical methods and strategies that fall in between.

Because it concerns memory, emotions, social arrangements, the distribution of beliefs and practices, and numerous other factors, the modes theory is a veritable treasure trove of potential studies. But where to begin? In this chapter, I offer a tentative framework prioritizing the empirical needs of the modes theory. I sketch seventeen different predictions of the modes of religiosity theory and tentatively suggest which of three different classes of empirical methods (experimental, naturalistic, and ethnographic) seems to be most appropriate for each specific prediction.[1]

By *experimental* methods, I mean studies that take place with samples from populations using artificially produced materials and measures. For instance, an experimenter might take a group of college sophomores and randomly assign them to two groups. To one group the experimenter might show a list of twenty one-syllable words projected on a large screen, each word appearing for two seconds then vanishing, and the next word being given after a two-second delay. After the final word presentation and a five-minute delay, the participants might be asked to recall as many of the words as possible and write them down. The second group might perform the exact same task but with Handel's "Hallelujah Chorus" playing in the background. The number of words each group remembers may then be compared, and any resulting differences attributed to the influence of Handel's "Hallelujah Chorus"—the experimental manipulation. Such experimental methods are common to the psychological sciences, because of their potential for great precision and control over variables of interest. Experimentation, however, remains fairly uncommon in explaining religious phenomena because of the impracticality of manipulating such variables as religious beliefs, practices, and commitments, or the "random assignment" of participants to the theist versus the atheist group or the Hindu versus the Mormon group. Experimental studies may also suffer from a lack of ecological validity—an ability to accurately generalize to naturally occurring conditions. Just because listening to Handel in a laboratory may improve memory for a list of monosyllabic words does not necessarily mean that playing Handel while reading a book at home will improve reading comprehension. Too many factors may differ.

What I call *naturalistic* methods are those studies that seize upon naturally occurring comparison groups within the same population. My favorite examples of naturalistic studies were conducted by Ulric Neisser and colleagues (Neisser et al. 1996) and bear upon one aspect of the modes theory. Neisser and colleagues questioned college students in the San Francisco Bay Area of California, and students in Atlanta, Georgia, immediately following the large Bay Area earthquake of 1991, which led to the collapse of the San Francisco Bay Bridge and the Major League Baseball World Series being postponed. Students in both locations were asked details about how they first heard about the earthquake (what they were doing, who they were with, etc.) and when they learned of the Bay Bridge's collapse. Experimenters then requestioned these same students months later to check for lapses in accuracy. Neisser found that students who experienced the earthquake had quite vivid and accurate memories of the event after enormous delays, whereas those who merely heard about the event were typically confident but mistaken in their memories. Though borrowing from experimental designs, experimenters could not manufacture the event to be remembered (an earthquake), nor assign participants to their condition (experiencing the earthquake versus only hearing about it). Consequently, the validity of the conclusions rest upon the assumption that the student samples from California and Atlanta were similar on all potentially relevant dimensions. If this assumption is granted, the study enjoys tremendous ecological validity because of its real-world setting.

The most ecologically sensitive sorts of methods are those I call *ethnographic*. By ethnography, I mean broadly the observation and measurement of human behavior (including speech acts as in conversations) in the course of normal day-to-day activities. Whitehouse's own participant/observation-based description of the Pomio Kivung over the course of approximately two years of field research is an excellent relevant example (Whitehouse 1995). I also include in this group sociological studies that would amount to tabulating the distribution of various explicitly held feelings or ideas and their correspondence to group identification or other demographic variables. Thus, for the sake of the present discussion, I term a study that, for instance, tabulates the proportion of Nigerian Muslims who approve of polygamy an "ethnographic" study.

Note that these ethnographic studies may be conducted on existing groups of people or using historical materials. Hence, studies I call experimental or naturalistic are those most likely to be conducted using psychological methods, whereas those labeled ethnographic are those falling under the methodological expertise of anthropologists, sociologists, historians, and even archeologists.

UNIT OF ANALYSIS

One potential difficulty in empirically testing Whitehouse's theory is the potential for both imagistic and doctrinal dynamics to be active in a single village, city, or congregation. For instance, within a village that would seem to be easily classified as doctrinal (e.g., a Catholic village in Mesoamerica), a subgroup of the residents might also identify with a religious group that would be best characterized as imagistic (e.g., only the men of the Mesoamerican village participate in an indigenous forest-spirit cult). A single individual could hold membership in more than one religious community. Because of this potential for "co-present modes," and because many of the predictions of the theory have to do with individual cognitive, affective, and behavioral processes, I do not favor an empirical approach that treats a geographic unit (e.g., village, town, island) as a unit of analysis. Rather, studies should begin with *individuals* and the community or communities to which they belong as the operative units of analysis. Individuals may be members of more than one religious community even if the individuals themselves do not recognize the fact of their joint membership.

FOUNDATIONAL CLAIMS

In developing his theory, Whitehouse makes four general, foundational claims. First, he asserts that religious traditions are materially constrained. By materially constrained he includes constraints imposed by physical materials in the environment, human biology, and characteristics of human minds. Second, to explain religious phenomena, one must consider selective dynamics that shape them. It is not as if any ideas or behaviors can become part of any culture. Some ideas and behaviors have better fitness to be stored in human minds or behavioral repertoire than others; and so some ideas and behaviors get forgotten or mistransmitted. Looking at just which ideas and behaviors are most readily accommodated by human minds goes a long way toward explaining recurrent cultural patterns. Third, Whitehouse maintains that this selective process of some ideas and behaviors being forgotten or mistransmitted is context dependent. Though some generalization may be made about cognitive factors impacting selection (e.g., that remembering a large number of kinship terms presents more difficulty than remembering a few), much of the observed variation in religious phenomena can only be accounted for by including contextual factors in explanatory models. Finally, Whitehouse insists that explicit religious concepts at least partly motivate religious transmission. That is, often people act based on their claimed religious beliefs. I summarize these claims and their empirical needs in table 6.1.

The cognitive science of religion has generally emphasized only the first two of these foundational claims, but also generally accepts the third. What is debated is not whether religion is materially constrained, but how it is constrained; not whether religious phenomena are selected, but the nature of the selective factors and dynamics; and not whether transmission is context dependent, but just how context matters and how much. Of the four foundational claims, the fourth raises mild controversy and need for empirical support.

Though sounding like common sense, the assertion that explicit religious beliefs motivate any behavior, let alone transmission, has remarkably little direct support. Even in more general studies of motivation, psychologists generally conclude that explicit beliefs or attitudes only serve as strong predictors of behavior when they are quite specific and consciously available at the time of the behavior (Ajzen and Fishbein 1977; Kallgren and Wood 1986). As applied to religion, this finding would imply that explicit religious beliefs

Table 6.1

Foundational Claims	Need for Empirical Assessment		
	Experimental	Naturalistic	Ethnographic
Religion is materially constrained	none	none	none
Religion results from selection.	none	none	none
Transmission of religion is context dependent	none	none	none
Explicit religious concepts motivate transmission.	strong	strong	strong

might only meaningfully impact transmission when they are beliefs specifically about an act of transmission *and* salient to the actors in question. If and
when these conditions are satisfied may be worthy of empirical attention using experimental, naturalistic, and ethnographic studies.

Existing studies that seem to account for religious behavior and transmission without strong appeal to explicit beliefs prompt this need for empirical
attention (e.g., Atran 2002; Boyer 2001; McCauley and Lawson 2002). To illustrate, I have shown that much of American Christian petitionary prayer
might be explained in terms of implicit cognition that contradicts explicit religious beliefs at points (Barrett 2001). In naturalistic studies involving prayer
journals and experimental methods requiring consideration of hypothetical
prayers, American Protestants demonstrated a strong tendency to avoid
prayers that asked God to act through mechanistic means (e.g., fixing cars)
even though their explicit theologies embraced such petitions as legitimate.
Similarly, colleagues and I found that American and Indian theists used implicit theological concepts in contradiction of explicit ones to interpret stories featuring religious characters (Barrett 1998, 1999; Barrett and Keil 1996;
Barrett and Van Orman 1996). Many other areas of religious thought and action, such as ritual (McCauley and Lawson 2002), transmission of ideas
(Boyer 2001), and "theologically incorrect" thinking about chance and luck
(Slone 2004), have been explained without a prominent role of explicit religious cognition. Common sense notwithstanding, perhaps explicit cognition
only plays a minor role in the transmission of religious phenomena. Hence,
we have a need for more direct empirical study.

In addition to the four foundational claims, each of Whitehouse's two
"modes" demands the testing of a number of empirical questions. Though
discussing the two modes in contrast makes for good rhetoric, in terms of
empirical challenges, the predictions relating to doctrinal and imagistic
modes may be considered independently.

DOCTRINAL CLAIMS

Whitehouse's account of the doctrinal mode of religiosity prompts at least
eight specific predictions, as captured by table 6.2.

*Doctrinal Claim #1: Frequent repetition of doctrinal information is re-
quired to develop explicit memory for religious teaching.*

According to the modes theory, one of the functions of the repetitive religious gatherings in many religious systems is the opportunity to explicitly
communicate complicated doctrine. Repetition far outstrips mnemonic requirements for replicating the rituals conducted as part of these gatherings,
but may be required to ensure accurate doctrinal replication and sustenance
of orthodoxy.

Table 6.2

Doctrinal Claims	Need for Empirical Assessment		
	Experimental	Naturalistic	Ethnographic
#1: Repetition → Explicit memory for doctrine	weak	moderate	none
#2: Theological knowledge ↔ Teaching religious leaders	none	weak	strong
#3: Teaching religious leaders → Orthodoxy	none	weak	weak
#4: Orthodoxy checks → Centralization	weak	weak	strong
#5: Repetition → Procedural memory	none	weak	none
#6: Procedural memory → Reduced personal innovation → Acceptance of Orthodoxy	strong	strong	strong
#7: Explicit memory for doctrine + Procedural memory → Anonymous community	weak	moderate	moderate
#8: Religious leaders → Spread of religion	none	weak	moderate

This prediction rests on a fairly solid experimental foundation: repetition of ideas (rehearsal) certainly helps ensure their accurate transmission. What remains in doubt and a question worthy of further investigation is just how much repetition is really required to transmit and maintain ideas of the sort of complexity characteristic of doctrinal systems. Is once a week the magic frequency, or is this excessive or too little repetition? At stake is determining just what about these repeated ceremonies requires explanation. If around once-a-week repetition is required for most people to accurately learn theological notions in doctrinal traditions using such transmission cycles, then it would appear Whitehouse's doctrinal mode theory is on the right track. If such repetition is insufficient or excessive, more factors must be implicated.

As replicating the motivational force of religious teaching in an experimental setting may be impractical, naturalistic studies may be appropriate. For instance, recent converts' theological knowledge might be monitored over various iterations in presently occurring worship gatherings. Because this prediction concerns individual explicit memory, typical ethnographic studies may be only marginally helpful without naturalistic studies.

Doctrinal Claim #2: Larger bodies of explicit theological knowledge required of participants and the prominence of recognized religious leaders/authorities mutually reinforce each other.

The thinking behind this prediction proceeds as follows. The presence of people recognized as religious experts who spend time communicating complex doctrinal systems enables the spread of theological ideas more efficiently than completely egalitarian arrangements. Likewise, consistent and accurate transmission of large bodies of complex ideas almost requires a smaller number of specialist teachers.

As this prediction squarely involves social organization patterns, ethnographic or sociological methods would likely be most fruitful. The extent that members of various communities possess complex doctrinal knowledge could be measured alongside the prominence of recognized religious leaders in those communities. Sampling across many different religious groups and finding a relationship between possessed doctrinal complexity and the prominence of religious leaders would go a long way toward supporting this claim.

It might also be possible to discover naturally occurring "experiments" in which a community suddenly finds itself infused with a more complex body of theological information from outside sources (e.g., from missionaries or reformers). Would religious leaders suddenly become more prominent? Similarly, when communities bring in new religious leaders (e.g., when evangelists, missionaries, or pastors move in), does the body of explicit theological knowledge expand?

Doctrinal Claim #3: The presence of religious leaders/teachers encourages orthodoxy maintenance.

This prediction may amount to a natural extension of the previous one. If religious specialists play a role in transmitting complex doctrine, almost certainly part of that transmission is instruction on what does not count as legitimate doctrine.

If doctrinal claim #2 gains empirical support, #3 may not require any.

Doctrinal Claim #4: The presence of orthodoxy checks in a religious community encourages centralization of power structures.

As a question of social structure rather than simple interpersonal dynamics, I see this prediction best addressed by ethnographic means. I also place this prediction as a higher-priority one for investigation, for I wonder if the claim is generally true. Do some groups check orthodoxy and orthopraxy through relatively distributed social mechanisms instead of centralized hierarchy? At least across North American Christianity, those with the least centralization seem to have some of the strictest restraint on theological innovation, whereas those with fairly strong centralization (such as "mainline" Protestants) seem to be among the most permissive and least concerned with orthodoxy. A broad survey of the degree of centralization versus the degree of freedom for theological innovation would be helpful in more clearly supporting or falsifying this prediction. Likewise, careful ethnographic descriptions of the policing of orthodoxy in communities with varying degrees of centralization could bear directly on this prediction.

The relationship between orthodoxy maintenance and tendency for people to organize themselves hierarchically might be explored experimentally.

For instance, an experimenter might ask groups of adults to successfully learn and transmit a certain body of information, permitting them to devise ways to ensure the accuracy of the material. In half of the groups, the need for precise accuracy might be stressed, whereas in the other half, no such need for total accuracy would exist. Under such conditions, the strict-accuracy groups might be expected to organize some kinds of hierarchies for ensuring orthodoxy at a higher rate than the comparison groups. As potentially valuable as such results might be, ecological validity might remain a formidable criticism.

Doctrinal Claim #5: Frequent repetition of religious ceremonies leads to implicit memory for the procedures involved in the ceremonies.

Available ethnographic information regarding the enormous repetition of many religious acts and the clearly automatic character of their performance supports this prediction. Similarly, this prediction rests on solid experimental ground. Certainly heavy repetition of a series of behaviors leads to implicit memory or learning of the procedure, as in riding a bicycle or driving a car. Nevertheless, I am not aware of any naturalistic investigations connecting repetitive motor activity with implicit learning of religious actions, and such studies could be fruitful for establishing how much repetition is needed to yield implicit memory for religious actions.[2]

Doctrinal Claim #6: Implicit memory for the procedures of ceremonies reduces individual reflection and innovation regarding theological justifications for the ceremonies, thereby increasing acceptance of orthodox interpretations.

This two-part prediction may be a relatively high priority in terms of needing empirical support. I am not aware of any experiments or naturalistic studies that establish that mastery of a symbolic procedure (as in religious rituals or ceremonies) reduces reflection on why it is performed the way it is or why it is performed at all. Indeed, anecdotally, I have had practitioners in religions with highly routinized ceremonies report to me that the predictability of the routine allows for reflection on the meanings, whereas unfamiliar behavioral sequences consume too much concentration to allow for exegetical reflection. Alternately, the relationship between repetition and reflection could prove to be curvilinear, with some procedural mastery enabling an increase in reflection, but too much repetition decreasing motivation in reflection.

Ethnographic studies could carefully examine the correspondence of uniform (orthodox) explanations for religious routines that have presumably become part of implicit memory because of repetition. For instance, Roman Catholics' explanations for self-crossing might be contrasted with explanations for elements of wedding ceremonies. Presumably, when and how to cross oneself is fully implicit in adult Catholics. Consequently, explanations for the practice should either be uniformly orthodox or absent. Whereas, for weddings, Catholics should readily produce interpretations that show relatively high levels of interpersonal variation.

Of comparable or greater value would be experimental and naturalistic studies. Under experimental conditions, the relationship between procedure learning and reflection could be directly examined. Though motivational problems and other pragmatic concerns lurk, participants might be taught to perform a mock ritual over a series of meetings. Participants might be asked to journal their thoughts or reactions to the mock ritual, a fraction of the participants answering after the initial training (before they have implicit memory for the procedure), another fraction after several more trials, another fraction after several more trials, and so on.

Naturalistic studies could avoid motivational and pragmatic problems of experiments by examining religious participants' reflections at various stages of acquiring procedural knowledge. The exegetical reflections of recent converts or juveniles who have recently qualified to participate in repeated actions might be examined as they acquire procedural knowledge of the tasks.

Doctrinal Claim #7: Explicit memory for teachings, combined with implicit memory for ceremonial procedures, encourages "anonymous" religious communities.

Generally, the notion that implicit procedural memory leads to a certain disregard for players in the procedure strikes me as fairly well-grounded in terms of experimental psychological research. Particularly, work on *scripts* has shown that familiar routines often lead us to replace individual identities with role markers (Schank and Abelson 1977). For instance, for people who have often visited restaurants, typically little effort is made to engage the server as an individual. The server is the server and nothing else. By analogy it seems reasonable that a lifelong Catholic might understand Mass in terms of the roles that the congregation plays, the altar boys play, and the priest plays, but pay relatively little attention to the particular identities of any of the players. Hence, an "anonymous" religious community is produced.

Though the experimental footing for a connection between procedural memory and anonymity of players is solid, a naturalistic extension to religious scripts and procedures would be helpful. For instance, if both expert churchgoers and novice churchgoers attended the same worship meeting, would the novices tend to pay more attention to individual characteristics of the principal players in the ceremony than would the experts?

What is less clearly supported experimentally or naturalistically is that acquisition of a body of explicit teachings contributes to an anonymous community. Whitehouse reasons that once teachings have become well learned over successive iterations, they become divorced from particular learning episodes or any specific episodic memory that ties them to a fixed set of coparticipants. Consequently, this abstract body of beliefs may be shared with any number of unknown others. Though sensible sounding, is it true? Perhaps one way to get at this notion would be to compare new believers' estimates of how many others believe what they do with older believers' estimates. A sixteen-year-old with very little theological knowledge who goes to an evangelical retreat and suddenly converts to a faith might not extend common belief much beyond the people at the retreat. Whereas this same sixteen-year-old three years later, or a long-term-believing sixteen-year-old who has considerably more solid theological knowledge, might have a more expansive vision of who shares membership in the faith.

Ethnographically, I would like to see it more clearly documented that feelings of belonging to a broad religious community correspond to repetitive explicit teachings and implicit memory for event procedures. Does the salience of other particular members of the religious community actually decrease with the repetition of religious teachings and events, or is this anonymity a function of the size or transience of the community? That is, perhaps the doctrinal nature of some traditions encourages their numerical growth (see the next doctrinal prediction below), and it is this size that leads to a sense of anonymity to members, and not explicit memory for teachings or the formation of scripts.

Doctrinal Claim #8: The presence of religious leaders contributes to beliefs spreading beyond original communities.

This claim readily lends itself to promising empirical investigation, particularly through ethnographic and naturalistic methods. Though a sensible claim, mitigating factors may render trivial the relationship between religious leaders and religious spread. Some religions, even having prominent religious specialists, may not readily spread because they are tied to a particular ethnicity or geography. Or some religions without any strong leadership may spread effectively because of communication tools such as written materials. Empirical study of this question could help tease apart these other factors and distill the unique contribution of prominent religious specialists.

Demographically, is it the case that a higher number and geographically more distributed number of people identify with religious traditions with religious specialists as compared with relatively egalitarian religions? The relative success of different strains of the same general religious tradition might be predicted from the relative prominence of religious leaders. To illustrate, it might be possible to analyze the various Christian groups in North America by modeling their spread based on church organization, factoring out covariates such as the general theological tradition of the group, the size of immigration that brought the particular faith to North America, and so forth.

Could ethnographic study reveal the importance of strong leadership when neighboring religions compete for converts? Are those religions that have active missionary efforts distinguished by having more prominent religious leaders than those religions that have shown no interest in converting others?

The generation of new religious movements in various places (such as California) may provide opportunities for naturalistic studies. Perhaps the growth rate of these new faiths could be predicted on the basis of the presence or absence of hierarchical leadership. Those with religious leaders might be expected to grow faster than those possessing more egalitarian organizations.

IMAGISTIC CLAIMS

Whitehouse's account of the imagistic mode of religiosity generates at least eight empirical predictions that may be considered independent of the doctrinal mode. These claims appear in table 6.3.

Imagistic Claim #1: Infrequently performed, emotionally arousing religious events create episodic memories for the events.

This fundamental prediction of the imagistic mode of religiosity springs directly from psychological research (including naturalistic and experimental studies) of so-called "flashbulb memories" (Brown and Kulik 1982). Though this labeling has become somewhat controversial, that unique and personally important events leave accurate and vivid episodic memories lasting for decades is well documented. Additionally, moderate to high physiological

Table 6.3

Imagistic Claims	Need for Empirical Assessment		
	Experimental	Naturalistic	Ethnographic
#1: Infrequent and high-arousal ceremonies → Episodic memory	none	strong	moderate
#2: Episodic memory → SER	moderate	strong	moderate
#3: SER → Exegetical pluralism	none	strong	none
#4: SER + Exegetical pluralism → Discouragement of religious leaders	none	weak	strong
#5: Lack of religious leaders ↔ Centralization ↔ Orthodoxy ↔ Lack of religious leaders	none	none	strong
#6: High-arousal ceremonies → Intense cohesion	moderate	strong	weak
#7: Intense cohesion + Episodic memory → Exclusive community	none	moderate	moderate
#8: Exclusivity + Lack of leadership → Little spread	none	none	moderate

arousal has been shown to contribute to accurate memory for many different types of information including images, narrative, and spatial configurations (Cahill et al. 1994; McGaugh 2003). Of the many specific factors that psychologists have suggested play a pivotal role in long-term episodic memories, the majority of religious rites that are infrequently performed and highly emotional seem to include these factors. Hence, I see this prediction as resting on solid experimental ground.

Where ethnographic or naturalistic studies might be helpful is in extending these psychological findings to religious events or ceremonies with comparable features. As revealing as Neisser's earthquake study was (described above), are religious events earthshaking enough to produce these vivid memories? Similar to Neisser's studies, investigators could systematically examine the memories for initiation rites of inductees to a religion (or comparable social group). It may be valuable to see whether participants in these rarely performed but emotional rites have detailed-enough and mutually-convergent-enough memories that they could collectively recreate the rite with enough similarity to previous ones that the community recognizes them as examples of the same ritual.

Not only have "flashbulb"-like memory effects not been extended to religious ceremonies, but the bulk of work on these long-lasting episodic memories has considered only events with negative valence (e.g., earthquake, assassinations, space program disasters, and rape). Would positive religious events such as weddings or bar mitzvahs yield similar mnemonic effects?

Imagistic Claim #2: Episodic memory for religious events promotes spontaneous exegetical reflection (SER).

The reasoning behind this prediction goes as follows. If my community conducts a highly emotional religious event directed at me (e.g., as an initiate), it must be for some important reason. The unshakable conscious memory for the event provides me many opportunities to ponder just why this event was conducted and why it was performed the way it was. That is, as compared with a fairly boring event or events that I might not remember well, these very emotional ones prompt me to exegetically reflect.

Ethnographic work, such as that by Whitehouse (1995) and Barth (1975, 1987), seems to support these predictions, but documenting *spontaneous* reflection may be outside the typical methods of ethnographic observation or interviews. After all, once a researcher asks an informant for an interpretation, it may no longer be spontaneous.

Experimental methods seem a difficult course. Replicating the personal meaning of a religious event would present enormous pragmatic difficulties and concerns of ecological validity, but if these obstacles could be surmounted, the work would be beneficial.

Naturalistic studies of religious initiations and other comparable events (such as fraternity or military hazing) may prove the most productive way to nail down the connection between the memories for these events and spontaneous exegetical reflection. For instance, participants in qualifying ceremonies (and those from the same community who have not undergone the ceremony) might be asked to keep a daily journal or diary that later could be mined for SERs.

As this imagistic-mode prediction is not obviously true and fairly fundamental to the dynamics of the imagistic mode, I consider it a fairly high-priority prediction to empirically test.

Imagistic Claim #3: SER spawns a diversity of understandings of the same religious events.

A corollary of the previous prediction is that individuals who have undergone the same religious event might have quite idiosyncratic interpretations of the event, and one orthodox interpretation may not exist in the religious community. As a corollary, it may be investigated in the same manner as the previous prediction, with naturalistic studies holding the most promise to reveal any new insights. The ethnographic support appears solid.

Imagistic Claim #4: SER along with a diversity of understandings discourages dynamic, specialist leaders in a religious community.

Though a diversity of interpretations of rituals may encourage a certain theological permissiveness, it need not follow that religious leadership would suffer. The contrary prediction could be the case. Perhaps in communities in which individuals generate idiosyncratic ideas about religious events, strong leadership becomes even more necessary for holding the group together than in communities with a strong uniformity of experiences and beliefs. Clearly these are empirical issues requiring empirical evidence.

As a prediction prefaced upon a number of existing conditions (participation in highly emotional and personally meaningful events, formation of episodic memories, and the generation of SERs), experimenters would be hard pressed to meaningfully reproduce these conditions in the lab. Hence, ethnographically establishing the relationship of these variables would be helpful.

Imagistic Claim #5: Lacking strong leadership, centralization of authority, and a lack of orthodoxy mutually reinforce.

A lack of leadership implies a lack of centralization, and it seems obvious that having little or no orthodoxy would take away at least part of a reason for leadership. Nevertheless, ethnographic work could better quantify the co-occurrence of these three variables as compared with their disjunction. After all, at least to this lay observer, many conservative Christian groups such as the Amish appear to have relatively little centralization or dynamic leadership but a strong sense of orthodoxy and orthopraxy that is enforced socially and not hierarchically. Surely other examples of this disjunction exist, but are they merely outliers that may be explained through alternate mechanisms against a backdrop that supports the prediction?

I see no compelling need for experimental or naturalistic studies of this prediction.

Imagistic Claim #6: Participants in a high-arousal religious ceremony tend to enjoy relatively intense social cohesion after the fact.

Finding anecdotal and ethnographic evidence supporting this prediction is not difficult. The dynamics this prediction implicates are the same as for those who survive disasters, torture, hazing, or brutal initiations together. As compelling as these data may seem, they may often be confounded with other variables relevant to social cohesion such as size of groups and isolation from outsiders. Perhaps a small group of people who were on a resort island playing canasta for days on end would show similar after-the-fact cohesion as plane-crash survivors. Standard ethnographic studies may not offer the precision to tease apart the impact of high emotional arousal from these other variables.

Similarly, experimental and naturalistic work in the psychology of group dynamics has identified a number of variables that contribute to group cohesion that may commonly occur within the religious groups Whitehouse identifies as in the imagistic mode. For instance, not only do plane-crash survivors experience a harrowing event together, they also have a *superordinate goal* of survival. Superordinate goals, or goals that override individual desires and differences and force cooperation, have been shown to be pivotal in creating group cohesion. Similarly, establishing an out-group against whom we define ourselves is a fine way to promote intense group cohesion. Initiation rites, especially those that include an air of secrecy or exclusivity, play upon this in-group/out-group dynamic. Might the presence of superordinate goals or in-group dynamics be more common factors driving the sort of group cohesion Whitehouse points to than emotional arousal?

Careful naturalistic or even experimental work examining various groups differing along these lines could be valuable for pinpointing the most important factors. For instance, hazing and other emotionally arousing initiation ceremonies have been parts of university fraternities in the United States for decades. In recent years, such practices have come under close scrutiny and institutional bans. Consequently, the degree of emotional arousal at play during fraternity initiations varies, but competing factors such as in-group/out-group dynamics, size of group, and so on may be matched or statistically factored out when examining feelings of group cohesion after the initiation.

As this prediction actually masks fairly complex cognitive-emotive factors influencing social dynamics, and as it plays a central role in Whitehouse's imagistic mode, I rate the urgency of empirical substantiation on this topic fairly high.

Imagistic Claim #7: Intense social cohesion along with episodic memories for central religious ceremonies encourages exclusive religious communities.

Intense social cohesion presumably makes it difficult for outsiders to enter the fold. Couple this with a binding memory of a particular episode shared by members of the group, and the religious community may be even more resistant to including outsiders. If, as suggested above, part of the cohesion-making dynamics includes setting one's own group against an out-group (e.g., during the course of an initiation ceremony), this exclusivity would likely be even stronger.

As creating this sort of exclusive community through experimental manipulation would be impractical (and probably unethical), naturalistic or ethnographic methods are advisable, much as concerning the previous prediction. A relevant measure would be the degree of movement into or out of these cohesive groups once they are formed. Presumably, one hallmark of exclusivity is the difficulty of adding to the groups' number.

Imagistic Claim #8: Exclusive religious communities with a lack of dynamic leadership tend to show very little spread within or between populations.

This prediction seems reasonable, especially in comparison with the relatively anonymous and hierarchical religions (such as Islam and Christianity) that have shown remarkable spread over time. Nevertheless, after factoring out population density and how transient the initial religious group is, perhaps this prediction no longer holds. In other words, delete reference to sailors and ports (though such maritime merchants and their ports of call were significant in the spread of the Isis cult). Ethnographic and sociological studies might be necessary to demonstrate that cases such as the Roman Mithras cult (Martin 2004) are exceptions to the general pattern and occur only under special conditions. (For instance, the Mithras cult seems to have been spread around the Roman Empire by the military deployment of soldiers, who made up a significant proportion of Mithraic membership—a historically unrepresentative transient lifestyle.)

As a large-scale social prediction, I see little room for experimental or naturalistic work.

SUMMARY

One of the refreshing features of many of the new cognitive scientific theories of religion is that they offer testable hypotheses that may be empirically supported or falsified (e.g., Barrett 2004; Boyer 2001; McCauley and Lawson 2002). They cannot indefinitely weather contradictory evidence from ethnography or from more controlled studies.

Whitehouse's modes of religiosity theory produces at least seventeen empirical predictions demanding investigation. For those with expertise in ethnographic, demographic, historical, or sociological methods, the most pressing needs are to test the following:

- the foundational claim that explicit theology motivates religious behavior (especially concerning transmission of religious beliefs and practices);
- the doctrinal claim (#2) that larger bodies of explicit theological knowledge required of participants and the prominence of recognized religious leaders/authorities mutually reinforce each other;
- the doctrinal claim (#4) that the presence of orthodoxy checks in a religious community encourages centralization of power structures;
- the doctrinal claim (#6) that implicit memory for the procedures of ceremonies reduces individual reflection and innovation regarding theological justifications for the ceremonies, thereby increasing acceptance of orthodox interpretations;
- the imagistic claim (#4) that spontaneous exegetical reflection along with a diversity of understandings discourages dynamic, specialist leaders in a religious community; and
- the imagistic claim (#5) that a lack of strong leadership, centralization of authority, and a lack of orthodoxy mutually reinforce.

I direct those with expertise in experimental and naturalistic methods to explore the following:

- the foundational claim that explicit theology motivates religious behavior (especially concerning transmission of religious beliefs and practices);
- the doctrinal claim (#6) that implicit memory for the procedures of ceremonies reduces individual reflection and innovation regarding theological justifications for the ceremonies, thereby increasing acceptance of orthodox interpretations;
- the imagistic claim (#1) that infrequently performed, emotionally arousing religious events create episodic memories for the events;
- the imagistic claim (#2) that episodic memory for religious events promotes spontaneous exegetical reflection (SER);
- the imagistic claim (#3) that SER spawns a diversity of understandings of the same religious events; and
- the imagistic claim (#6) that participants in a high-arousal religious ceremony tend to enjoy relatively intense social cohesion after the fact.

Though pared down from seventeen empirical predictions, this list of projects remains daunting. Given the size and diversity of these projects, contributions from numerous scholars from many disciplines are desperately needed to move forward this ambitious and exciting theoretical framework.

NOTES

1. In this sketch, I assume that the reader has familiarity with Whitehouse's modes of religiosity theory. Consequently, I spend little time placing the seventeen empirical predictions in their theoretical framework.

2. Throughout I make my evaluations based upon my (limited) knowledge of relevant literatures. If experiments or ethnographic work relevant to these questions exist and I have claimed none such do, I apologize and look forward to being corrected. The modes theory, let alone the cognitive science of religion, is much too interdisciplinary for any one person to have mastery of all the relevant literature. Collaborative effort is desperately needed.

REFERENCES

Ajzen, I., and M. Fishbein. 1977. Attitude–Behavior Relations: A Theoretical Analysis and Review of Empirical Research. *Psychological Bulletin* 84: 888–918.

Atran, S. 2002. *In Gods We Trust: The Evolutionary Landscape of Religion.* Oxford: Oxford University Press.

Barrett, J. L. 1998. Cognitive Constraints on Hindu Concepts of the Divine. *Journal for the Scientific Study of Religion* 37: 608–19.

———. 1999. Theological Correctness: Cognitive Constraint and the Study of Religion. *Method & Theory in the Study of Religion* 11: 325–39.

———. 2001. How Ordinary Cognition Informs Petitionary Prayer. *Journal of Cognition & Culture* 1: 259–69.

———. 2004. *Why Would Anyone Believe in God?* Walnut Creek, CA: AltaMira Press.

Barrett, J. L., and F. C. Keil. 1996. Anthropomorphism and God Concepts: Conceptualizing a Non-natural Entity. *Cognitive Psychology* 31: 219–47.

Barrett, J. L., and B. VanOrman. 1996. The Effects of Image Use in Worship on God Concepts. *Journal of Psychology and Christianity* 15: 38–45.

Barth, F. 1975. *Ritual and Knowledge among the Baktaman of New Guinea.* New Haven: Yale University Press.

———. 1987. *Cosmologies in the Making: A Generative Approach to Cultural Variation in Inner New Guinea.* Cambridge: Cambridge University Press.

Boyer, P. 2001. *Religion Explained: The Evolutionary Origins of Religious Thought.* New York: Basic Books.

Brown, R., and J. Kulik. 1982. Flashbulb Memory. In *Memory Observed: Remembering in Natural Contexts*, ed. U. Neisser. San Francisco: W. H. Freeman.

Cahill, L., B. Prins, M. Weber, and J. McGaugh. 1994. Beta-Adrenergic Activation and Memory for Emotional Events. *Nature* 371: 702–4.

Kallgren, C. A., and W. Wood. 1986. Access to Attitude-Relevant Information in Memory as a Determinant of Attitude–Behavior Consistency. *Journal of Experimental Social Psychology* 22: 328–38.

Martin, Luther H. 2004. Performativity, Narrativity and Cognition: Demythologizing the Roman Cult of Mithras. In *Rhetoric and Reality in Early Christianity*, ed. Willit Braun. Waterloo: Wilfrid Laurier Press.

McCauley, R. N., and E. T. Lawson. 2002. *Bringing Ritual to Mind*. Cambridge: Cambridge University Press.

McGaugh, James L. 2003. *Memory and Emotion: The Making of Lasting Memories*. London: Weidenfeld and Nicolson.

Neisser, U., E. Winograd, E. Bergman, C. Schreiber, S. Palmer, and M. S. Weldon. 1996. Remembering the Earthquake: Direct Experience versus Hearing the News. *Memory* 4: 337–57.

Schank, R. C., and R. Abelson. 1977. *Scripts, Plans, Goals, and Understanding*. Hillsdale, NJ: Lawrence Erlbaum.

Slone, D. J. 2004. *Theological Incorrectness: Why Religious People Believe What They Shouldn't*. New York: Oxford University Press.

Whitehouse, H. 1995. *Inside the Cult: Religious Innovation and Transmission in Papua New Guinea*. Oxford: Oxford University Press.

———. 2000. *Arguments and Icons: Divergent Modes of Religiosity*. Oxford: Oxford University Press.

———. 2004. *Modes of Religiosity: A Cognitive Theory of Religious Transmission*. Walnut Creek, CA: AltaMira Press.

7

Memory and Analogical Thinking in High-Arousal Rituals

Rebekah A. Richert, Harvey Whitehouse, and Emma Stewart

Imagine that you are a teenage boy calmly sleeping one night. You are suddenly awakened and dragged from your bed to a dark location on the periphery of the settlement, along with other terrified boys. Your head is covered with a hood, and you are brutally attacked by the senior males of the village and herded onto a ceremonial platform. You are whipped with nettles and forced over a fire so that your skin is licked by the dancing flames before strange concoctions of disgusting substances are forced into your mouth and daubed over your skin. You are given no indication of the purpose of these experiences; you are simply required to endure whatever comes next. Such behaviors are quite typical of male initiation rituals in Papua New Guinea (see Whitehouse 2000). Moreover, rituals like these are found all around the world. This chapter sets out to explore how participants in highly emotionally arousing rituals make sense of their unique experiences.

In addressing this issue, we need to appreciate at the outset that *ritual* actions differ from nonritual actions by virtue of being irreducible to means-end technical motivations or to the intentional states of the actor. Reaching out to catch a ball is a qualitatively different kind of action from making the sign of the cross. It is different in part because there is a direct means-end connection between stretching out one's hand and the stopping and grasping of a ball, whereas self-crossing could be a means to almost any end, but never in a way that conforms to intuitive ideas about mechanical causation. People might cross themselves as an expression of relief or fear, or to show respect or piety. Sometimes they might have no idea why they do it. Of course, they might belong to a religious tradition that specifies exactly what this action means as well as when and why it should be carried out. But whatever ritual actors tell you about the meanings of their behavior, it will not be based on the same kinds of cognitive operations that lead us to expect a ball to stop when a hand gets in the way.

Further, rituals involve alterations to our normal intuitive inferences about
the *intentions* that lie behind actions. When somebody catches a ball, we
naturally assume that the behavior is motivated by intentions located inside
the catcher. By contrast, ritual actors are not the authors of their actions in
any usual sense (Humphrey and Laidlaw 1994; Bloch 2004). They are not the
ones who decided that the procedures should take this particular form rather
than that, or what clothes should be worn, or any of the myriad other features of the ritual that are prescribed (as well as the things that are forbidden). Rituals are constructed out of clusters of actions that are stipulated in
advance, rather than expressing the intentionalities of those who carry them
out. It is not intuitively obvious why the particular stipulations take the form
that they do, rather than some other form. Who was it who first came up with
these rules for performing the ritual, and (even more puzzlingly) *why?*

The question of who made up the rules for a given ritual practice might
elicit standard answers: it was God, or a messianic leader, or the ancestors,
or "the tradition" (conveniently construed as an agent, for this purpose), or
some such entity. But the why-type question can present more of a challenge
to ritual participants. Whitehouse (2004) argues that the challenge is only
taken on in rather special circumstances. If you perform the same ritual
many times over to the extent that you can carry it out competently without
having to reflect on how it is done, you are less likely to worry about why it
has to be done in a certain stipulated way rather than in some other fashion.
If, on the other hand, the ritual is performed in such a way that causes you
to think a great deal at an explicit level about the nature of the procedures
involved, then you are likely to be more exercised by the problem of what it
means. Both hypotheses are potentially testable. The second, however, is the
main focus of this chapter.

Whitehouse (e.g., 1992, 1995, 2000, 2004) has argued that the lower the
frequency of a ritual, the more arousing it is likely to be, because if it were
not arousing it would fail to elicit the right kinds of memories and motivations and would either die out or come to be more frequently performed. In
response to this argument, much debate has focused on the question of what
constitutes the "right kinds" of memories and motivations. Most researchers
in this area agree that low-frequency, high-arousal rituals give rise to enduring episodic memories. In some of his early work, Whitehouse argued that
the survival of rarely performed rituals depended on episodic memory for
the procedures involved. More recently, McCauley and Lawson (2002) have
developed a highly instructive theory of religious ritual transmission that is
based partly on the same premise. Others, however, have criticized this line
of argument on the grounds that low-frequency rituals are seldom reconstructed wholly (or even largely) with reference to episodic memory, and

more commonly depend on the guidance of elders and experienced experts who have developed general scripts for the rituals through repeated involvement (see, for instance, Barth 2002 and Houseman 2002). In light of these arguments, Whitehouse has started to focus his attention instead on the consequences of episodic recall for the way people think about the *meanings* of high-arousal rituals (e.g., Whitehouse 2002a, 2002b, 2004).

According to Whitehouse, a major effect of vivid, enduring episodic memory for rituals is that it encourages long-term rumination on what it all means. We may assume that there is intelligent agency behind it all, but that is not what really commands our attention. What preoccupies participants in high-arousal rituals is the question of *why* the originator of the rituals insisted on certain prescriptions and proscriptions with regard to conduct, demeanor, dress, speech, and so on, as opposed to all the other possible ways of doing the ritual that could easily be imagined. Answers to this question constitute what anthropologists call "ritual exegesis." Exegesis presents a considerable challenge for human memory. Whitehouse argues that it may be quite easy to remember ritual procedures (what you must and mustn't do), but people have great difficulty remembering the official *meanings* of the acts unless these meanings are frequently repeated. In the case of high-frequency rituals, there are many opportunities to rehearse official exegesis, and this fact (combined with low rates of spontaneous reflection on the matter) explains why standardized authoritative exegesis is mainly found in routinized religious traditions. It simply could not survive in conditions of very low-frequency transmission. In the case of rarely performed rituals, exegesis is based not on verbal testimony but on independent reflection. What typically drives this reflection is episodic memory for intrinsically puzzling actions, that is to say, for *ritual* actions. According to Whitehouse, elaborate ritual exegesis generated in this way takes on the character of a body of revelations—that is, of initially surprising insights into esoteric mysteries that, over time, develop great motivational force. What drives the elders and ritual experts to reproduce the tradition is their deeply held conviction that the knowledge they have gained is valuable and necessary to preserve.

In his contribution to this book, Pascal Boyer expresses doubts about the capacity of low-frequency, high-arousal rituals to stimulate elaborate exegetical thinking and to motivate subsequent transmission. He argues that ritual ordeals may well "focus the mind," in the sense of causing people to pay attention to what is happening during the rituals. They may also give rise to vivid and haunting episodic memories. But what evidence is there, he asks, that these experiences give rise to revelatory religious knowledge based on personal rumination about the meanings of the rituals?

Whitehouse has based his case mainly on ethnographic evidence. Many social and cultural anthropologists have tried to show that participants in rare, traumatic rituals (such as violent initiation rites) gradually develop elaborate esoteric insights into their meaning, culminating in cosmological expertise on the part of cult leaders (see Whitehouse and Laidlaw 2004). This view has more recently been reinforced to some extent by reports from historians, archaeologists, and classicists (see Whitehouse and Martin 2004). Still, evidence of this kind is not as precise and comprehensive as any of us would like. Ritual participants may be very reluctant to talk or write about their private ruminations on matters of ritual exegesis, particularly in traditions that regard rituals and their meanings as secret. If mystery cults are founded on personal revelations rather than publicly transmitted teachings, as Whitehouse maintains, then how are we to access those "private moments" of reflection? Ethnographic and historiographical evidence does this only indirectly, by pointing to cryptic hints from those involved, their insistence that they are driven by "deeper" forms of knowledge and insight, the often astonishing profusion and systematicity of cultic iconography, and patterns of behavior that seem to imply "hidden" generative schemes shared only by experts but never explicitly divulged. But all of this remains less than convincing if we cannot demonstrate the exact psychological mechanisms involved in the production of this kind of exegesis and the way in which it unfolds over time.

Whitehouse has argued that one of the most prominent psychological mechanisms involved in the production of exegesis is *analogical thinking* (see Whitehouse 2002a, 2002b, 2004). Psychological research on analogical thinking traditionally draws a distinction between source and target analogs. Analogies postulate links between a particular object, event, or state of affairs (the "target" analog) and some previously independent object, event, or state of affairs (the "source" analog). Analogical reasoning has been defined as "the process of understanding a novel situation in terms of one that is already familiar" (Gentner and Holyoak 1997, 32), suggesting that source analogs consist of familiar situations and target analogs consist of novel ones. This definition has serious drawbacks, however. Some instances of analogical thinking are based on the recognition of connections between two situations that are both novel or that are both familiar. We maintain that what is characteristic of spontaneous analogical thinking is that the *connections it proposes are novel*, insofar as the person is drawing parallels that he or she has not recognized before (even if others have already done so at least partly by independent means).

As is outlined below, research suggests that the production of analogies is a natural cognitive process and seems to be used often to impart information that is less easily conveyed in other ways. Although until very recently no attempt has been made to examine the role of analogical thinking in relation to emotionally salient *rituals*, we suspect that analogical reasoning plays a significant role in ritual participants' attempts to make sense of their experiences, at least in highly arousing rituals. Whitehouse refers to this process as "spontaneous exegetical reflection" (or SER).

SER AND ANALOGICAL THINKING

A key defining feature of SER is that of "analogic depth." According to Holyoak and Thagard's (1997) *multiconstraint theory*, there are three general constraints that guide the selection of analogical comparisons. These constraints are similarity, structure, and purpose. The constraint of similarity requires that analogies be guided by perceptual commonalities between the source and target. For instance, a spider web and a fishing net are similar in appearance insofar as both are comprised of interconnected strands of material. In terms of the ritual context, a superficial analogy might connect red paint used to cover a ritual instrument to blood—as both are red. Analogies based exclusively on similarities of this sort may be described as "superficial," in the sense that they have common outward appearances or visceral connotations rather than because they are formally or functionally similar. Source-target pairings based on *structure and purpose*, however, are capable of delivering much greater *depth* to analogical thought.

Deep analogies capitalize on parallels in the *relational structure* of elements in the source and target domains (Gentner 1983; Gentner and Markman 1997; Holyoak and Thagard 1997). Although there may be many surface similarities between two analogs, the most meaningful and informative ("deep") analogies are those in which the source and target analogs share connected systems of relations, resulting in more elaborate parallels. A spider web and a fishing net may have superficial (perceptual) similarities, but deeper connections might be made between their trapping functions, allowing further analogical connections between spiders and fisherman, or between flies and fish, air and sea, and so on. In the case of the web–net analogy, superficial similarities might draw attention to "deeper" functional parallels. But since ritual behavior is not functional in the same way as spiders' webs and fishing nets (i.e., is not reducible to technical motivations), deep analogical thinking in relation to problems of ritual meaning cannot be triggered by a simple surface analog, taken in isolation. In puzzling over the question of what a particular ritual action means, we have to look for intentionality *not* in the functional properties of the action but in its place in a *wider nexus* of ritualized behaviors. If the instruments of ritual torture, for instance, are painted in random colors (or not painted at all), then their color is unlikely to be considered salient. If, however, such instruments used in rituals are always the same color, then a search for something rather like (but not of course the same as) a "function" is more likely to be activated. Perhaps the hooks and knives are red because they can draw blood, in which case they might be analogous to the teeth of carnivores that draw blood from their victims, or (more extravagantly) analogous to drawings of reddish waxing discs in the temple, alluding to lunar cycles that "draw" menstrual blood from women.

Purpose (in the sense of "motivation") also appears to contribute to the depth of analogical connections. A considerable body of experimental research on analogical thinking focuses on the question of what conditions make it likely for people to apply a given source analog to various target situations. Recently, Blanchette and Dunbar (2001) have studied the use of analogy in natural settings. In one study, they explored the types of source analogs people will choose in political debates, by extracting and coding political analogies from several newspapers (Blanchette and Dunbar 2001). The analogies were coded for the source category (the source of the analogy, which is then mapped onto the current situation, or target), the range (within-domain vs. other-domain), the goal of the analogy creator, and the emotional connotation. They found significant differences in the types of newspaper articles that contained analogies. In general, they found that analogies were most often used in opinion articles rather than articles meant to impart information. The large majority of the analogies (77 percent) were from domains other than politics, and these analogies tended to be more strongly emotionally charged than analogies that remained within the domain of politics. Furthermore, the large majority of analogies that were employed to support a given position had a positive emotional connotation, and analogies used to oppose a position had a negative emotional connotation. The findings suggested that analogies offer more than just factual information on a topic and seem to be well suited to the communication of emotionally colored meanings.

Whitehouse (2004) hypothesizes that ritual actions constitute a domain of activity in which the potential for the formation of deep analogical connections is considerable; the extent to which this potential is realized, however, depends on whether the ritual procedures become a focus of conscious rumination. The tendency for ritual procedures to spark conscious rumination is likely enhanced in high-arousal rituals by the prominence and diversity of what McCauley and Lawson call "sensory pageantry" (2002). But, according to Whitehouse, levels of conscious rumination are *also* determined by the relative frequency and emotionality of rituals. Frequently performed rituals give rise to implicit procedural fluency but low rates of explicit reflection. More rarely performed ritual actions, especially if they are arousing and personally consequential, are likely to be remembered consciously as unique episodes in one's life experience. In these conditions, problems of exegetical meaning cannot be so easily ignored and intermittently thrust themselves upon consciousness like a nagging puzzle that refuses to be solved. But these experiences are also different from profane puzzles. Participants in high-arousal rituals generally believe that the mysteries confronting them originate in powerful otherworldly agents, and that the consequences of misunderstanding the rituals are dire. So the motivation to gain some sort of mastery over problems of ritual exegesis, however provisional and speculative, is much greater than that which drives us to tinker with crossword puzzles.

In general, we predict that levels of arousal during ritual performances will correlate directly with volume and structural depth in exegetical thinking. This prediction requires that our elements of SER be potentially measurable. We argue that they are. In any given ritual, it is possible in principle to determine what proportions of the actions are accorded exegetical meanings based on verbal testimony as opposed to independent inference, assuming one can determine exactly what participants are told about the ritual *and* that they are willing to report their conscious interpretations of it. We could measure the structural depth of SER by scoring exegetical commentaries according to whether or not they contain analogies. Given the minimal amount of research on this topic, we have no clear prediction about what, other than the creation of an analogy, should constitute depth in these circumstances. Depth could of course be defined in a number of ways: within-domain (e.g., one part of a ritual is analogous to another part of it) versus cross-domain (e.g., one part of a ritual is analogous to some process, object, or event in a nonritual setting), or concrete (e.g., ritual procedures that resemble other kinds of procedures) versus abstract (e.g., ritual cohesion resembles relations based on kinship). Combinations of these principles are also possible, of course (within-domain/concrete, within-domain/abstract, cross-domain/concrete, and cross-domain/abstract). Since the range of possible ways of categorizing structurally deep analogs is quite considerable, and the consequences of this for the construction of expert exegetical knowledge are not fully known, it is hard to determine appropriate scales of measurement in advance. Thus, in developing new methods of testing Whitehouse's predicted correlation between SER and arousal, we began by measuring sheer volume of reflection, as well as depth in the form of any analogic comparison. We report below on two experiments designed to test whether participants who have a strong emotional reaction to a ritual demonstrate greater volume and depth of spontaneous exegetical reflection than participants experiencing lower levels of arousal.

PROPAGATION RITUAL EXPERIMENT

In this study, participants enacted a particular ritual in one of two groups: a high-arousal form of the ritual or a blander version of the same ritual. To control for type of exegesis, both groups were provided the same minimal amount of information about the ritual. To recruit participants, announcements were made in large lectures that a study of rituals was being conducted and students could earn £20 for their help in reconstructing a ritual. Interested students were then contacted to participate on a given day and

Table 7.1   Source Analog Levels

Level	Definition
0	Repeats the symbolic meaning given in the ritual (e.g., rubbing earth on hands was a cleansing process)
1	Attributes a functional purpose to the action or element (e.g., rubbing earth on hands was preparing for the ritual)
2	Provided an analog in the same domain after a prompt (e.g., rubbing earth on hands was becoming one with nature)
3	Provided an analog in the same domain without a prompt
4	Provided an analog in a new domain after a prompt (e.g., rubbing earth on hands was cleansing your soul)
5	Provided an analog in a new domain without a prompt

participated in a large group with the other participants in that condition. We had a total of 29 participants (mean age = 21, 15 male, 14 female) broken into two groups (14 high arousal, 15 low arousal).

The ritual was conducted outdoors in a large field fringed by trees, owned by the university where the authors work. The participants gathered in a parking lot next to the field and were given a brief introduction to the project. Participants were told that they would be directed through some simple ritual actions and then asked to fill out some questionnaires following. They were also told that they would be asked to return at two other times to meet with one of the experimenters for follow-up interviews. They were told that they would receive £10 at the completion of the first follow-up interview, in one week, and an additional £10 upon completion of the second follow-up interview, two months later. Participants were then told some information about the ritual itself. The experimenter mentioned that he was interested in testing the efficacy of certain ritual procedures. Participants were told that this particular ritual was derived from propagation rituals in Amazonia, often conducted to increase hunting success. Participants were asked to maintain an attitude of respect toward the ritual procedures and not to discuss the ritual with anyone until after the final interview, scheduled two months later.

Following this introduction, participants were led through the ritual itself. Participants in the low-arousal condition performed the ritual in the afternoon, and participants in the high-arousal condition performed the ritual at dusk. Both groups of participants were instructed to stand in a line and then follow one of the authors (hereafter referred to as the "leader") across a field. As they were walking across the field, the leader shook a rattle. Participants were led into a circle of tree stumps and asked to bend down and "wash" their hands in the rotting leaves on the ground. Next, they were given cloaks made of Hessian fabric to wear. The leader then led the participants, again in a line, out of the trees and back into the field. As they walked toward the field, participants were handed a long stick. Participants were instructed to break a small piece off the top of the stick and throw it behind them. They were then asked to draw a circle around themselves with the stick. At this point, the leader gave each participant a small stone and instructed him/her to grind it into the earth. After all participants received their stone, the leader told them to the plant their "spear" (i.e., stick) into the ground between their feet.

The next phase of the ritual varied for low- and high-arousal groups. Following the stick planting, the participants in the high-arousal group were given blindfolds to wear. Participants in the low-arousal group did not wear blindfolds. In both conditions, participants were led individually to a hole in the ground, beside which a torch was lit. As participants walked toward the hole, drums were played. Once participants reached the hole, the drumming stopped and participants were asked to kneel at the hole and place their hands on a piece of fur that was in the hole. The leader chanted the meaningless utterance "wadih nyalu ama asumga," and then participants were led back to their original position. Once all participants were back in line, they were instructed to remove the blindfolds (in the case of the high-arousal participants), throw their sticks as hard as possible into the trees, and follow the leader in a line back out of the field.

After the ritual, all participants were given two questionnaires: an emotional rating form and a feedback form. Our analysis here is based on the emotional rating form, which asked participants to indicate whether they had at any point felt any of six emotions (frightened, nervous, relaxed, confused, uncomfortable, and bored) and the intensity of that emotion. Two and a half months after their original participation, participants returned for a final follow-up interview. Six participants did not return for the follow-up interview, and thus the final sample consisted of 23 participants (mean age = 22 years). In the high-arousal group, there were eight women and four men. In the low-arousal group, there were four women and seven men.

For the purposes of this chapter, only one aspect of these interviews will be reported. Participants were asked to recall freely the events of the evening or afternoon that they participated in the interview. They were also asked to indicate what thoughts crossed their mind while performing the ritual and if any aspect of the ritual struck them as especially significant or important. If participants did not expand on the possible meanings of a ritual action, the interviewer questioned them directly on whether that action seemed important and for what reason.

Participants' responses to these questions were coded for volume of reflection and use of analogies. Volume was assessed by tallying the number of actions to which participants attributed meaning. To establish a measure of depth, each meaning was then coded as to whether it was a specific analog (e.g., the stone symbolized a seed, and pushing it into the ground was like planting it to grow) or not. The specific analogs were given a score of 2 each, and all other meanings were given a score of 1. These scores were then totaled for a cumulative SER score for the final interview.

Results and Discussion

Participants' responses to the initial emotional rating were analyzed to establish that our two groups of participants (high-arousal ritual condition and low-arousal ritual condition) indeed had significantly different emotional experiences. Immediately following the ritual experience, participants in the high-arousal ritual condition reported a significantly greater intensity of fright ($M = 1.83$, $SD = 1.90$) than participants in the low-arousal ritual condition ($M = .45$, $SD = .82$; $t[21] = 2.22$, $p < .05$). There was also a trend toward significance in reported levels of relaxation. Participants in the high-arousal ritual condition ($M = 1.50$, $SD = 1.57$) reported lower levels of relaxation than participants in the low-arousal ritual condition ($M = 2.73$, $SD = 1.56$; $t[21] = 1.88$, $p = .07$). Thus, our two groups reported different emotional reactions to the ritual experience, indicating that our two ritual experiences offered opportunities for varied emotional reactions to the ritual.

However, a key element of our hypothesis is that individual emotional reactions will predict volume and depth of reflection on the experience. Given that some of the participants in the low-arousal ritual condition reacted with fear to the ritual, and some participants in the high-arousal ritual condition reported no emotional reaction to the ritual, we created *post-hoc* arousal groups based on participants' original reports of intensity of fright. If participants reported not being frightened at all, they were placed in the low-arousal group ($n = 11$; mean age = 20; 4 female, 7 male), and all other participants were placed in the high-arousal group ($n = 12$; mean age = 24; 8 female, 4 male).

Since there were different gender breakdowns for the two groups (in the high-arousal group there were eight women and four men, compared to the low-arousal group where there were four women and seven men), we needed to ensure that any differences between our ritual conditions were not attributable to gender differences. Thus, all the following analyses were first conducted by comparing the two gender groups and revealed no significant differences by gender. The remaining analyses compared the two *post-hoc* arousal conditions.

To assess differences in SER for the two groups, the mean number of actions attributed meanings, as well as the cumulative SER scores themselves, were compared using independent-samples *t*-tests. The mean cumulative SER scores for the final interviews are demonstrated in figure 7.1. First, participants in the high-arousal group ($M = 11.25$, $SD = 8.44$) on average attributed meanings to a significantly greater number of actions than did participants in the low-arousal group ($M = 6.27$, $SD = 3.61$; $t[21] = 1.81$, $p < .05$).

Thus, participants in the high-arousal group demonstrated a greater volume of reflection than did participants in the low-arousal group.

To assess depth of reflection, the cumulative SER interview scores were compared for the two groups and again revealed a significant difference in the cumulative SER interview scores ($t[21] = 1.69, p = .05$). The mean score for the high-arousal group ($M = 18.92, SD = 15.07$) was significantly higher than the mean score for the low-arousal group ($M = 10.45, SD = 2.02$). In sum, participants who reported experiencing a stronger emotional reaction to the ritual experience also demonstrated greater volume and depth of reflection on that experience in an interview two months later.

There were two key limitations to this study. One limitation of this method was that our measure of participants' emotional arousal relied on participants' self-reports of their emotional reaction. It is conceivable that participants may have over- or underestimated their emotional reactions. In addition, our hypothesis was that participants with greater emotional arousal during the ritual would demonstrate a greater increase in volume and depth of reflection *over time*. In this case, however, we were only able to compare the final interview scores for the groups, rather than the *change* in reflection

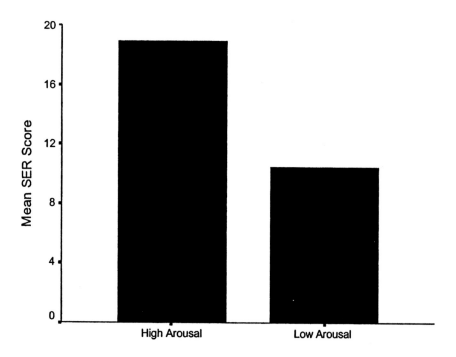

Figure 7.1   Mean SER score by arousal condition for propagation ritual

between the groups. To correct for these two issues in the propagation ritual experiment, a second experiment was designed.

ALTAR RITUAL EXPERIMENT

Our second experiment was designed to correct for some of the problems in the first experiment, more specifically group sizes, measurement of arousal level, and interviewing techniques. To address the issue of group size, we recruited over twice as many participants for this study. To correct for uncertainties about arousal level, we used extreme sound and lighting differences at Queens's Sonic Arts Research Centre (SARC) to vary arousal level, and we assessed participants' actual emotional arousal levels while performing the ritual through a galvanic skin response (GSR) measure that could then be compared to their subjective reports of emotion. GSR is a measure of skin conductivity. It is obtained by sending a small electric pulse between two fingers and measuring the skin's resistance to the pulse. Higher GSR levels mean that the skin is conducting greater levels of electricity, which constitutes a well-established indication of emotional arousal. Third, the interviews were designed to be more probing about participants' thought processes and were conducted at two different time points.

As in the propagation ritual experiment, participants performed a ritual in one of two conditions: high arousal ($n = 26$) or low arousal ($n = 27$). Participants were recruited by a paid recruiter through posters, e-mail announcements, and by word of mouth. In total, there were 53 participants ranging in age from 19 to 32 ($M = 22$). There were 29 women and 24 men (high arousal: 14 women and 12 men, low arousal: 15 women and 12 men). In contrast to the propagation ritual, participants performed the ritual alone, not in groups. Furthermore, the ritual was performed indoors in a sonic-arts research facility. This location, while admittedly not ideal for ecological validity, was chosen because of the extensive capabilities for manipulating sound and lighting.

Before performing the ritual, participants were told that the purpose of the experiment was to get their feedback about what purpose they thought this ritual may have served in its original cultural setting. They were told that while we knew the actions of the ritual, we were as yet uncertain about their meanings or the purpose of the ritual as a whole. Participants were then brought into a large room at the SARC and were led to the center of the room, where an altar had been placed. The altar was a table covered in a cloth made from Hessian fabric. Already on the altar were a round, flat piece of clay; a small bowl of oil; and a shell necklace. In front of the altar hung a sheet on which was back projected the instructions that participants followed. The index and middle fingers on the participant's left hand were connected to two sensors that measured the GSR. For baseline comparisons, participants were asked to stand still for three minutes before the ritual actually began, and participants were instructed to use their right hand to perform all ritual actions, while keeping their left hand still. Once the three minute baseline was completed, participants were told that they should pay attention to the screen for instructions on how to carry out the ritual. In the high-arousal group, at this point the house lights were turned off, and the room became red. For the low-arousal group, the house lights remained on, and red lights were turned on at a very low setting.

The Altar Ritual

The actual steps of the ritual were quite basic. First participants were instructed (via projection on the screen) to dip their index finger in the oil and rub oil on their forehead and throat. They were then asked to draw a triangle around the necklace and recite a chant. After reciting the chant, participants put the necklace on, recited another chant, and were then instructed to keep their eyes focused on the object that would appear on the screen. At this point, some music was played, which constituted another key difference between the high-arousal and low-arousal groups. For the low-arousal group, the music was played quite softly through one small speaker in front of the participants. For the high-arousal group, the music was played very loudly and in surround sound.

While the music played, a man covered in cloth resembling fur entered the room carrying a box. The man approached the table and set down the box. In the high-arousal condition, he walked slowly, stood at the table until the music had ended, and then proceeded to walk behind the participant and shake a rattle. In the low-arousal condition, he walked more quickly and shook the rattle while standing in front of the participant. After the man left the room, some drums were played. Again, in the high-arousal condition, the sound emanated loudly from many speakers, whereas in the low-arousal condition, the sound was played at lower volume from just one speaker. In addition, for the high-arousal condition, the drumming steadily increased in intensity and pace. In contrast, in the low-arousal condition, the drumming maintained an unvarying tempo.

After the drumming stopped, participants were instructed to place their hand inside the box. In the case of the high-arousal ritual, the lid of the box could not be removed, and participants had to access the interior of the box by inserting their right hand through a hole in the side. In the case of the low-arousal ritual, the box was open (the lid removed) and participants could simply reach inside. All participants were instructed to remove the item from inside the box, which was a smooth, black stone. They were asked to place the stone in the clay, wrap the clay around the stone, and place the stone back in the box. They were then instructed to remove the necklace and place it in the box.

The Interviews

Immediately following their performance of the ritual, participants responded to questions in a one-on-one verbal interview with a trained interviewer. Participants were asked to rate the intensity of nine emotions on a scale of 1 to 5. The two emotional ratings most relevant to this chapter were fright and surprise. Following the reports of their emotional reaction, participants were asked to recall freely the procedures of the ritual and to offer some suggestions as to what they thought the purpose of the ritual might have been and what the various steps of the ritual might have meant. In addition to being asked these same questions in the one-month follow-up interview, participants were also asked if they had any significant moments of insight about the ritual, and to reflect on the process by which they came to decide on particular ritual meanings.

Responses to these interview questions were then coded as a measure of participants' spontaneous exegetical reflection (SER) on the ritual. The coding system used was the same as that used in the propagation ritual experiment. Each meaning attribution was given a score of 1, and specific analogic connections were given a score of 2. These scores were then tallied for a cumulative SER score. In contrast to the propagation ritual experiment, however, both the initial and follow-up interviews were coded in this way, and a change score for each participant was also derived by subtracting the follow-up interview score from the initial interview score.

Results and Discussion

The first step in analyzing the results was to ensure that our two arousal groups actually demonstrated different levels of arousal. This was assessed through the GSR measures, participant self-reports, and the relation between the two. In order to compare the GSR readings from the two groups, a baseline average was established for each participant by taking the average of the last minute (60 s) of the initial three-minute period where participants were asked to stand still for the baseline readings. Two other segments of GSR readings were also averaged for each participant: the 50 seconds while the music was playing and the man entered the room and the 20 seconds while the drums were playing. These two segments were chosen because in both cases participants were motionless while staring at an object on the screen (thus minimizing interferences to the GSR readings attributable to bodily movements), and because these particular aspects of the ritual were in place specifically to increase arousal for our high-arousal group. Participants' baseline averages were then subtracted from each segment average for a measure of the average change in GSR for each of those segments.

For both segments, participants in the high-arousal ritual condition had a significantly greater increase in GSR than did participants in the low-arousal ritual condition. For the music segment, participants in the high-arousal ritual condition demonstrated a large mean increase ($M = 142.65$, $SD = 89.58$), which was significantly greater than the increase for the low-arousal ritual participants ($M = 87.69$, $SD = 75.84$) over the same time interval ($t[51] = 2.43$, $p < .05$). The same pattern was true for changes in GSR during the drumming. Participants in the high-arousal ritual condition ($M = 125.73$, $SD = 91.51$) had a significantly greater change in GSR than did participants in the low-arousal ritual condition ($M = 71.30$, $SD = 63.22$; $t[51] = 2.52$, $p < .05$).

These differences in GSR changes were mirrored in participants' self-reports on their emotional reaction. Participants were asked if they ever felt frightened or surprised over the course of the ritual. For each time point that participants reported being frightened or surprised, they were asked to rate the intensity of that emotion on a 5-point scale, with 1 being very low and 5 being very high. The intensities for each time point were then summed for a total measure of fright and surprise for each participant. Participants in the high-arousal ritual condition reported significantly greater intensities of fright ($M = 7.19$, $SD = 3.23$ v. $M = 1.13$, $SD = 1.48$) and surprise ($M = 4.15$, $SD = 3.72$ v. $M = 1.73$, $SD = 1.66$) than did participants in the low-arousal ritual condition ($t[51] = 8.78$, $p < .001$ and $t[51] = 3.13$, $p < .01$, respectively). Furthermore, the changes in GSR at the music segment were significantly correlated with both reports of fright ($r[50] = .33$, $p < .05$) and of surprise ($r[50] = .36$, $p < .05$), as were changes in GSR at the drum segment (fright: $r[50] = .32$, $p < .05$; surprise: $r[50] = .36$, $p < .01$). Based on the strength and consistency in these differences, we are confident that our two ritual-procedure conditions provided the opportunity for varied emotional reactions to the ritual itself.

Given that our hypothesis claims that an individual's personal emotional reaction to the ritual will affect their reflection on the experience, we again created *post-hoc* low-and high-arousal groups based on our three measures of emotional reaction (i.e., the two GSR difference scores and participants' self-reports of fright intensity). To create these groups, the three measures were compared for consistency. A participant was placed in the low-arousal group if at least two of the three measures indicated an emotional reaction below average in intensity, and a participant was placed in the high-arousal group if at least two of the three measures indicated an above-average emotional reaction. This *post-hoc* division was done with the participants who returned for the follow-up interview one month after participation ($N = 41$, mean age = 23; 23 female, 18 male). The low-arousal group ($n = 21$; mean age = 23) consisted of 11 women and 10 men; the high-arousal group ($n = 20$; mean age = 22) consisted of 12 women and 8 men.

As was described above, participants' reflections during both the initial and follow-up interviews were coded by rewarding general interpretive reflections each with a score of 1 and analogic connections with a score of 2. These scores were then summed for an initial-interview score and a follow-up-interview score. As the hypothesis is that there should be a greater increase in reflections for those participants with high-arousal emotional reactions to the experience, a difference score was computed by subtracting participants' initial-interview scores from their follow-up-interview scores. The mean changes in cumulative SER scores are shown in figure 7.2.

In terms of volume of reflection, an independent samples t-test comparing the change in the number of meanings that participants reported indicated a significant difference in the change in volume of reflection ($t[39] = 2.38, p < .05$). Participants in the high-arousal group ($M = 4.85, SD = 3.36$) demonstrated a greater increase in the mean number of meaning attributions than did participants in the low-arousal group ($M = 2.38, SD = 3.28$). In terms of cumulative SER scores (which reward analogic comparisons), participants in the high-arousal group ($M = 5.15, SD = 3.90$) again demonstrated a significantly greater increase in reflection than did participants in the low-arousal

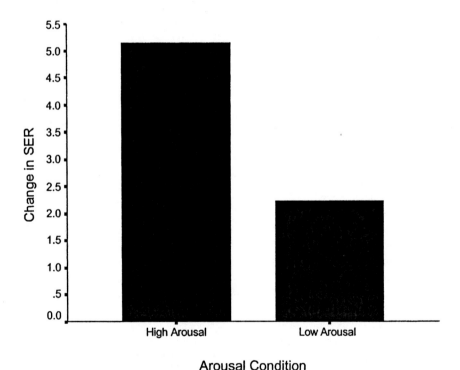

Figure 7.2   Mean change in SER score by arousal condition for altar ritual experiment

group (M = 2.23, SD = 4.13; $F[1, 39]$ = 5.37, p < .05). In other words, as was predicted, participants who had a stronger emotional reaction to the ritual also demonstrated a greater increase in their volume and depth of reflection on the ritual between their initial interview and the follow-up interview.

CONCLUSION

The purpose of this chapter was to operationally define Whitehouse's concept of spontaneous exegetical reflection (SER) and to test Whitehouse's prediction that high-arousal rituals spur deep SER on ritual experiences. SER, which Whitehouse claims occurs following participation in low-frequency, high-arousal rituals, has implications not only for an individual ritual participant's life, but also for the motivation to continue to transmit low-frequency, high-arousal rituals across generations. According to Whitehouse, spontaneous exegetical reflection is characterized by sudden insights into ritual meanings, which eventually contribute great motivational force in transmission. In other words, elders and ritual experts reproduce rituals because they are deeply convinced that they must preserve the knowledge and insight gained by performing the ritual.

Boyer (this volume) questions whether there is any evidence that low-frequency, high-arousal rituals actually stimulate this form of elaborate exegetical thinking that could motivate subsequent transmission. To address this concern, we designed two experiments to directly assess participants' reflections on rituals. Participants' emotional reactions to the rituals were assessed both through self-report and biological methods (i.e., GSR). The volume and depth of participants' reflections on the rituals were assessed by coding face-to-face interviews for the volume of meanings that participants attributed to the rituals as well as the analogic connections that participants made in their meaning attributions. In the first experiment, we found that participants with stronger emotional reactions to the ritual demonstrated greater volume and depth of reflection on the meaning of the ritual two months later. Furthermore, in the second experiment, we found that participants with stronger emotional reactions to the ritual demonstrated a greater *increase* in volume and depth of reflection on the ritual over a one-month time period. These findings suggest that indeed both volume and depth of reflection on rituals vary with level of emotional arousal.

Admittedly, there were some limitations to this research. First, one could argue that the participants in our rituals lacked any sense of personal consequentiality, given that the rituals were not "real" rituals and that the social circumstances for participants were quite different from those we would expect in more natural settings. However, we expect that personal consequentiality would increase the volume and depth of reflection, not decrease it. Thus, the fact that we found significant differences based on emotional arousal even in the absence of personal consequentiality is quite suggestive. Whether personal consequentiality would indeed increase the volume and depth of SER is a question for future research. Second, our results do not speak directly to the issue of motivation for transmission. We have begun to develop an answer to the first half of the puzzle. High-arousal rituals do indeed appear to encourage spontaneous exegetical reflection, at least as defined in terms of volume of reflection and analogic depth. But whether spontaneous exegetical reflection is a motivating force in itself is another question to be explored in the future. Lastly, further analysis of these reflections will seek to tease apart whether certain kinds of analogic comparisons (e.g., cross-domain, abstract) are more likely to be reported by participants with strong emotional reactions to a ritual experience, and what features of reflections may provide more fine-tuned indications of SER.

Despite these limitations, we found that participants who had strong emotional reactions to rituals were more likely to engage in the process of reflecting on exegetical meaning. They exhibited more and deeper reflections on their ritual experiences, which evolved over time, as compared with participants who experienced little emotional arousal while performing the ritual.

ACKNOWLEDGMENTS

The research reported in this chapter was supported by a National Science Foundation International Post-doctoral Research Fellowship (Richert), a British Academy Research Readership (Whitehouse), and a Research Studentship from the Department of Employment and Learning, Northern Ireland (Stewart). The authors would like to thank the director of the Sonic Arts Research Centre at Queen's, Michael Alcorn, for making the facilities of his facility available to us and for his collaborative contributions to the experiments conducted there. We would also like to thank Claire Cooper for her substantial work in recruiting participants, Renato Cohen for his help with the management of sound and lighting systems, and Jason E. Geistweidt for recording parts of the music used in the artificial rituals.

REFERENCES

Barth, F. 1987. *Cosmologies in the Making: A Generative Approach to Cultural Variation in Inner New Guinea*. Cambridge, UK: Cambridge University Press.
———. 2002. Review of *Arguments and Icons. Journal of Ritual Studies* 16: 14–17.
Blanchette, I., and K. Dunbar. 2001. Analogy Use in Naturalistic Settings: The Influence of Audience, Emotion, and Goals. *Memory and Cognition* 29: 730–735.

Bloch, M. 2004. Ritual and Deference. In *Ritual and Memory: Toward a Comparative Anthropology of Religion*, ed. Harvey Whitehouse and James Laidlaw. Walnut Creek, CA: AltaMira Press.

Gentner, D. 1983. Structure-Mapping: A Theoretical Framework for Analogy. *Cognitive Science* 7: 155–70.

Gentner, D., and K. J. Holyoak. 1997. Reasoning and Learning by Analogy: Introduction. *American Psychologist* 52: 32–34.

Gentner, D., and A. B. Markman. 1997. Structure Mapping in Analogy and Similarity. *American Psychologist* 52: 45–56.

Gick, M. L., and K. J. Holyoak. 1983. Schema Induction and Analogical Transfer. *Cognitive Psychology* 15: 1–38.

Goswami, U. 2001. Analogical Reasoning in Children. In *The Analogical Mind: Perspectives from Cognitive Science*, ed. D. Gentner, K. J. Holyoak, and B. N. Kokinov. Cambridge, MA: The MIT Press.

Holyoak, K. J., and P. Thagard. 1997. The Analogical Mind. *American Psychologist* 52: 35–44.

Houseman, M. 2002. Dissimulation and Simulation as Forms of Religious Reflexivity. *Social Anthropology* 10: 77–89.

Humphrey, C., and J. Laidlaw. 1994. *The Archetypal Actions of Ritual: A Theory of Ritual Illustrated by the Jain Rite of Worship*. Oxford: Oxford University Press.

McCauley, R. N., and E. T. Lawson. 2002. *Bringing Ritual to Mind: Psychological Foundations of Cultural Forms*. Cambridge: Cambridge University Press.

Spellman, B. A, and K. J. Holyoak. 1996. Pragmatics in Analogical Mapping. *Cognitive Psychology* 31: 307–46.

Whitehouse, H. 1992. Memorable Religions: Transmission, Codification, and Change in Divergent Melanesian Contexts. *Man*, n.s., 27: 777–97.

———. 1995. *Inside the Cult: Religious Innovation and Transmission in Papua New Guinea*. Oxford: Oxford University Press.

———. 2000. *Arguments and Icons: Divergent Modes of Religiosity*. Oxford: Oxford University Press.

———. 2002a. Conjectures, Refutations, and Verification: Towards a Testable Theory of "Modes of Religiosity." *Journal of Ritual Studies* 16: 44–59.

———. 2002b. Modes of Religiosity: Towards a Cognitive Explanation of the Sociopolitical Dynamics of Religion. *Method & Theory in the Study of Religion* 14: 293–315.

———. 2004. *Modes of Religiosity: A Cognitive Theory of Religious Transmission*. Walnut Creek, CA: AltaMira Press.

Whitehouse, H., and J. Laidlaw, eds. 2004. *Ritual and Memory: Toward a Comparative Anthropology of Religion*. Walnut Creek, CA: AltaMira Press.

Whitehouse, H., and L. Martin, eds. 2004. *Theorizing Religions Past: Archaeology, History, and Cognition*. Walnut Creek, CA: AltaMira Press.

III

WIDER APPLICATIONS

8

Religious Conversion and Modes of Religiosity

Ilkka Pyysiäinen

Whitehouse's theory of the modes of religiosity is a good analytical tool. But it is also easy to misunderstand the point. When I, for example, use the theory in my teaching, a frequent comment is that no known religion seems to be imagistic or doctrinal; the features rather mix and mingle. It is then difficult to try to argue that the modes theory actually is meant only as an analytical distinction, not a typology. It may thus be helpful to forget the labels of "imagistic" and "doctrinal" altogether for a while and only focus on the way the differing contents of the twelve modal variables (Whitehouse 2002b) may "excite" or "inhibit" each other. We must remember that "imagistic" and "doctrinal" only refer to ideal types, that is, to purely abstract clusters of variable contents. A single ritual, belief, or any other single feature cannot be imagistic or doctrinal, because being imagistic or doctrinal depends on all 12 variables simultaneously. It is only a larger combination of features that can be more or less imagistic or doctrinal. But also these are seldom simply imagistic or doctrinal.

Let us substitute the letters from *a* to *l* for the imagistic contents of the 12 variables and the letters from *m* to *x* for the doctrinal contents of the same variables (the actual contents are discussed below one by one). The theory now seems to presuppose that in practice {*a* . . . *l*} are not the singly necessary and jointly sufficient characteristics of imagistic religiosity, and that {*m* . . . *x*} are not the singly necessary and jointly sufficient characteristics of doctrinal religiosity. As the distinction is only an analytical one, we can always find *some* of the {*a* . . . *l*} in otherwise doctrinal constellations and some of the {*m* . . . *x*} in imagistic ones.

The question now follows *how many* of the features {*a* . . . *l*} can we find in an otherwise doctrinal constellation and still be able to recognize/regard it as doctrinal? Or, how many of the features {*m* . . . . *x*} can we find in an otherwise imagistic constellation and still be able to recognize/regard it as imagistic? Also, if the contents of the variables in the sets of {*a* . . . *l*} and of {*m* . . . *x*} mix in practice, what might be the "evolutionarily stable strategy," that is, the most fit combination of {*a* . . . *x*}? In other words, which combination of features from the two sets results in a religious tradition that has the best potential for cultural survival? This would be the real attractor position; pure imagism and pure doctrinality are not attractor positions since they do not canalize actual religiosity. Pure imagism and pure doctrinality, rather, are ideal types.

Still another question is how many of the features {*a* . . . *x*} must be present in order for the transmission to count as modal (assuming that also non-modal transmission exists)? Or, perhaps, the question cannot be framed in quantitative terms and we should rather look for some specific contents of the twelve variables that are necessary for a transmission process to count as modal? It also seems that the distinction between modal versus nonmodal transmission is more important in Whitehouse's theory than the distinction between imagistic and doctrinal itself (see Whitehouse 2000, 2002a, 2000b).

CONVERSION

I shall here discuss the case of religious conversion in the light of the above questions. I mean by religious conversion a sudden change in one's religious convictions, behaviors, and affiliations. These may then also have repercussions other than for religious beliefs and behaviors. "Sudden" here means that the person in question is able to point out a specific moment when "everything changed" in his or her life (see Miller and C'de Baca 2001). Even if the conversion experience is a doctrinal construct, one can point out a specific moment in his or her life when the import of the doctrine supposedly was personally realized. To the extent that it is a real event, its suddenness does not exclude the possibility that the change may have been preceded by a longer period of restlessness, doubt, seeking, and so forth. Yet I am primarily interested in the moment at which all this culminates in an experience of a dramatic change (real or imagined). By "change" I mean the fact that some beliefs, concepts, and practices that one previously either has ignored or actively opposed suddenly begin to seem both true and relevant (see Miller and C'de Baca 2001). "Relevant" here means that one is able to perceive some positive connection between the target information and the knowledge one already possesses; one is able to combine it with one's existing knowledge and to form new premises on that basis. This, then, allows for new inferences (Sperber and Wilson 1986, 46–50, 118–71). By "religious" I refer to anything that involves counterintuitive representations, is an object of belief, is shared by a group, and is used in management of life (see Pyysiäinen 2001, 9–23; 2002a; Boyer 2001, 51–91, Atran 2002). A conviction is a metarepresentational attitude that takes certain concepts and beliefs to be more important than others as premises in reasoning.

"Conversion" is a predominantly Christian and Protestant theological concept, although its application has been extended to other religious traditions as well (see Taves 1999; Malony and Southard 1992). It has been studied from varying angles, yet the phenomenon seems to escape definition as well as explanation. The actual process of conversion, as well as the effects of conversion processes on the self, have so far not been properly specified; neither have different types of conversion processes been adequately differentiated (Zinnbauer and Pargament 1998, 161). Conversion has been explored mainly from sociological, psychological, and theological perspectives, identifying the phenomenon mainly by its effects, that is, transformations in the contents of beliefs, behaviors, and religious affiliations. The neurocognitive mechanisms of conversion have been by and large ignored in research (see Brown and Caetano 1992; Miller and C'de Baca 2001, xi–xii, 3–7, 156). As far as I know, there is currently no evidence indicating the existence of a separate neurocognitive (or socioneurocognitive) mechanism responsible for the sudden transformations taking place in a conversion (cf. Miller and C'de Baca 2001). The concept of "conversion" has mostly received its coherence from underlying theological assumptions (see, e.g., Rambo 1993, 1998).

Atran (2002, 165–169) summarizes some of the work on religious conversion, arguing that linked feelings of guilt, anxiety, and social alienation are good predictors of a religious conversion; in large-scale industrial societies, socially marginal individuals, especially adolescents, whose stress levels are high and levels of self-esteem low are likely to pursue a religious identity. Kirkpatrick (1997, 1998, 1999), for example, argues on the basis of empirical studies that insecure-anxious and insecure-avoidant adult social-attachment styles were more likely predictors of finding a new relationship with God than a secure attachment style. Women who were initially anxious were significantly more likely than either avoidant or secure women to report having had a "religious experience or conversion" during the four-year period that the study covered. (The attachment-theoretical approach, however, is elsewhere [71–78] criticized by Atran.)

Pargament (2002a) argues from a coping perspective that religious converts have experienced great difficulty in their lives, so much so that existence itself has become a problem. In realizing that something is wrong, the would-be convert sees his or her "old self" and way of life as inadequate and regards a radical change that would transform his or her entire life as the only possible solution (see Miller and C'de Baca 2001). Zinnbauer and Pargament (1998) found that both a sudden spiritual conversion and a gradual conversion markedly changed the self-definition of the converts. When compared to a group of religious subjects who had not experienced religious change, the sudden-conversion group showed more preconversion perceived stress, a greater sense of personal inadequacy and limitation prior to the conversion, and also greater pre–post improvement, together with a greater increase in postconversion spiritual experiences. Paloutzian and colleagues (1999), however, suggest that spiritually transforming experiences can result in profound changes in life mostly at the level of goals, feelings, attitudes, and behaviors. Also, such self-defining personality functions as identity and meaning of life change dramatically after a spiritual experience. Yet the elemental functions of personality (whether one is open to experience, conscientious, extroverted, agreeable, or neurotic) change only minimally. These are also the dimensions of personality that are strongly heritable; in a typical population, 40 to 50 percent of the variation in them seems to be tied to genes (Pinker 2002, 50).

Atran (2002, 176–79) suggests a mechanism based on the finding that posttraumatic stress disorder (PTSD) is accompanied by heightened amygdala activation in response to fearful stimuli. He speculates that the overly stimulated amygdala goes into undirected hyperactivity, being unable to process the emotional significance of individual stimuli. The hypothalamus then receives a confounding flood of information and relays it to the autonomic nervous system; this then provokes increased discharges in the sympathetic and parasympathetic nervous systems (see also Pyysiäinen 2001, 114–15). PTSD is characterized by uncontrollable arousal mediated by adrenergic dysregulation. However, adrenergic blockers, such as beta blockers and possibly antidepressants, can reduce terror and arousal and interrupt the neuronal imprinting leading to long-term symptoms, if administered in the first hours after the terrifying incident. Patients also may benefit from cognitive-behavioral therapy (see MacReady 2002). Atran then argues for the possibility that heightened expressions of religiosity can serve a similar blocking function. This is supported by Atran and Norenzayan's (in press) result that the strength of belief in God and in the efficacy of supernatural intervention are reliably stronger after exposure to death primes than to a neutral or religious prime.

Atran's (2002, 169) tentative conclusion about conversion (based on a somewhat different sample of studies than here) is that "the more traditionally and continuously religious the person, the less likely to suffer depression and anxiety in the long run." However, religion provides not only comfort but also is a source of fear. Many religious concepts, images, and beliefs can be interpreted either as fearful or as comforting, depending on how one relates to them. Gods, for example, have counterintuitive potency to punish and to reward alike; the course of action is determined by the nature of the relationship. (See Pyysiäinen 2001, 136–37.) Thus religion can both increase fears and anxieties and resolve them. The mechanisms work in both ways: a very difficult life situation may trigger the fear of extinction and lead to a religious solution, or religious stimuli may trigger the emotions of fear, anxiety, and hope; that is, religion may be both "the sickness and the cure" (see Thorson 1998; Guthrie 1993).

This entails that the emotions of fear and hope are closely allied both cognitively and religiously, just as Atran (2002, 68) argues. They may be cognitively (but not physiologically) composed of identical elements, differing only in valence. There is, for example, some empirical evidence to support the hypothesis that an increase in fearfulness is accompanied by heightened faith in God as well as hope for a providential outcome in a difficult situation. Hope is here understood as the subjective sense of having a meaningful future, despite obstacles (Post 1998, 24).

Fear is also related to anxiety, which is an internal state that generates multiple fast scenes in the mind, as though they were occurring in the external world. The turnover of neural constellations at the basis of anxiety is as high as in fear, although the mental contents are as internalized as in depression (Greenfield 2000, 152–53). Anxiety has no clear object; it is dominated by internal reasoning processes, not by sensation; yet it also involves emotions. It may also not be easy in practice to differentiate between anxiety and depression; some common cognitive and behavioral features may underlie the apparent differences (see Craig and Dobson 1995). There is, for example, some empirical evidence for anxiety as a sequel to depression (MacDougall and Brown 1984). Information may also be misattributed to substitute objects, the information about which is derived from affective states. This happens when an affective state lacks a salient object, as is the case in anxiety. An anxious mood is turned into an emotion when an object is provided by focusing on whatever happens to be most salient to the experiencer (Clore and Gasper 2000, 10–11.) Thus, for example, indefinite feelings of guilt can be turned into religious emotions by connecting them to religious objects. This may make it easier to handle them (see Thorson 1998).

But, as Emmons and Paloutzian (2003, 394) observe, almost all studies of conversion suffer from various kinds of methodological shortcomings, such as for example near total reliance on measures of self-perceived change. This is no minor issue in the study of religion (cf. Barrett and Keil 1996). Many extensive literature reviews have shown that results from studies on religion and mental health are mixed and even contradictory. Bergin (1983), for example, found that in 23 percent of the reviewed studies there was a negative relationship between religion and mental health, in 47 percent of the studies the relation was positive, and in 30 percent there was no relationship. This is close to what one would expect by chance. Another alternative is that the results are skewed because of methodological difficulties. For example, Gartner (2002, 187–88), who is suspicious about the existence of such difficulties, yet acknowledges the fact that the very concept of "religious concept" has no generally accepted definition. Krymkowski and Martin (1998), for instance, found that in papers published in the *Journal for the Scientific Study of Religion*, beginning from 1986, religion was prominently taken to be an independent causal factor, affecting such things as abortion attitudes and alcohol consumption. They claim that such explanations are highly problematic because no sufficient attention has been paid to the mechanisms by which "religion" supposedly exercises influence, the direction of causality is not always clearly established, and controls are not always used. Often it is not too clear what is meant by religion (see Pyysiäinen, in press).

Gartner (2002, 200), for his part, claims that much of the discrepancy in the findings may be explained by differences in the ways mental health is measured. Thus we actually are dealing with variables too vaguely defined; it is therefore very difficult to find unequivocal causal relationships. Gartner (2002, 201) argues that the studies reporting a negative relationship between religion and mental health typically employed personality tests with only limited reliability and validity, whereas the studies that found a positive correlation were based on real-life observations concerning such things as drug abuse, delinquency, and so forth. It should, however, be specified what it is in religion that contributes to mental health: professing certain counterintuitive beliefs, performing rituals, the social relationships among believers, or what (see Levin and Chatters 1998)? Thus George and colleagues (2002) conclude that "we are far from understanding the mechanisms by which religious involvement promotes health," and Pargament (2002b, 169) says that, even when significant results are obtained, they provide only little insight into how religion works. Moreover, many of the relevant studies have been made in the United States, and the results cannot necessarily be generalized to other cultural contexts (see Pyysiäinen, in press).

Thus, although traditionally and continuously religious individuals may report less stress and anxiety than nonreligious or unconventionally religious individuals, this may be because they have more enduring social relationships and because they have conceptual and other cognitive-affective means to deal with their negative experiences. They do not necessarily lack these negative experiences; they only are better equipped to deal with them.

In the following section, I present the 12 modal variables systematically according to Whitehouse (2002b; cf. Whitehouse 1995), trying to evaluate their relevance for explaining conversion phenomena.

CONVERSION AND THE MODES

1. Frequency of Transmission

In the imagistic ideal type, the transmission of a given ritual takes place once every year at the most. More frequent transmission means a decisive move toward the doctrinal position, although we cannot say that increased frequency *makes* the ritual doctrinal (doctrinality depending on all the other variables as well). It is also problematic to measure only the frequency of one single ritual, as some rituals may be embedded in other rituals; an individual ritual always works in that wider context (Lawson and McCauley 1990; McCauley and Lawson 2002; cf. Lévi-Strauss 1979). Moreover, what counts as participation in a ritual is not always clear (McCauley and Lawson 2002, 55, 127–30; Atran 2002, 160–61). Third, what is learned in a ritual may also be learned from other sources; myths and doctrines are recounted not only in rituals.

With these caveats in mind, we can say that religious conversion may take place in both frequently and infrequently performed rituals. Sometimes a single event may trigger a conversion; sometimes it happens only after participation on a regular basis. It all depends on so many other things.

2. Level of Arousal

The imagistic ideal type is characterized by high emotional arousal, the doctrinal one by low. Whitehouse does not suggest any exact method of measurement, but he seems to mean the type of arousal that can, in principle, be registered by physiological measures (saliva samples, galvanic skin responses, etc.). The scale to be used should be a universal one: what is high among American Protestants is also high among the Haitian practitioners of voodoo, as well as everywhere. We are not talking only about the external expression of emotion and its cultural interpretation but rather about basic physiological facts. The argument is clearly different from that advanced by McCauley and Lawson (2002), which deals with relative levels of arousal across the repertoire of rituals found in any single religious tradition (rather than across traditions).

Conversions typically involve high emotions by both standards. It could even be said that this is one of the defining characteristics of conversion as here understood.

3. Memory

One of the central characteristics of the imagistic ideal type is episodic memories for personally experienced events, the doctrinal ideal type relying more heavily on semantic memory for teachings codified in language. While the cognitive contents of doctrinal religions are largely based on semantic knowledge organized into abstract scripts and schemata, conversions are personal experiences encoded in episodic memory. They take place at a specified time and place and are remembered as such: it happened to me then and there. For Tulving, episodic encoding actually depends on prior semantic encoding and vice versa, episodic and semantic memory working in a parallel fashion in storing information: it is only retrieval of information from these two stores that happens independently (Tulving 1995; Frith and Dolan 2000; Brown and Craik 2000; see Atran 2002, 159–61). Semantic memory, based on the lateral temporal cortex, and episodic memory, based on the medial temporal lobe, need to cooperate for us to be able to recognize surprising and exceptional events and phenomena: semantic memory represents what is common across situations, while episodic memory represents the exceptions. This means that situations requiring more conscious control tend to give rise to stronger episodic memories (Lieberman et al. 2002, 228, 233–34; see Zola and Squire 2000; Schacter et al. 2000; Pyysiäinen 2004c).

Klein, Cosmides, Tooby, and Chance (2002), for example, present strong empirical evidence to support the hypothesis that decision rules designed to render judgments about the self and others recruit information both from episodic and semantic memory stores. Episodic memories are about specific events and behaviors involving a target, while semantic memories consist of summaries of the target person's personality traits abstracted from a set of particular events. Once a "trait summary" has been formed, judgments about a person's traits are made on this basis. However, if there are episodic memories that are inconsistent with the trait summary, they will always be activated when a piece of summary information is retrieved. Thus, we might speculate that also in their religious judgments people draw information both from episodic and semantic memory stores, with semantic information consisting of summaries of what has been acquired in cultural transmission. It is the interaction between episodic memories and summaries that needs to be considered in developing a theory of religious conversion.

4. Ritual Meaning

In the imagistic ideal type, ritual meanings are internally generated in contrast to the doctrinal position typified by learned or acquired meanings. In the doctrinal position, persons can interpret the rituals using concepts and beliefs that can be inferred from cultural communication without much effort, whereas in the imagistic mode, the interpretative concepts are arrived at through a lengthy and laborious process of "spontaneous exegetical reflection" (see Sperber and Wilson 1986; Barrett and Keil 1996).

In a conversion, what Barrett and Keil (1996, 612) call "rehearsed, nonintegrated attributes that have no causal efficacy" might suddenly be invested with a very personal meaning; what previously seemed like unconnected bits and pieces that could not be connected to one's database without very costly cognitive processing, suddenly appear as a coherent whole that can be combined with what one already has in mind. Thus, although one is processing familiar (partly at least) and "rehearsed" concepts, they acquire a new meaning that is somehow internally generated, doctrinal summaries and episodic memories being simultaneously activated. The difference between imagistic and doctrinal is that in learning meanings one merely uses some commonly accepted concepts without much reflective thought or feeling of personal relevance, whereas in the case of internal generation one consciously ponders over the meanings and arrives at an interpretation that seems to have personal relevance. Thus conversion is typified by internally generated meanings, although they can be arrived at by reinterpreting learned concepts.

5. Revelation Techniques

Whitehouse's way of differentiating between two kinds of "techniques of revelation" may be problematic. He argues that whereas imagistic religions are typified by iconicity, multivocal imagery, and analogic reasoning, doctrinal religiosity is characterized by "logical integration" and rhetoric. This might lead a psychologist to think that Whitehouse is actually distinguishing between intuitive/spontaneous/automatic processing and systematic/rational/controlled processing. This, however, is not his point; the two types of cognitive processing certainly belong to both imagistic and doctrinal religion, although in varying degrees (Bargh 1994; Pyysiäinen 2003, 2004d). Atran (2002, 155–57) correctly remarks that there is no evidence to support the claim that the doctrinal mode tends toward some "logically integrated and coherent ideology" connected by implicational logic. This is only true of theology as an ideational artifact that exists in the collective book–minds interaction (Pyysiäinen 2004a, 2004d). If, on the other hand, we step back from this argument and define logical integration more loosely, we risk blurring the difference between imagistic and doctrinal (see Pyysiäinen 2004c).

6. Social Cohesion

The imagistic ideal type is characterized by intense social cohesion and the doctrinal one by diffuse cohesion. It seems, on the basis of relevant literature, that conversion takes place from a diffuse group to a more cohesive one (see Malony and Southard 1992).

7. Leadership

In imagistic religion, leaders are either passive or totally absent; doctrinal religiosity is characterized by dynamic leadership. Conversion seems to necessitate, somewhat paradoxically, both intense group cohesion *and* dynamic leadership. The leader in a way represents the whole group, which gets personified in the leader. However, it might be that these two variables are complementary in the sense that a conversion requires either a coherent group or a dynamic leader (of a diffuse group). If both are absent, there can be no concrete doctrinal expectations to trigger the conversion.

8. Inclusivity/Exclusivity

Imagistic religions are exclusive, doctrinal religions inclusive. Yet it seems that there are important differences in inclusiveness/exclusiveness between various types of doctrinal movements: conversions are more typical in doctrinal movements such as Pentecostalism than in the more hierarchical religions of Lutheranism or Catholicism. As Weber (1965) argued, in institutionalized religions, an "official grace" (*Anstaltsgnade*) replaces personal piety; personal piety can even be considered a threat to the institution's capacity to bestow salvation to anyone it chooses. This, however, only excludes conversion *to* inclusive religions; conversion *within* an inclusive religion but *to* a more exclusive one seems to be common.

9. Spread

The spread of imagistic religions is slow and inefficient in contrast to doctrinal religions that spread fast and efficiently. As conversion is a means of entering a religion, rapid spread also means great potential for conversions. Conversions cannot take place in stable movements that can only be entered by being born into the group.

10. Scale

Imagistic religions are small-scale phenomena, whereas doctrinal religions are large-scale phenomena. It seems that conversions most typically happen within large-scale movements but lead to smaller-scale movements. Although for example Pentecostalism is a large-scale movement worldwide, its noncentralized nature may make it appear locally as a small-scale movement.

11. Degree of Uniformity

The degree of uniformity is supposed to be low in imagistic religions and high in doctrinal religions. In the imagistic ideal type there is no binding doctrine, whereas in doctrinal religions everybody is supposed to subscribe to the same doctrine in principle. Yet at the same time, the way of life in imagistic religions may be at least as uniform as in doctrinal religions. It seems to be specifically the ideal of a *doctrinal* unity that is the catalyst for conversions.

12. Structure

The structure is noncentralized in imagistic religions and centralized in doctrinal religions. Such centralization seems to be a catalyst for conversions that, however, happen toward noncentralized groups (see below).

CONVERSION IN THE MODES DYNAMICS

There are now four possibilities:

- Conversion within imagistic religiosity (rare)
- Conversion from imagistic to doctrinal religiosity (tedium follows)
- Conversion within doctrinal religiosity (typically happens)
- Conversion from doctrinal to imagistic religiosity (might happen?)

The first option seems like a rather unlikely event; it is very difficult to "convert" from a local cult to another such cult. Or, if it happens, one usually does not substitute one cult for another but simply joins one more cult (as in the Greek mystery cults, for example; see Martin 2004).

As to the second option, conversion from an imagistic religion to a doctrinal religion is often a reaction to missionary efforts. Koskinen (1953, 91–94) argues that when the Pacific Islanders were converted to Christianity en masse, they still did not discard their old beliefs and practices. The influence of Christianity "remained superficial"; the natives "had none of the ambition of real Christians." At first Christianity was popular, but "disappointment and tedium soon made their appearance." The natives felt that Christianity had promised more than it had been able to give and that they did not gain the expected this-worldly advantages from "white man's magic" (see Whitehouse 2000 44–45, 142–43). Thus, in this type of conversion, one adopts something of a doctrinal tradition, trying to combine it with one's imagistic religion with varying degrees of success.

The most typical conversion seems to be a conversion within the doctrinal ideal type. It is possible, for instance, to have a Christian belief environment and yet be relatively ignorant about Christian doctrine. Conversion then revitalizes the known (if only vaguely) doctrinal beliefs.

The fourth option might be realized when someone for example converts from Christianity to an imagistic cult. It is, however, doubtful that one could really totally abandon one's doctrinal way of thinking about religion. The result may rather be some kind of hybrid religion.

Summarizing the analysis, we see that conversions seem to belong to religiosity that is more typically imagistic on the basis of the variables of 2, 3, and 4. In the variables 1 and 4, both imagistic and doctrinal content allows for

160   *Ilkka Pyysiäinen*

conversions. The fifth variable is undetermined because it fails to differentiate between the two modes. In the variables 6, 7, 10, 11, and 12, it is doctrinal contents that are more likely to lead to conversions. In the variables 8 and 9, something like a mixture of imagistic and doctrinal contents leads to conversions. It thus seems that although conversion is a phenomenon that typically happens in a doctrinal context, it is nevertheless a phenomenon that does not quite fit with Whitehouse's description of the doctrinal ideal type. It is a sort of imagism within doctrinality: the psychological variables (of the 12) have an imagistic content, while the social variables have a doctrinal content.

Pyysiäinen (2001, 2004c) and Tremlin (2002) have emphasized on the basis of Boyer's (1994, 2001) and Barrett's (Barrett and Keil 1996; Barrett 1998) studies that because theological traditions are an epiphenomenal overlay on natural religiosity (also McCauley 2000), doctrinal religiosity thus is constantly threatened by the fact that its concepts seem irrelevant and are difficult to use in everyday reasoning. Yet only doctrinal religions have the potential to spread beyond the boundaries of the local community and unite large masses of people. Tremlin (2002) thus argues that imagistic-like phenomena provide individual motivation, while doctrinal-type phenomena offer systems-level tools for the preservation of stable traditions (see also Pyysiäinen 2004a).

In this perspective, conversion might be said to be a reaction to a situation where doctrinal development has produced such abstract religious concepts and beliefs that they no longer can motivate people. Their abstractness makes them difficult to process and also makes it difficult to see their relevance: what for example concretely follows from the view that God is "The Ground of Being?" (see Boyer 2001, 320–22). It seems that when theology gets really abstract, religious institutions also tend to become all-encompassing but "empty" (see Pyysiäinen 2004a). Weber (1965) described such a process in his argument about new movements gradually getting institutionalized and then giving birth to revivalist movements that aim to restore the lost original spontaneity. At first the religious virtuosity of leaders may be important, but as institutionalization proceeds they become suspect because they seem not to trust the institution's capacity to bestow salvation freely to all. Weber takes as an example the Scholastic distinction between *fides implicita* and *fides explicita*: ordinary people were not supposed to know the whole doctrine; it was enough for them to accept it on the grounds that the specialists know it and have rational reasons to believe it. The specialists had to know the doctrine explicitly. Ordinary people thus have only implicit belief, whereas specialists have explicit belief.

This kind of development is evident in the Reformation that broke the doctrine of implicit faith (although similar phenomena, like the "New Devotion," were known also before). Christianity now was understood to be an intimate matter between God and the individual believer. Luther's emphasis on an individual believer's right to judge matters in the light of his personal understanding of the Bible is well known. Yet Luther did not want radically to depart from the Catholic Church or the scholastic tradition, the presuppositions and methods of which he shared to a certain extent. Some of his followers, however, went much further in their individualism, rejecting hierarchical authority both on institutional and doctrinal levels (Williams 1962; Saarinen 1988; Lohse 1999).

But, as the Weberian hypothesis predicts, the Reformation itself was in due course institutionalized; this led the so-called Lutheran orthodoxy and its rigid dogmatism. A new kind of revival then took place in the Pietistic movement(s) that had their earliest beginnings in the early seventeenth century; the word *Pietism*, however, came to be known only in 1677, two years after the publication of Philipp Jakob Spener's *Pia desideria*; Spener's followers were now called "Pietists." In the various forms of Pietism, great emphasis was put on the personal life of piety (Brecht 1996).

In Finland, for example, the first appearance of radical Pietism is personified in the mysterious figure of Lars Ulstadius. He was a Lutheran minister and a schoolteacher who came to be tormented by religious doubt, guilt, and general anxiety. He fell ill, and for about two years he neither washed himself nor had his hair or beard cut. In his agony he turned to the local vicar, asking for public absolution for his sins. The vicar explained to him that such scruples were merely the work of the devil and he should not pay attention to them. On July 22, in 1688, Ulstadius then in due course appeared in the Dome of Turku in his rags, with his hair hanging long and with a huge matted beard, interrupting the service by starting to read aloud the radical theses he had written down. When two men grabbed him to throw him out of the Dome, what was left of his humble dress fell off, and poor Ulstadius stood there naked, only covered by his long hair and beard. Like some Old Testament prophet, he proclaimed that the Lutheran doctrine was to be doomed, that prayer books and postillas were a bunch of lies, and that the ministers were not endowed with the Holy Spirit (Akiander 1857, I 3–30; Odenvik 1940). The revivalist movements that then emerged in Finland in the eighteenth and nineteenth centuries all protested against a too-liberal and too-abstract interpretation of the doctrine, emphasizing both correct doctrine and an individual believer's responsibility of his or her religious choice: baptized members of the Lutheran Church were now expected to make a personal decision in favor of faith (see Pentikäinen 1975; Pyysiäinen 2004c).

Ulstadius's dramatic appearance in the Dome might have marked the beginning of a new imagistic movement, but that did not happen; the revivals took a very doctrinal form despite the emphasis on emotional experience. We may thus make the prediction that doctrinal religiosity develops slowly but has strong staying power: revivalism does not undermine doctrinal religiosity but supports it. Conversions are reactions to inherent problems in doctrinal religiosity; they derive their motivational power from imagistic-like phenomena but combine them with elements of doctrinality. The important thing is that one experiences an intimate connection with some counterintuitive agent. Episodic memories of conversion experiences are then always activated when a doctrinal summary is activated, as they contradict what one previously thought about the doctrine. Yet the episodic memories may themselves in due course develop into schemata in semantic memory, due to the doctrinal context of interpretation and numerous retellings of the episodes. Thus the intimacy may also be lost to an extent.

In my opinion, the amount of emotional arousal in religious rituals and other religious situations depends precisely on whether such intimacy is experienced or not (Pyysiäinen 2001, 80–97). Ritual form (McCauley and Lawson 2002) is one way of producing it, ritual frequency is another (Whitehouse 1995, 2000, 2001, 2002), and there are others still (see also Atran 2002, 290–91). Let me emphasize, however, that I am here speaking of the actual experiences of real people, not of rituals' potential to arouse emotions—*ceteris paribus*—in an ideal participant. Thus, from the modes point of view, the strong emotional component in conversions is explained by the fact that a sudden conversion is a unique and personal event that creates strong episodic memories that seem to fulfill the criteria of flashbulb memory (see Whitehouse 2000, 7–9, 119–22; Conway 1995). The "spontaneous exegetical reflection" that supposedly follows is constrained by the doctrine, however. Therefore it may gradually develop into fixed schemata.

Conversion also is a way of establishing a personal relationship with the counterintuitive agent(s) as presented in the doctrine. Thus, from the point of view of the ritual form hypothesis (McCauley and Lawson 2002), the emotional component is explained by the logical form of the event: when one experiences a conversion, one supposedly is the direct object of action of some counterintuitive agent; this creates the intimacy that triggers the emotions. Such conversion also often leads to frequent participation in various kinds of services and devotions, and thus revitalizes doctrinal religiosity. Occasionally conversions may also form "epidemics" and spread like wildfire, as in the case of the Great Awakenings in the United States (see Taves 1999; Slone 2004, 85–102).

CONCLUSION

To the extent that the modes theory is meant as an empirical theory, its worth can only be judged by the range of phenomena it helps explain. We must ask how and for what purpose this theory can be used in the empirical study of religions. In the case of conversions, the modes theory helps draw attention to the interplay between psychological and social factors in canalizing religious transmission into differing feedback systems. They are not independent from each other. This, then, helps explain, for example, why there can be no conversions in the imagistic ideal type. In imagism there is no need for conversions because the problem is not motivation but the coherence and durability of the tradition. In doctrinal religiosity, the problem is motivation, not preservation. The attractor position thus cannot be imagistic or doctrinal, but precisely in between the two ideal types. Living religiosity always seems to combine features of the two modes; pure imagism and pure doctrinalism are abstract ideals only. Conversion is one example of how religious phenomena tend to oscillate in the middle position; magic might be another (see Pyysiäinen 2004b, 90–112). Conversions thus represent an attempt at an evolutionarily stable strategy in cultural transmission. Although a conversion is a psychological phenomenon, that is, something that happens in the mind, an increase or a decrease in conversions at some time or in some sociocultural context is a social phenomenon. The modes theory, albeit in a somewhat modified form, can help analyze the mutual interdependence of the psychological and social variables here.

REFERENCES

Akiander, Matth(ias). 1857. *Religiösa rörelserna i Finland i ålder och senare tider*, vol. 1. Helsingfors: J. Simelii arfvigar.

Atran, Scott. 2002. *In Gods We Trust: The Evolutionary Landscape of Religion.* Oxford: Oxford University Press.

Atran, Scott, and Ara Norenzayan. In press. Religion's Evolutionary Landscape: Counterintuition, Commitment, Compassion, Communion. *Behavioral and Brain Sciences.*

Bargh, John A. 1984. The Four Horsemen of Automaticity: Awareness, Intention, Efficiency, and Control in Social Cognition. In *Handbook of Social Cognition*, ed. Robert S. Wyer and Thomas K. Srull. Hillsdale, NJ: Erlbaum.

Barrett, Justin L. 1998. Cognitive Constraints on Hindu Concepts of the Divine. *Journal for the Scientific Study of Religion* 37: 608–19.

Barrett, Justin L., and Frank Keil. 1996. Conceptualizing a Nonnatural Entity: Anthropomorphism in God Concepts. *Cognitive Psychology* 31: 219–47.

Bergin, A. E. 1983. Religiosity and Mental Health: A Critical Revaluation and Meta-Analysis. *Professional Psychology: Research and Practice* 14: 170–84.

Boyer, Pascal. 1994. *The Naturalness of Religious Ideas: A Cognitive Theory of Religion.* Berkeley: University of California Press.

———. 2001. *Religion Explained: The Evolutionary Origins of Religious Thought.* New York: Basic Books.

Brecht, Martin. 1996. Pietismus. *Theologische Realenzyklopädie* 26: 606–31. Berlin: Walter de Gruyter.

Brown, Scott C., and Fergus I. M. Craik. 2000. Encoding and Retrieval of Information. In *The Oxford Handbook of Memory*, ed. Endel Tulving and Fergus I. M. Craik. Oxford: Oxford University Press.

Brown, Warren S., and Carla Caetano. 1992. Conversion, Cognition, and Neuropsychology. In *Handbook of Religious Conversion*, ed. H. N. Malony and S. Southard, 147–58. Birmingham, AL: Religious Education Press.

Clore, Gerald L., and Kasper Gasper. 2000. Feeling is Believing: Some Affective Influences on Belief. In *Emotions and Beliefs: How Feelings Influence Thoughts*, ed. Nico H. Frijda, Anthony S. R. Manstead, and Sacha Bem. Paris: Editions de la maison des sciences de l'homme & Cambridge: Cambridge University Press.

Conway, Martin A. 1995. *Flashbulb Memories*. Hove, UK: Lawrence Erlbaum.

Craig, Kenneth D., and Keith S. Dobson, eds. 1995. *Anxiety and Depression in Adults and Children*. Thousand Oaks, CA: Sage.

Emmons, Robert A., and Raymond F. Paloutzian 2003. The Psychology of Religion. *Annual Review of Psychology* 54: 377–402.

Frith, Chris, and Raymond J. Dolan. 2000. The Role of Memory in the Delusions Associated with Schizophrenia. In *Memory, Brain, and Belief*, ed. Daniel L. Schacter and Elaine Scarry. Cambridge, MA: Harvard University Press.

Gartner, John. 2002. Religious Commitment, Mental Health, and Prosocial Behavior: A Review of the Empirical Literature. In *Religion and the Practice of Clinical Psychology*, ed. E. Shafranske. Washington, DC: American Psychological Association.

George, Linda K., Christopher G. Ellison, and David B. Larson. 2002. Explaining the Relationships between Religious Involvement and Health. *Psychological Inquiry* 13: 190–200.

Greenfield, Susan. 2000. *The Private Life of the Brain: Emotions, Consciousness, and the Secret of the Self*. New York: John Wiley.

Guthrie, S. 1993. *Faces in the Clouds*. New York: Oxford University Press.

Kirkpatrick, Lee A. 1997. A Longitudinal Study of Changes in Religious Beliefs and Behavior. *Journal for the Scientific Study of Religion* 36: 207–17.

———. 1998. God as a Substitute Attachment Figure: A Longitudinal Study of Adult Attachment Style and Religious Change in College Students. *Personality and Social Psychology Bulletin* 24: 961–73.

———. 1999. Attachment and Religious Representations and Behavior. In *Handbook of Attachment Theory: Research, and Clinical Applications*, ed. J. Cassidy and P. R. Shaver, 803–22. New York: The Guilford Press.

Klein, Stanley B., Leda Cosmides, John Tooby, and Sarah Chance. 2002. Decisions and the Evolution of Memory: Multiple Systems, Multiple Functions. *Psychological Review* 109: 306–29.

Koskinen, Aarne A. 1953. *Missionary Influence as a Political Factor in the Pacific Islands*. Helsinki: Suomalainen tiedeakatemia.

Krymkowski, Daniel H., and Luther H. Martin. 1998. Religion as an Independent Variable: Revisiting the Weberian Hypothesis. *Method & Theory in the Study of Religion* 10: 187–98.

Lawson, E. Thomas, and Robert N. McCauley. 1990. *Rethinking Religion: Connecting Cognition and Culture*. Cambridge: Cambridge University Press.

Lévi-Strauss, Claude. (1958/1979). *Structural Anthropology*. Trans. C. Jacobson and G. Schoepf. Harmondsworth: Penguin.

Levin, Jeffrey S., and Linda M. Chatters. 1998. Research on Religion and Mental Health: An Overview of Empirical Findings and Theoretical Issues. In *Handbook of Religion and Mental Health*, ed. Harold G. Koenig. San Diego: Academic Press.

Lieberman, Matthew D., Ruth Gaunt, Daniel T. Gilbert, and Yaacov Trope. 2002. Reflexion and Reflection: A Social Cognitive Neuroscience Approach to Attributional Inference. *Advances in Experimental Social Psychology* 34: 199–249.

Lohse, Bernhard. 1999. *Martin Luther's Theology: Its Historical and Systematic Development*. Ed. and trans. Roy A. Harrisville. Edinburgh: T&T Clark.

MacDougall, Mary Ann, and Robert S. Brown. 1984. The Temporal Order of Depression and Anxiety. In *The Self in Anxiety, Stress, and Depression*, ed. Ralf Schwarzer, 341–51. Amsterdam: Elsevier Science Publishers.

MacReady, Norra. 2002. Adrenergic Blockers Shortly after Trauma Can Block PTSD. *Clinical Psychiatry News* 30: 9.

Malony, H. Newton, and Samuel Southard, eds. 1992. *Handbook of Religious Conversion*. Birmingham, AL: Religious Education Press.

Martin, Luther. 2004. Cognitive Science, Historiography and the Study of So-Called Folk Religions: The Case of the Eleusinian Mysteries of Demeter. *Temenos* 39/40: 81–100.

McCauley, Robert N. 2000. The Naturalness of Religion and the Unnaturalness of Science. In *Explanation and Cognition*, ed. Frank C. Keil and Robert A. Wilson. Cambridge, MA: MIT Press.

McCauley, Robert N., and E. Thomas Lawson. 2002. *Bringing Ritual to Mind: Psychological Foundations of Cultural Forms*. Cambridge: Cambridge University Press.

Miller, William R., and Janet C'de Baca. 2001. *Quantum Change: When Epiphanies and Sudden Insights Transform Ordinary Lives*. New York: The Guilford Press.

Odenvik, Nathan. 1940. *Lars Ulstadius*. Stockholm: Förlaget Philadelphia.

Paloutzian, Raymond F., James T. Richardson, and Lewis R. Rambo. 1999. Religious Conversion and Personality Change. *Journal of Personality* 67: 1047–79.

Pargament, Kenneth I. (1996/2002a). Religious Methods of Coping: Resources for the Conservation and Transformation of Significance. In *Religion and the Practice of Clinical Psychology*, ed. E. Shafranske. Washington, DC: American Psychological Association.

———. 2002b. The Bitter and the Sweet: An Evaluation of the Costs and Benefits of Religiousness. *Psychological Inquiry* 3: 168–81.

Pentikäinen, Juha. 1975. Revivalist Movements and Religious Contracultures in Finland. In *New Religions (Scripta Instituti Donneriani Aboensis, 7)*, ed. Haralds Biezais. Åbo: The Donner Institute for Research in Religious and Cultural History.

Pinker, Steven. 2002. *The Blank Slate: The Modern Denial of Human Nature*. New York: Penguin.

Post, Stephen G. 1998. Ethics, Religion, and Mental Health. In *Handbook of Religion and Mental Health*, ed. Harold G. Koenig. San Diego: Academic Press.

Pyysiäinen, Ilkka. 2001. *How Religion Works: Towards a New Cognitive Science of Religion*. Leiden: Brill.

———. 2003. Dual-Process Theories and Hybrid Systems: A Commentary on Anderson & Lebiere. *Behavioral and Brain Sciences* 26: 617–18.

———. 2004a. Folk Religion and Theological Correctness. *Temenos* 39/40: 151–65.

———. 2004b. *Magic, Miracles and Religion: A Scientist's Perspective*. Walnut Creek, CA: AltaMira Press.

———. 2004c. Corrupt Doctrine and Doctrinal Revival: On the Nature and Limits of the Modes Theory. In *Theorizing Religions Past: Archaeology, History, and Cognition*, ed. Harvey Whitehouse and Luther H. Martin. Walnut Creek, CA: AltaMira Press.

———. 2004d. Intuitive and Explicit in Religious Thought. *Journal of Cognition and Culture* 4: 123–50.

———. In press. Religion is neither Costly, nor Beneficial: A Commentary on Atran and Norenzayan. *Behavioral and Brain Sciences* 27, no. 6.

Rambo, Lewis. 1993. *Understanding Religious Conversion*. New Haven, CT: Yale University Press.

———. 1998. The Psychology of Conversion. Paper delivered at the International Coalition for Religious Freedom Conference on "Religious Freedom and the New Millennium," Berlin, Germany, May 29–31. *http://www.religiousfreedom.com/conference/Germany/rambo.htm* (accessed 22 August 2002).

Saarinen, Risto. 1988. *Gottes Wirken auf uns. Die transzendentale Deutung des Gegenwart-Christi-Motivs in der Lutherforschung*. Reports from the Department of Systematic Theology, University of Helsinki, IX. Helsinki: University of Helsinki.

Schacter, Daniel L., Anthony D. Wagner, and Randy L. Buckner. 2000. Memory Systems. In *The Oxford Handbook of Memory*, ed. Endel Tulving and F. I. M. Craik. Oxford: Oxford University Press.

Slone, Donald Jason. 2004. *Theological Incorrectness: Why Religious People Believe What They Shouldn't*. New York: Oxford University Press.

Sperber, Dan, and Deirdre Wilson. 1986. *Relevance: Communication and Cognition*. Cambridge, MA: Harvard University Press.

Taves, Ann. 1999. *Fits, Trances, & Visions: Experiencing Religion and Explaining Experience from Wesley to James*. Princeton, NJ: Princeton University Press.

Thorson, James A. 1998. Religion and Anxiety: Which Anxiety? Which Religion? In *Handbook of Religion and Mental Health*, ed. Harold G. Koenig. San Diego: Academic Press.

Tremlin, Todd. 2002. A Theory of Religious Modulation: Reconciling Religious Modes and Ritual Arrangements. *Journal of Cognition and Culture* 2: 309–48.

Tulving, Endel. 1995. Organization of Memory: Quo Vadis? In *The Cognitive Neurosciences*, ed. Michael S. Gazzaniga et al. Cambridge, MA: MIT Press.

Weber, Max. (1922/1965). *Sociology of Religion*. Ed. and trans. E. Fischoff. London: Methuen.

Whitehouse, Harvey. 1995. *Inside the Cult: Religious Innovation and Transmission in Papua New Guinea*. Oxford: Clarendon Press.

———. 2000. *Arguments and Icons: Divergent Modes of Religiosity*. Oxford: Oxford University Press.

———. 2001. Transmissive Frequency, Ritual, and Exegesis. *Journal of Cognition and Culture* 1: 167–81.

———. 2002a. Conjectures, Refutations, and Verification: Towards a Testable Theory of "Modes of Religiosity." *Journal of Ritual Studies* 16: 44–59.

———. 2002b. Modes of Religiosity: Towards a Cognitive Explanation of the Sociopolitical Dynamics of Religion. *Method & Theory in the Study of Religion* 14: 293–315.

Williams, George Huntston. 1962. *The Radical Reformation*. Philadelphia: The Westminster Press.

Zinnbauer, Brian J., and Kenneth I. Pargament. 1998. Spiritual Conversion: A Study of Religious Change among College Students. *Journal for the Scientific Study of Religion* 37: 161–80.

Zola, Stuart, and Larry R. Squire. 2000. The Medial Temporal Lobe and the Hippocampus. In *The Oxford Handbook of Memory*, ed. Endel Tulving and F. I. M. Craik. Oxford: Oxford University Press.

9

Charisma, Tradition, and Ritual: A Cognitive Approach to Magical Agency

Jesper Sørensen

The relation between ritual actions and dogmatic systems is of central concern to both anthropology and to the academic study of religion. Because of its philological roots, the study of religion has tended to focus on systems of beliefs as coherent worldviews most evidently affecting behavior in ritual action. Anthropology, on the other hand, has been more concerned with actual behavior and therefore, to a large extent, focused on ritual and its relation to social organization, and only subsequently turned its attention to beliefs as systems legitimizing and explaining the origin and form of both ritual action and social structure. Two types of explanations have emerged from this: Either systems of beliefs are seen as the primary thing causing the performance of ritual, or rituals are seen as the primary thing causing the construction of systems of beliefs. One of the problems common to both approaches is the lack of psychologically plausible theories explaining exactly how belief and action are related in religious traditions. How do people actually become motivated to perform ritual actions? How are these motivations related to structures of beliefs? What cognitive mechanisms are involved in both representations of beliefs and in ritual performance (e.g., what role is played by basic cognitive mechanisms such as memory and categorization)?

Harvey Whitehouse (1992, 1995, 2000, 2004) has addressed these questions by means of a cognitive theory. Whitehouse argues that religions gravitate toward two attractor positions, which he describes as "imagistic" and "doctrinal" modes of religiosity that respectively entail contrasting relations between ritual and beliefs. He argues that fundamental aspects of human cognition, especially memory, must be taken into account in order to explain why rituals tend to conform to either an imagistic mode based around low-frequency, high-arousal ritual performances, or a doctrinal mode with high frequency of performance but lower levels of arousal. It is of central importance to the project that these two modes support different types of social and political organization: imagistic rituals support the cohesion of small groups based on face-to-face interaction, whereas doctrinal rituals support larger, anonymous groups, thus facilitating the emergence of large-scale political structures. The theory thus proposes a direct relation between modes of ritual performance, doctrinal belief systems, and social organization and bases this on properties of the human cognitive system.

My concern in this chapter will not be to provide a comprehensive description of Whitehouse's theory, nor to discuss the recent and very thorough critique offered by McCauley and Lawson (2002). I will focus instead on three questions that are germane to the modes theory and that may help us to develop a more complete picture of the relationship between ritual action, religious traditions, and political organization.

The first question concerns the role of charisma. Since the pioneering work on this topic by Max Weber (1947, 1976), charisma has played a prominent role in the analysis of religious organization in general, and in particular in the study of the emergence of new religious movements. In this chapter, I will discuss what role charismatic authority has in instigating new religions, both imagistic and doctrinal. When investigated from a cognitive angle, the human proclivity to ascribe charisma to certain persons, actions, or objects points to features of human categorization of great importance in the study of religion and the development of ritual traditions.

The second question concerns the function of certain aspects of rituals, and in particular whether rituals, as a special behavioral modality, generate distinctive cognitive responses by their mere performance. I will argue that this is indeed the case. Rituals involve representations of magical agency understood as entities infusing the force necessary for ritual efficacy.

This naturally leads to a third question, concerning the role of participants' interpretations of ritual actions in the development of ritual form. Ritual actions can be interpreted using two hermeneutic approaches. In the first, attention is directed toward perceptible features of ritual actions in an attempt to relate these to the overall goal or *purpose* of the ritual. I will refer to this as "magical interpretation" focusing on ritual efficacy or instrumentality. The second is "symbolic interpretation" in which participants relate ritual actions to external dogmatic structures in order to construct ritual *meaning*. Religious institutions invest much energy in controlling these interpretations in order to ensure institutional coherence. Extended symbolic interpretations of ritual action, however, seem to correlate inversely with representations of ritual efficacy. The more elaborate symbolic interpretation of a ritual becomes, the less efficacy is accorded to it. This in turn has significant implications for the further development of ritual structures. Such processes can take place over considerable time periods, extending beyond the lifetime of individuals. The processes affecting ritual form are thus understood as involving an opposition between social dynamics pressing toward control of ritual force by means of symbolic interpretation, on the one hand, and more intuitive responses to the formal properties of ritualized actions, on the other.

RELIGIOUS LEADERSHIP AND THE CHARISMATIC PROCLIVITY

In his vast sociological study of world religions and their intimate relationship to political and economic structures, the German sociologist Max Weber accorded a prominent role to religious leaders endowed with so-called charisma. In Weber's thinking, charisma confers a special type of authority based on the attribution of a more-or-less direct link with superempirical agency and powers deriving from this connection.[1] In contrast to traditional and legal-rational authority, which are both based on constitutive rules, charismatic authority is a revolutionary force that enables the abolition of conventional rules of conduct and the construction of new ones, in particular of new ritual structures. Thus, Weber is concerned with how new religious groups and thereby new ritual traditions get started in the first place, and this might fruitfully be related to the theory of modes of religiosity, proposed by Whitehouse (2000, 2004) and discussed throughout this book. Whitehouse's most detailed example of a doctrinal tradition, the mainstream Pomio Kivung religion in Papua New Guinea, started out firmly grounded in charismatic authority (Whitehouse 1995). Its deified founder, Koriam, was able to abolish existing practices and establish new ones with divine sanction. By the same token, questions of charismatic authority were a central concern in Kivung splinter groups, dominated by the imagistic mode of religiosity, both in terms of their complex relations to the centralized authority of the Pomio Kivung movement, but also internally, as demonstrated by Whitehouse's description of the rise of splinter-group leaders.

That charismatic authority is basic to the foundation of religions operating in both doctrinal and imagistic modalities naturally raises two further (interdependent) questions. The first concerns the temporal aspects of charismatic authority, in relation to which Weber's concept of *routinization* becomes especially important. For various reasons, ascription of charismatic authority is highly unstable.[2] If the new movement is to survive, it must become routinized, for instance through the establishment of bureaucratic religious offices, stipulated ritual actions, or authorized ritual instruments. The Pomio Kivung movement succeeded in making this transition, whereas the splinter groups described by Whitehouse did not.

The second question concerns the emotional aspects of charismatic ascription. Whitehouse is correct when he points out that Weber emphasized the emotional and communal aspects of charismatic movements, but he overstates his case when he connects these emotions solely to imagistic ritual practices. This leads to some strange results, as when Protestant acts of iconoclasm during the Reformation must be described as doctrinally motivated and thereby less emotionally arousing. Surely the very *process* of wiping out pictures and destroying images in churches must have been highly emotionally arousing, at least more so than the ordinary Catholic Mass. That these actions subsequently rendered the Protestant traditions more vulnerable to the tedium effect may be correct, but should not be confused with the fact that the *beginning* of new religious traditions involves both charismatic agents and emotionally arousing actions.[3] Even a tradition seeking the abolition of certain imagistic practices itself, such as most Protestant sects, will use highly emotional actions producing lasting and vivid memory in participants. (Recall also the radically doctrinal Taliban's destruction of Buddhist sculptures as a vivid and ritual demonstration of authority.) In a similar manner, oratorical performance using vivid and moving imagery produces intense emotional arousal, especially if this oratory conveys new conceptual structures (for instance predicting an imminent eschaton).

Weber's theory of charismatic authority suggests that all new religious formations draw extensively on imagistic practices (and perhaps other means of producing emotional arousal), but that this phase of religious innovation is extremely unstable and therefore must be controlled by other forms of authority connected to some sort of doctrinal encoding and orthodoxy. Further, as Weber argued with respect to charismatic groups, the initial excitement surrounding novel religious revelations must be controlled or at least coordinated with everyday activities, for instance those necessary for subsistence, either by becoming routinized (and thus combined with other everyday routines) or by becoming confined to specific and circumscribed periods. These issues loomed large for the splinter groups described by Whitehouse, as all economic activities were abandoned in favor of ritual actions concerned with bringing about the desired millennium, and the new activities ultimately proved unsustainable.

But why do humans everywhere apparently spontaneously attach charismatic qualities to certain individuals? In *The Naturalness of Religious Ideas*, Pascal Boyer argues that ascription of charisma is found everywhere in relation to religious offices, and that this "charismatic proclivity" occurs even where official doctrines downplay or outrightly condemn such beliefs. Protestant priests are for instance appointed only if they fulfill certain standardized criteria, but even in these cases people tend to ascribe certain personal characteristics to priests, even regarding them as necessary qualities. Persons in religious offices are attributed a special essence that connects them to the office, and this goes even for Protestant priests. We need to look more closely at this psychological essentialism (Medin and Ortony 1989) in order to understand the nature of personal charisma.

Two types of reasoning underlie the ascription of essentialized characteristics to individuals. First, perceptual features, especially behavior, are understood as iconic signs that they belong to a certain category of persons. Car dealers, professors, and priests all exhibit perceptual characteristics that lead to their classification as belonging to these social categories. Second, these perceptual features are understood as outward manifestations of essential characteristics generally ascribed to this category of people. By means of abductive inference, these two processes mutually enforce each other, as the presence of perceptual characteristics indicates internal essence that in turn explains perceptual characteristics, which confirm the possession of internal essence, and so forth.

We are especially prone to ascribe essentialized qualities to holders of religious offices. This is partly because ritual actions deliver salient perceptual features indicating underlying essence. In contrast to university theologians who are usually not ascribed any special religious essence, priests performing ritual actions are categorized as containing the "right stuff." This observation fits neatly with the fact that Weber originally based his observation of charismatic authority on Paul's first letter to the Christian congregation in Corinth. The background for the letter is a crisis that apparently risks jeopardizing the unity of the congregation. Among other things, Paul warns the congregation against placing undue emphasis on charismatic expressions such as speaking in tongues, healing, and prophetic utterances as means of authority. If everybody can appeal to charismatic authority, how can early Christianity avoid splintering into thousands of competing factions, each with its own heavenly sanctioned version of the teachings of Christ and competing ritual techniques? Of importance in this context is that these actions are performed in a ritual context. Paul seems aware that ritual performances, such as speaking in tongues, healing, and prophesying, are a direct means to ascription of special essence, and thereby to a charismatic authority that might hinder the unification of the early Christian movement. Ritual actions are one of the primary mechanisms by which charismatic authority is acquired, and this has serious consequences for the temporal development of ritual forms in any given social formation.

To summarize, perceptual features producing great emotional intensity seem to be an inherent aspect in the initial phase of all new religions. The ascription of personalized charismatic authority enables the replacement of existing constitutive rules with new rules legitimized by the leader's direct relation to superempirical agencies. Rituals are the primary means to produce this superempirical connection, and at the same time rituals are among the first structures to crystallize as new constitutive rules are constructed.

RITUAL AND MAGICAL AGENCY

But why are ritual actions so important in this respect? Why are they a forceful way to produce representations of charismatic authority? And why does the routinization of charisma almost always entail the construction of new stipulated ritual structures? In order to answer these questions, we need to take a closer look at some of the inherent aspects of ritual action itself, and especially, as noticed by McCauley and Lawson, the role of agency in ritual action (McCauley and Lawson 2002).

That rituals form a special category of actions seems to be evident to everybody involved, performers and observers alike. Rituals, for instance, elicit symbolic interpretations, often exhibit extreme redundancy, and are performed with nonapparent and often downright obscure relations to their purported goals. As should be clear by now, however, rituals are first of all *actions* and therefore make use of the same cognitive mechanisms used in ordinary actions. They contain representations of *purposeful* bodily movements usually performed for more-or-less specific purposes; they entail representations of *agents* responsible for what goes on in the ritual; and in relation to agents they contain schematic representations of a *force* necessary for the fulfilment of the action. Especially representations of force have been unaccounted for in recent cognitive theories of ritual action, despite their importance in theories of ordinary actions. Cognitive linguist Leonard Talmy argues that representations of force, or *force dynamics*, are pervasive in language, where they are found in grammaticalization (such as modals), in lexicalization, in metaphor (such as social and psychological forces), and in discourse. Force dynamics are based on a basic-level perception of the physical world, where entities interact through force and counterforce, and thus constitute a preconceptual domain of cognition used to organize several other domains (Talmy 2000). Representations of force are thus fundamental in representations of agency and intentionality, where psychological dispositions are represented as a force that drives outward actions. In a similar vein, Alan Leslie argues that the possession of an internal and renewable force is a defining characteristic of agency. According to Leslie, force is a basic schematic structure of perception: "(a) when objects move they possess or bear force, and (b) when objects contact other objects, they transmit, receive or resist force" (Leslie 1995, 124). When such motion is represented as based on an internal source of energy, we find a very basic representation of agency. This not only enables physical objects (such as bodies) to instigate motion on their own, but also furnishes the necessary energy to change trajectory as a contingent response to other elements in the immediate surroundings without any physical contact (cf. Blakemore et al. 2003). Leslie argues that representations of such mechanical agency form the first of three levels constituting representations of intentional agency. In order to have a full-fledged intentional agent, two higher levels of agency are added: (a) "actional agency" that construes agents as having immediate goals (i.e., relating the motions to productions of a future state) and (b) the cognitive "attitude" to information (i.e., the belief states underlying the action process). When observing an action, all three levels interact to produce a complex notion of agency, as the lower levels feed information into the higher (Leslie 1995, 137).

The ability to exert force is not only a necessary condition in the ascription of agency to elements in the surroundings, but it is exactly the force dynamical properties that make agents cognitively relevant (cf. Baldwin and Baird 2001). Agents that do not influence the world (whether physically, psychologically, or socially) can be ignored without any costs, and it is doubtful whether such entities are regarded as agents at all. A cognitive system with the ability to correctly judge not only that agents are entities exerting forces, but what kind and what amount of force is likely, will have a great advantage over a system without this ability. This goes for physical force, but also for psychological and social forces. Seen from another angle, the expenditure of energy is a necessary condition for reaching a goal through an action. Reaching a goal without any use of force does not constitute an action but rather an event. Thus representation of force is an implicit part in both understanding entities in the world as agents with intentions and in being an agent oneself when acting with specific goals in mind based on beliefs.

This has important ramifications for the study of ritual action. Being actions, rituals are generally performed in order to change some aspect of the world, and as such, rituals involve the exertion of force. This is, of course, a very banal observation implied by most theories that envisage rituals as displays of social relations of power or of more general social and religious commitments (cf. Boyer 2002; Bulbulia 2004). Besides obvious parameters such as expense and pain, investment of force is a reliable indication for evaluating the depth of such social and religious commitment. Representations of force, however, have another and more direct influence on ritual actions. Rituals themselves exert or canalize forces, and these interact with counterforces. This is manifest in rituals of exorcism and protection in which (often malignant) counterforces are more or less directly represented and interacted with in the ritual procedure. But other types of ritual are also embedded in force-dynamic schemata. In the final parts of a Christian wedding, the groom *may* kiss the bride; that is, by ritual intervention a social and religious ban against sexual interaction is lifted. Other rituals expose the same modal aspects of prohibiting, allowing, permitting, preventing, and so on. When seen in such a force-dynamical perspective, it becomes clearer why certain parameters in rituals can be manipulated in order to enhance or decrease the force of the ritual performed. Saying 50 instead of 25 Ave Marias intuitively entails a relative increase of ritual power. This also makes sense of many so-called secondary elaborations used to explain why certain ritual procedures were unsuccessful. They simply could not overcome the opposition they faced (both aspects are discussed in Sørensen 2000).

Of particular interest in this context is *how* such force is invested in the ritual action. As we shall see below, ritual is a very peculiar kind of action, and it is therefore far from obvious how participants represent the force necessary for ritual efficacy. An obvious possibility is that the ritual agent, that is, the agent performing the ritual, invests the ritual with the necessary force to produce its desired effect. Many rituals, however, do not seem to live up to this form, as the elements invested with ritual force (or "magical agency," discussed below) are not the ritual's logical agent.

Rituals differ from ordinary actions on at least two accounts, and this has important consequences for representations of the source of the force necessary for ritual efficacy. First, as noted in ethological definitions of ritual (e.g., Lorenz 1966; Burkert 1979), ritualization entails that actions are removed from their ordinary instrumental domain and thereby gain other functions. When bread and wine are consumed during the Eucharist, this is not in order to satisfy hunger and thirst. Actually these functions are often subverted by the sheer amount and quality of the products, and by the context of the actions. This might seem like an obvious point of little interest, but, as noted by Sperber (1975), it has important cognitive consequences. Whereas ordinary actions are processed very quickly by means of a number of causal expectations related to domain-specific ontologies, these are of little help in making sense of or ascribing purpose to ritual actions. There is no inherent, domain-specific relation between eating sanctified bread and receiving grace, even though there is a fundamental schematic structure in "giving" and "receiving" that is common to both. Rituals in that respect violate or transform automatically ascribed causal properties of actions.

The second distinguishing feature of ritual action concerns intentionality. In *The Archetypal Actions of Ritual*, Humphrey and Laidlaw argue that in ritualized actions the intentional stance relating the agent performing the actions and the particular actions found in the ritual are radically transformed. Compared with ordinary intentional actions, where the agent can alter any specific subset of actions if failing to reach the desired goal, ritualized actions are nonintentional in the sense that the acts are stipulated and cannot be changed in order to achieve the goal in question. Either one performs a ritual by doing the prescribed action, or one does not perform the ritual at all (see related point in Boyer 1994). This stipulated character of ritualized actions follows naturally from causal underspecification, but it has important cognitive consequences of its own. It points to the presence of an underlying (superhuman) agency that has stipulated the ritual action, and as such is intentionally related to it. This agency might, or might not, be present in the ritual, but will in both cases function as the intentional instance *legitimizing* the ritual action.[4] As we saw in the last section, this is exactly one of the main aspects of charismatic authority, as it enables both the deconstruction of old constitutive rules and the stipulation of new ones.

However, if the intentional agent need not be present in the ritual and ordinary causal presumptions are violated, how does the ritual work? How do participants represent the ritual as containing the necessary force to be an effective action if the intentional agent is not present? Again we must attend to the peculiar features of ritual combined with the human proclivity to ascribe agency to all types of events and happenings. The absence of direct causal connections (based on intuitive ontological assumptions) between ritual and purpose and the transformation of intentionality entails that the agent performing the actions need not be represented as the source of the necessary force. Often the logical agent is not represented as the carrier of the agency involved in the action, but the hyperactive agency-detection device entails that ritual actions *must* be ascribed agency (Boyer 2002). This leads to representation of one or several ritual elements as invested with "magical agency." As mentioned above, the technical term "magical agency" refers to a ritual element or elements represented as a necessary condition for the ritual to have any efficacy. In fact, the ritual has no force if magical agency is absent. Often these agencies are gods or spirits that act more or less directly in rituals, whether as agents, patients, or instruments (as described by McCauley and Lawson), but as indicated by the immense volume of magical rituals performed around the world, other ritual elements can play a significant role as well. In strongly stipulated ritual traditions, magical agency often resides in the very actions performed. By performing the right actions, such as pronouncing a powerful spell, the ritual result is ensured no matter who performs it. Malinowski describes how the Trobrianders accord ritual efficacy to the actual saying of the spell, and ownership of spells is invested with great prestige (the long and complicated structure of the spells meanwhile limiting unauthorized spread) (Malinowski 1935; Evans-Pritchard 1929). In other cases, magical agency rests in the ritual or religious office, and only rituals performed by a correctly appointed person will be deemed efficacious. Often, however, links to office are combined with other means of ensuring magical agency. For instance, both the presence of an ordained priest *and* the performance of the correct linguistic actions are necessary prerequisites for the rite of transubstantiation in the Roman Catholic Mass (McCarthy 1956). Finally, even objects can be endowed with magical agency, as seen in the many instances of magical objects working without rules guiding agents or specific actions. According to anthropologist Evans-Pritchard, the Zande represent magical agency as resting solely in the ritual objects (or medicine): "It is the material substance which is the occult and essential element in the rite, for in the substance lies the mystical power which produces the desired end" (Evans-Pritchard 1937, 44).

Thus, ritual actions produce representations of magical agency, allowing otherwise nonspecial agents (e.g., the fellow next door) to perform special actions by virtue of either position of office, stipulated actions, or special objects. By virtue of their very form, ritual actions provoke a search for magical agency as the necessary source of force enabling ritual efficacy, and all ritual elements, persons, actions, and objects are potentially ascribed this property. Lawson and McCauley (1990) argue that the object-agency filter will effectively block representations of objects and actions from having agency. By virtue of basic ontological intuitions, objects (and actions) cannot fill the role of agent unless these are embedded in enabling rituals that endow them with the quality of agency, or unless they are defined as a special type of object with agentive properties in the conceptual system informing the ritual action. Ritual elements can thus be seen as the source of force in ritual actions by means of a ritually or conceptually established connection to a superhuman agent.

A basic problem that the theory does not account for is *how* rituals can invest agency into objects (except by sheer participation). According to Lawson and McCauley, participants' ascription of agency to otherwise nonagentive ritual elements is solely a result of their knowledge of prior enabling rituals. Ultimately all ritual elements owe their ability to function as agents to their role in earlier performed rituals ultimately connecting them to the actions of superhuman agents, but it is a question whether ritual participants actually have representations of the embedded rituals. There must be important cognitive structures that facilitate the transfer of agency in ritual settings, and it seems likely that there is a limit to how many embedded ritual structures the cognitive system will incorporate. Further, all participants most likely won't share the same knowledge of prior ritual structures. Some participants will represent objects as containing magical agency by virtue of their mere appearance in a ritual setting and as a result of the immediate event frame the ritual takes part in. This, of course, threatens a conceptual distinction between magic and religion based on *types* of rituals (i.e., whether or not their power is represented as stemming from a god, spirit, ancestor, or by necessity). It is, however, possible to maintain a distinction between magic and religion as different *modes of interpretation* (i.e., how people use and understand the rituals they participate in). Such difference in approach to ritual action would explain how one and the same ritual in one situation is seen as an efficacious action working as an instrument addressing specific problems, and in another context as a symbolic reference to a system of doctrines (this is further discussed below). This position does not question the fact that we find enabling rituals as described by Lawson and McCauley. It merely poses the question of whether such ritual histories are means to ensure institutional control over participants' ritual interpretation, rather than spontaneous intuitions held by participants in the absence of explicit tuition. Lawson and McCauley's structural theory of ritual competence might then be a description of institutionally developed religious traditions with elaborate systems to control ascription of magical agency, rather than a general theory of participants' intuitive understanding of religious rituals. This is in line with Whitehouse's (2004) recent argument that the relation between ritual action and explicit religious knowledge is of crucial importance in understanding the historical development of religious traditions.

To summarize, we have seen that charismatic authority is a necessary condition for introducing new ritual and doctrinal structures. By a direct connection to superempirical agencies, charismatic persons can be considered the source of ritual force, but eventually such charisma must be routinized if the ritual and/or dogmatic tradition shall remain relatively stable and spread beyond the immediate vicinity of the charismatic person. Further, I have argued that even though rituals are actions involving agents with purposes using physical and psychological forces, rituals in a number of ways differ from ordinary actions by severing most domain-specific causal expectations, and by transforming the relation between participants' intentions and the actions performed. This provokes a cognitive search for ritual entities endowed with a force necessary for ritual efficacy, and for an intentional agent legitimizing the ritual action. A crucial question then is how religious and ritual institutions ensure that the magical agency ascribed to ritual actions is in general concurrence with the overall doctrinal system and how they prevent participants' representations of unauthorized magical agency. Obviously they often fail, but the mere attempt by institutions to control representations involved in ritual actions has serious consequences for the social and historical development of religious traditions.

THE INTERPRETATION OF RITUAL ACTION: MAGICAL OR SYMBOLIC

In order to account for these processes, we need to turn our attention to how participants interpret ritual actions, that is, how they relate the performance of ritual with any representation of purpose and meaning. This raises the important question of how motivations influence participants' representations of ritual actions.

We can discern two hermeneutic methods used by participants when interpreting ritual actions: the first can be called a "magical interpretation," as it focuses on the relations between ritual actions performed, representations of ritual force and magical agency, and the overall goal or *purpose* of their performance. As we shall see, this interpretation is to a large extent dependent on factors internal to the ritual action or its immediate context. In contrast to this method, "symbolic interpretation" directs attention to the issue of how ritual actions are connected to overarching symbolic or doctrinal systems, that is, to the *meaning* of the ritual actions. This interpretive stance depends more heavily on factors external to the ritual action itself and its immediate context. These two hermeneutic strategies are available to participants in all rituals, but religious traditions usually endorse one or the other, depending in part on the size and nature of social organization.

As already noted, an important feature of ritualized actions is the disconnection of cognitive processes otherwise used to interpret ordinary actions. The strong causal relations used in processing everyday physical actions are to a large extent suspended in rituals, provoking a cognitive search for other means to relate them to an overall purpose. It is a reasonable assumption that participants' attention is first and foremost directed toward the *perceptual features* of ritual action in order to extract such possible connections. Strong domain-specific assumptions are replaced by what ethologist Hans Kummer (1995) describes as weak causal assumptions based on perceptual relations of contagion, similarity, and contiguity. Basic perceptual features involving image-schemata, essence, and force are highlighted by participants' cognitive systems, thereby relating perceptible elements of the ritual actions performed to conditions, both prior to and following the ritual. Thus we find transfer of desirable and undesirable essence by means of contagious interactions (e.g., communion); we find iconic actions containing image-schematic structures of similarity by which one domain can be manipulated through actions performed in another domain (e.g., voodoo), and we find iconic representations of force by means of temporal duration and iteration (e.g., the night vigil of the Dadul splinter group). Further, we find great importance attached to the immediate spatial and temporal context surrounding the ritual performance (e.g., in how ritual as a whole functions as a causal force in strings of events). Magical interpretations further entail an enhanced focus on magical agency. Rituals with strongly defined goals entail a greater emphasis on the agency able to bring about this goal.

The schematic properties underlying magic, prototypically seen as manipulation of dolls, burning of hair, and ingestion of mysterious potions, can be found in all ritual actions. By focusing on the perceptual aspects of ritual actions, representations of weak causal connections can be constructed, leading to representations of ritual efficacy. Thus magical interpretations are involved when interpreting ritual actions as actually *doing* something in the world. This focus on purposefulness entails that internal features of the ritual are directly related to context-dependent parameters, such as the autobiography of individuals and groups, and thereby to episodic memory.

In contrast to this focus on ritual efficacy in immediate contexts, symbolic interpretations are more directly concerned with the relation between ritual action and doctrinal systems. Of course, doctrinal systems can contain descriptions of the how rituals work and thereby why and how they should be performed. But these must be of a rather general nature and therefore do not play a significant role in symbolic interpretations. Instead, the actions performed in the ritual are understood as symbols, allegories, and signs pointing to central dogmatic aspects of the tradition. Thus, according to a symbolic interpretation, the Eucharist is not so much about transferring a desirable essence infusing a state of grace as it is a symbolic act of, for instance, the self-sacrifice of Jesus on behalf of humanity.

Symbolic interpretations can take wholly idiosyncratic forms, and in principle each individual will construct his or her own interpretation. Thus in some traditions there are no explicit exegetical models available to participants, and explicit interpretations are strongly discouraged, leaving only rather idiosyncratic interpretations. More often, however, ritual actions are related to explicit and institutionally approved interpretational models that connect the ritual action to specific propositions.

As Whitehouse points out, a conventional relation between ritual action and dogmatic systems has several implications, such as the relative stability in time of both ideology and authority; the direct support for the conceptual and doctrinal system through repetition; the connections of bodily actions and beliefs, making otherwise rather abstract propositions something one acts upon; and the possibility of constructing larger, imagined communities based on behavioral commonalties. Whitehouse may be correct when he argues that the stability of doctrinal systems presupposes that rituals and symbolic interpretations are reiterated on a regular basis, that is, that the rituals are often performed and systematically related to verbal, dogmatic propositions. Thus, it can be argued that the primary function of institutionally endorsed symbolic interpretations is to constrain possible idiosyncratic interpretations and thereby prevent the emergence of competing charismatic authority threatening ritual, and thereby economic, privileges of religious guilds (Boyer 2001).

However, the attempt to control interpretations, relating these in a systematic manner to doctrinal systems, can be a source of serious instability if it is taken too far. Not only are ritual interpretations notoriously difficult to control because the actions found in rituals underdetermine subsequent interpretations. Symbolic interpretations further tend to downplay the internal source of purpose found in ritual actions in favor of an externally related ascription of meaning. Thus, instead of relating ritual actions to the immediate context through episodic memory, symbolic interpretation relates ritual actions to context-independent doctrinal systems, thus making them more stable, but less relevant.

Therefore, in order to highlight the relation between ritual actions and doctrinal systems, ascription of magical agency and the more directly perceived weak causal connections must be deemphasized or even eradicated. In Protestant churches, magical interpretations of Communion relating transfer of essence to individuals' degree of sin are explicitly deemphasized in favor of a symbolic interpretation based on dogmatic propositions. Nothing *really* happens when participants eat the sanctified bread, but the actions should be understood as pointing toward important aspects of the dogmatic system. Similarly, Pomio Kivung members have not experienced the promised effect of their repeated ritual actions, and the centralized religious institutions have deemphasized this aspect of the ritual actions as immoral, an interpretation in stark contrast to the feelings of eschatological imminence conveyed by the rituals of the Dadul splinter group (Whitehouse 1995, 86). Radical symbolic interpretations will in effect remove the action element from rituals and thereby make their performance causally irrelevant. Therefore doctrinal traditions are not only threatened by the tedium effect, as argued by Whitehouse (2000). They are equally threatened by a "triviality effect" where the performance of rituals is represented as having no causal consequences.

Undue emphasis on symbolic interpretations of ritual action can have at least two deleterious effects. First, reform movements will reritualize existing ritual actions, thereby reinvigorating representations of magical agency and ritual purpose. This in effect rejuvenates routinized magical agency by a process of desymbolization whereby actions are deprived of their conventional symbolic interpretations. This can be achieved in numerous ways, for instance by reintroducing archaic practices or exotic materials that do not have an established symbolic interpretation, or simply by emphasizing the actions themselves and restricting exegesis (Sørensen, forthcoming). In general, such reform movements do not pose a serious threat to established institutions, as no competing doctrinal system legitimized by charismatic authority is introduced. In the second development, the triviality effect will make people look elsewhere for ritual efficacy. This entails a search for charismatic authority outside established constitutive rules, thus facilitating a genuine breach of tradition.

The reformist development can be exemplified by the Dadul splinter group (Whitehouse 1995). The principal aim was to reenergize existing ritual structures by making them purposeful in an imminent sense. It never totally abandoned the constitutive rules legitimized by the central Pomio Kivung movement, but rather it raised the stakes in order to make the rituals work right away by inserting additional force into the ritual, iconically represented by the ring ceremony and the nightly vigils. This development was supported by the fact that the central leadership of the Pomio Kivung did not press the matter by forcing participants in the splinter group to choose between different sources of authority. Examples of the "revolutionary" development are to be found in numerous rituals competing with established Protestant institutions in Scandinavia. Ritual structures of this kind are based on charismatic authority or ritualized magical agency found outside established religious institutions, and even though very few have been able to crystallize into more widespread established institutions with extensive doctrinal systems, they have still to a large extent influenced beliefs. About 20 percent of the Danish population more or less believe in reincarnation, a belief strongly opposed by the majority Lutheran church and nonexistent two hundred years ago.

CONCLUSION

A graphic depiction of the dynamic interaction stemming from both cognitive and social pressures might be set out as depicted in figure 9.1.

In this idealized model, ascription of charismatic authority prompted by the charismatic proclivity facilitates the emergence of new constitutive rules. These will eventually be routinized into ritual structures with ascription of magical agency ensured by the agency-detection device and controlled by institutions. Direct relations to superempirical agencies will thus be upheld, and rituals can be represented as efficacious in a stable manner. In general, the performance of rituals provokes secondary symbolic interpretations

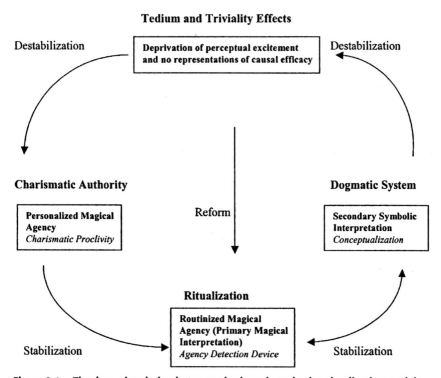

Figure 9.1   The dynamic relation between charismatic authority, ritualization, and dogmatic systems.

legitimizing and explaining the persistence of magical agency and relating ritual actions to emerging doctrinal systems. This entails further stabilization as the ritual actions are removed from context-dependent relations and are related to exclusive groups of ritual agents, or religious guilds (Boyer 2001). In the model, the two-way arrow connecting ritualization and dogmatic system indicates that religious systems often reach a stable state at this point, including both routinized magical agency (i.e., efficacious rituals) and dogmatic interpretations. The Catholic Church would seem to furnish an apposite example of such a relatively stable system incorporating individually relevant rituals, involving representations of magical agency and magical interpretations on the one hand, and extensive doctrinal systems giving rise to secondary symbolic interpretations and ritual control on the other. If rituals and dogmas are to have a stable relation, however, they must be frequently performed, which in turn will give rise to the tedium effect described by Whitehouse. Further, symbolic interpretations equally entail a deemphasis of ritual efficacy, eventually producing a triviality effect. The reason for performing the rituals disappears if they are neither emotionally arousing nor represented as having any causal effect. Of course, performance might continue for a while due to "tradition," but eventually ritual performance will either die out or take one of two courses. First, ritual actions can be reritualized, entailing a renewed ascription of magical agency to the ritual actions. This can be described as a "reform" of existing ritual structure. Second, further destabilization can found in cases where alternative sources of charismatic authority are sought after. A few of these new sources of ritual efficacy will eventually complete a routinization and thereby stabilize into institutionalized structures, eventually initiating a new round in the cycle.

This model is an attempt to describe how different modes of religiosity are related in a temporal sequence incorporating both social dynamics of institutionalization and political-economical control, and cognitive mechanisms relating to the charismatic proclivity, agency detection, and interpretation. It has the advantage of transgressing the temporal limitation of an individual's lifetime by arguing that social dynamics of institutional control and movements toward purely symbolic interpretations are long-term developmental trends intimately related to the cognitive consequences ritual actions produce. Imagistic and doctrinal modes of religiosity are thus not merely coexisting modes, but are related to each other through both cognitive mechanisms and social processes.

NOTES

1. Weber claimed the ascription of "ausseralltächlichen Kräfte," that is "nonordinary forces" as the primary means to distinguish charismatic from ordinary persons

(Weber 1976, 245). In line with cognitive theorizing about the counterintuitive aspects of religious ideas (Boyer 1994, 2002), the term "superempirical" is preferred in this context.

2. One reason is that ascription of personal charisma is a social process in which followers take certain perceptible clues (e.g., ritual success) as evidence of charismatic authority. Without strong institutions backing charismatic authority, such charisma is at risk of fading away if not constantly renewed by further perceptual evidence. But even if this fate is avoided, religious institutions based on personal charismatic authority face the inevitable fact that the person carrying personal charisma will eventually die, wherefore charismatic authority must be routinized if the religious/ritual institution is to persist.

3. Several Protestant reformers saw themselves and were seen by others as playing a pivotal *personal* role in the reform. In addition, Protestant reforms were widely understood as an imminent precursor to a new millennium (Baylor 1991; Scribner 1986).

4. Representations of intentionality involved in ritual actions are, of course, much more complex. Sørensen (2004) suggests that two types can be analytically discerned. The first type involves a basic recognition of intentionality involved in all types of actions, including rituals. Thus Gallese (2000a, 2000b, 2001) suggests that the human cognitive system includes so-called "mirror neurons" used both in the execution of actions and in perception of actions leading to ascription of intentionality. The second type of intentionality relates actions to each other in larger event structures and is attributed to ordinary actions involving human agents as a default. Whereas the first-order intention links motions in space to a proximate goal (e.g., using my hand in order to move a piece in a game of chess), the second-order intentionality transforms the first action into an instrument of achieving more ultimate goals (e.g., sacrificing the piece in order to win the game). In ordinary actions, these two levels are directly connected (Sommerville and Woodward 2005), contrary to ritual actions, where the relation between proximate and ultimate intentions is open to constant negotiation and reevaluation.

REFERENCES

Baldwin, Dare A., and Jodie A. Baird. 2001. Discerning Intentions in Dynamic Human Action. *Trends in Cognitive Sciences* 54: 171–78.

Baylor, Michael G. 1991. *The Radical Reformation*. Cambridge: Cambridge University Press.

Blakemore, S. J. et al. 2003. The Detection of Contingency and Animacy From Simple Animations in the Human Brain. *Cerebral Cortex* 13: 837–44.

Boyer, Pascal. 1994. *The Naturalness of Religious Ideas: A Cognitive Theory of Religion*. Berkeley: University of California Press.

———. 2002. *Religion Explained: The Human Instincts that Fashion Gods, Spirits and Ancestors*. London: Vintage.

Bulbulia, Joseph. 2004. Religious Costs as Adaptations that Signal Altruistic Intentions. *Evolution and Cognition* 101: 19–42.

Burkert, Walter. 1979. *Structure and History of Ancient Greek Mythology and Ritual.* Berkeley: University of California Press.

Evans-Pritchard, Edward E. 1937. *Witchcraft, Oracles and Magic among the Azande.* Oxford: Clarendon Press.

———. 1929. The Morphology and Function of Magic. *American Anthropologist* 3: 619–41. Reprinted in Levack, B. P., ed. 1992. *Anthropological Studies of Witchcraft, Magic and Demonology.* London: Garland Press.

Gallese, Vittorio. 2001. The "Shared Manifold" Hypothesis: From Mirror Neurons To Empathy. *Journal of Consciousness Studies* 8: 5–7, 33–50.

———. 2000a. The Acting Subject: Toward the Neural Basis of Social Cognition. In *Neural Correlates of Consciousness: Empirical and Conceptual Questions,* ed. T. Metzinger. Cambridge, MA: MIT Press.

———. 2000b. The Inner Sense of Action: Agency and Motor Representations. *Journal of Consciousness Studies* 710: 23–40.

Humphrey, Caroline, and James Laidlaw. 1994. *The Archetypal Actions of Ritual: A Theory of Ritual Illustrated by the Jain Rite of Worship.* Oxford: Clarendon Press.

Kummer, Hans. 1995. Causal Knowledge in Animals. In *Causal Cognition: A Multidisciplinary Debate,* ed. D. Sperber, D. Premack, and A. J. Premack. Oxford: Clarendon.

Lawson, E. Thomas, and Robert McCauley. 1990. *Rethinking Religion: Connecting Cognition and Culture.* Cambridge: Cambridge University Press.

Leslie, Allan M. 1995. A Theory of Agency. In *Causal Cognition: A Multidisciplinary Debate,* ed. D. Sperber, D. Premack, and A. J. Premack. Oxford: Clarendon.

Lorenz, Konrad. 1966. Evolution of Ritualization in the Biological and Cultural Spheres. *Philosophical Transactions of the Royal Society London,* series B, Biological Sciences, 251: 273–84.

Malinowski, Bronislaw. 1935. *Coral Gardens and Their Magic.* London: George Allen & Unwin Ltd.

McCarthy, John C. 1956. *Problems in Theology I: The Sacraments.* Dublin: Brown and Nolan Limited.

McCauley, Robert, and E. Thomas Lawson. 2002. *Bringing Ritual to Mind: Psychological Foundations of Cultural Forms.* Cambridge: Cambridge University Press.

Medin, Douglas L., and Andrew Ortony. 1989. Psychological Essentialism. In *Similarity and Analogical Reasoning,* ed. S. Vosniadou and A. Ortony. Cambridge: Cambridge University Press.

Scribner, Richard W. 1986. *The German Reformation.* London: MacMillan.

Sommerville, Jessica A., and Amanda L. Woodward. 2005. Pulling out the Intentional Structure of Action: The Relation between Action Processing and Action Production in Infancy. *Cognition* 95: 1–30.

Sperber, Dan. 1975. *Rethinking Symbolism.* Cambridge: Cambridge University Press.

Sørensen, Jesper. 2000. *Essence, Schema and Ritual Action: Towards a Cognitive Theory of Magic.* PhD dissertation, University of Aarhus.

———. 2004. Acts That Work: Cognitive Aspects of Ritual Agency. *Cognitive Semiotics* 18.

———. Forthcoming. The Problem of Magic: Or How Gibberish Becomes Efficacious Action. *Semiotic Inquiry.*

Talmy, L. 2000. Force Dynamics in Language and Thought. In *Toward a Cognitive Semantics,* ed. L. Tamy. Cambridge, MA: MIT Press.

Weber, Max. 1947. *The Theory of Social and Economic Organisation*. New York: Free Press.

———. 1976. *Wirtschaft and Gesellschaft*. 5. rev. Ausgabe, Tübingen: Johannes Winckelmann.

Whitehouse, Harvey. 1992. Memorable Religions: Transmission, Codification, and Change in Divergent Melanesian Contexts. *Man*, n.s., 27: 777–97.

———. 1995. *Inside the Cult: Religious Innovation and Transmission in Papua New Guinea*. Oxford: Clarendon Press.

———. 2000. *Arguments and Icons: Divergent Modes of Religiosity*. Oxford: Oxford University Press.

———. 2004. *Modes of Religiosity: A Cognitive Theory of Religious Transmission*. Walnut Creek, CA: AltaMira Press.

10

Why Religions Develop Free-Will Problems

D. Jason Slone

Cognitive scientists of religion have identified various features of religion that recur across cultures and eras. For one, religious systems generally involve systems of ritual actions that include culturally postulated "modestly counterintuitive agents" (henceforth MoCA[1]) such as gods, goddesses, witches, demons, ancestors, and so on (Lawson and McCauley 1990; Boyer 1994). For another, god and goddess concepts within religious systems typically lie on a continuum of complexity from explicit offline theology to intuitive online religion. Depending on the cognitive demands of the context, such as whether one has the time to recall learned theology, when representing god people rely upon either more basic intuitive religious concepts (e.g., God is a big guy in the sky) or more abstract and complex theological creeds (e.g., God exists everywhere at once). People are thus able to maintain parallel levels of understanding as a result of the cognitive capacity for multiple levels of representation (Barrett 1999; Barrett and Keil 1996). (See figure 10.1.)

That certain features of religion recur across cultures and that a conceptual pluralism exists within and between religions are both old news. That both are natural by-products of ordinary cognitive processes is a recent and important discovery for the scientific study of religion. For one, it helps guard against scholarly misrepresentation of the actual thoughts religious people have and against misleading comparisons of religion at different levels of thought. Barrett cautions wisely, "when doing comparative religion focusing on the theological level of understanding, one runs the risk of overestimating differences across faiths, cultures, generations, and individuals." And, "comparative studies can also suffer by mistakenly comparing the theological level of one group or tradition with the basic level of another . . . (for example)

187

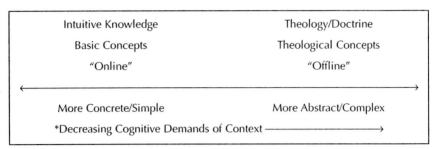

Intuitive Knowledge	Theology/Doctrine
Basic Concepts	Theological Concepts
"Online"	"Offline"

←——————————————————————————→

| More Concrete/Simple | More Abstract/Complex |

*Decreasing Cognitive Demands of Context ——————→

Figure 10.1   (from Barrett 1999: 325)

Christians have long ridiculed Hindus for their elaborate use of concrete images, citing this as evidence that Hindus worship human-like gods and not the true Supreme Being who is wholly different from the created world and cannot be represented by human-like forms" (Barrett 1999, 334).

Comparisons that focus entirely on the theological contents of religious systems certainly run the risk of overestimating differences between religions. However, focusing on similarities only at the level of online religion risks an overestimation of the differences between theological thought. Obviously the contents of theologies differ across systems, but if the central theoretical assumption of the cognitive science of religion is correct—that all religious thought is constrained by cognition—then theology should also be constrained by cognition. There ought to be, and there are, recurrent features of theology.

Two strands of research converge to support this claim. First, there is abundant empirical evidence from comparative studies of theology showing that there are recurrent features of theology across religious systems and eras. Second, H. Whitehouse's "modes of religiosity" hypothesis provides a framework for explaining why this is so; certain theological concepts—and conceptual problems—recur in religions operating in the "doctrinal" mode of religiosity because of this mode's tendency to use implicational logic as a way to maintain conceptual coherence across large groups of nonrelated members. Let us examine the empirical evidence first and Whitehouse's hypothesis second.

COMPARATIVE THEOLOGY

One recurrent feature of theology has been noted above, that the god concepts of theology are more abstract and complex (i.e., they violate more default expectations about the nature and properties of agents) than the gods of online religious thought (Barrett 1999; Barrett and Keil 1996). A second recurrent feature of theology, and the focus of this chapter, is the free-will problem of how to reconcile the existence of an omniscient and omnipotent deity with the existence of human agency.[2] A comparative survey of prominent theological schools in major world religions reveals that this conceptual problem is recurrent.

Christianity

In the West the free-will problem is, for obvious reasons, probably best known as formulated in its Christian forms. In Christian theology debates over numerous issues, like providing proof for the existence of God, resolving the problem of theodicy (i.e., explaining "God's justice" in a world that includes evil and innocent suffering), engendering a religious experience, justifying revelation as a source of knowledge, establishing ritual efficacy, and so on all turn on a more central conceptual problem that I shall call *the ambiguity of agency*. By postulating the existence of MoCA, which are said to have the power to influence or even control world events, theologians generate ipso facto an ambiguity of agency: who has power to control the world, we or them? Let me briefly summarize some Christian theological problems in order to show how an ambiguity of agency drives the debates.

First, a prominent argument for the existence of God is the "argument from design" made famous by W. Paley's (1838) watchmaker analogy. In Paley's thought experiment, the existence of a world that operates according to natural laws justifies the inference that the world has been designed by an intelligent designer just as the discovery of a functioning watch on a deserted island would imply the existence of a watchmaker. Although clever, there is a significant conceptual problem with Paley's argument. Paley argues that humans are like watches. Having been created by God, we act according to God's laws. But this raises serious questions about human control or free will. If humans act *totally* in accordance with God's laws, then we don't really act freely. Therefore an ambiguity of agency exists. Where is the "locus of control," in God's laws or in human beings?

Similarly, an ambiguity of agency exists in debates over theodicy, or the problem of how to explain the existence of evil and innocent suffering in a world created and governed by an omnipotent and benevolent God. Classically, if God is able but unwilling to eradicate evil and innocent suffering, then God must not be benevolent. In contrast, if God is willing but unable to prevent evil and suffering, then God must not be omnipotent. Typical solutions to the problem of theodicy invoke the human capacity to create and stop evil and suffering. Two prominent answers to the problem of theodicy include the doctrine of "Original Sin" (i.e., that Adam and Eve caused evil and suffering when they fell from God's grace in the Garden of Eden [Genesis 2.4b–3.24]) and that God allows evil and suffering as part of a teleological or eschatological plan (e.g., to teach us lessons, to allow us to perfect ourselves, etc.) (Hick 1963). Like arguments from design for the existence of God, arguments about evil and suffering reveal the tension between divine sovereignty and free will. Both answers to why evil and suffering exist are ambiguous with regard to the actual cause(s) of evil and innocent suffering—God (in His plan) or humans (Original Sin). Moreover, responses to these answers raise further tensions in the argument. If human free will is a part of God's plan, then God must have preordained it as a feature of life. On the other hand, if humans could sin against God, then we must have a significant degree of control over what happens in the world, thus making God effectively not sovereign.

Third, a great deal of theological debate has explored the nature of religious experience. In particular, theologians and philosophers of religion have debated what causes one to have a religious experience. William James noted that humans in all cultures engage in a variety of activities like singing, praying, dancing, and the like designed to engender religious experiences (James 1902). However, it is not clear whether or not a religious experience occurs as a result of the actions of the person or by the grace of God. In other words, does God give in to our requests, or are our activities largely irrelevant (i.e., does God choose when, where, why, and to whom such experiences are granted)? Suggesting that human activities cause religious experiences suggests that God can be coerced, and yet to say that our activities have no effect on God suggests that we have no ability to engender such experiences; they just come at the whim of God.

Fourth, theologians wrestle with the degree to which humans have the ability to reason effectively or if humans must rely on faith for knowledge of God. Generally, theological liberals in the post-Enlightenment West have embraced the notion that scripture is subject not only to interpretation but in some cases even to criticism (e.g., historicism, feminism, Marxism). The justification given for this stance is confidence in the rational powers of human thought. In contrast, theological conservatives tend to downplay the ultimate efficacy of human rational powers. In their view, humans have the capacity to reason as a component of understanding scripture, but we ought not go so far as to criticize and change scripture according to human standards. The debate is therefore one over agency: should we have faith in human ability to reason or stick to faith in literal readings of God's revelations (assuming a "literal reading" is possible)?

Fifth, theologians disagree over what is necessary for salvation. In Christianity, this issue, among others, split the Western church along Protestant–Catholic lines. Famously, Martin Luther argued that faith was necessary and sufficient for salvation, whereas Catholic traditions held that participation in the sacraments was also required. Interestingly, both positions reveal ambiguous stances on what causes salvation. Is salvation *achieved* by human faith/effort or *received* via God's grace? This question was systematically hashed out in the Reformed arguments between John Calvin and Jacobus Arminius. Calvin held that God preordained a group of "elect" that was saved by Christ's sacrifice on the Cross, whereas Arminius argued that by the grace of God Christ's sacrifice made it possible for all willing persons to achieve salvation. Note the theological tension in Arminius' theology. Is it God or human effort (i.e., grace or faith) that engenders salvation? Regardless of its conceptual difficulties, Arminianism has come to be the dominant theology of Western Protestant thought, even replacing Calvinism in the British colonies of North America where Puritanism originally reigned. This historical development is not surprising, however, given the maximally counterintuitive nature of Calvinism, which theologically precludes *any* and *all* human agency (Slone 2004, chap. 5).

Islam

Similar debates to Christian theology are found in Islam. A cursory review of contemporary Islam reveals that many issues revolve around tensions between liberals/modernists and traditionalists/conservatives (Esposito 1988). Whether the topic is the role of women, the legitimate invocation of *jihad*, legal interpretation of *sharia*, or rightful authority of interpretation, theological debates in modern Islam reflect ages-old stances with regard to divine sovereignty and free will and the subsequent issue of the human capacity for reason.

Islamic theological debate (Arabic: *kalam*) developed in two periods, each with central issues of concern. The earliest periods of debate occurred during the time of the civil wars that split the *ummah* (community) into Sunni and Shia sects after the death of Muhammad and later assassinations of leaders like Umar, Uthman, and Ali. Not surprisingly, the central theological issue concerned the rightful authority to lead the *ummah*. Over time, at least three leading theological schools emerged with different positions on the problem of free will and divine sovereignty: *Qadariya*, *Jabriya*, and later *Mu'tazila*. The Qadariya argued that humans have the ability (*qudra*) to determine the outcome of their acts. Therefore, humans are responsible for their behaviors. In contrast, the Jabriya argued that divine compulsion (*jabr*) determined human actions. Arriving at this position is a logical move in a conceptual scheme constrained by the foundational assumption that a MoCA created and controls the world. Like John Calvin, the Jabriya theologians insisted that the doctrine of *qudr* necessarily challenged God's sovereignty and therefore bordered on blasphemy. God, not humans, the Jabriya argued, was ultimately responsible for human actions since His compulsion created human actions in the first place.

As to be expected, debates over the issue of human responsibility eventually led to arguments over the human capacity for agency. By the eighth century CE, the theological school of the Mu'tazila emerged with a combinatorial position. First and foremost, the Mu'tazila professed faith in the supernatural properties and powers of God:

> The Mu'tazilites all agree that *Allah is One* ([Qu'ran] 2:158), there is *nothing like him* (42:9) and *he is the Hearing One, the Seeing One* (17:1), and is not a substance or an object or a body . . . nor does he move or rest; nor is he divided. He has not parts or atoms or limbs or members . . . he is not bound by the limitations of space and time . . . nor is he to be compared with mankind, or likened to creatures in any way at all. He is eternally first, antecedent, prior to contingent beings, existent before created things. He is eternally Knowing, Powerful and Living and thus he continues. Eyes do not seem him, nor does sight attain him. (Waines 1995, 117–18; italics in original)

Yet, the Mu'tazila also had confidence in the powers of human agency:

> A person is able in the first moment of time to perform an act in the second moment of time. Thus, before the moment exists, it is said that the act "will be done" in that second moment. When the second moment existed, it is said that the act "has been done." (Waines 1995, 119)

Thus they argued that God does not determine what people do. This combinatorial position, note, generates an inherent tension between the power of God and human agency (Elias 1999, chap. 3; Hourani 1985; Marmurra 1984; Morewedge 1979; Watt 1973; Wolfson 1976).

Hinduism

It is tempting to argue that Islamic theological debate mirrors Christian theological debate simply because they share the same basic conceptual scheme—that is, the same basic monotheistic belief in one sovereign deity. However, the same types of theological debates are also found in religious systems with different theological conceptual schemes such as Hinduism and Buddhism, each of which is polytheistic.[3]

Though not couched in the technical terms of divine sovereignty and free will, tension between the powers of the Hindu MoCA and human beings is present in Hinduism even in the earliest sacred texts, the Vedas. According to the Rig Veda, the world was created through a primordial sacrifice of the god-man Purusha:

> His mouth became the brahmin; his two arms were made into the rajanya; his two thighs the vaishyas; from his two feet the shudra was born.
> The moon was born from the mind, from the eye the sun was born; from the mouth Indra and Agni, from the breath the wind was born.

From the navel was the atmosphere created, from the head the heaven issued forth; from the two feet was born the earth and the cardinal directions from the ear. (Rig Veda 10.90, in Embree 1988, 18–19)

A common interpretation of this passage is that the world is a collection of many parts, each interconnected and operating as a whole. The key to maintaining order (Sanskrit: *rita*) in the world is to perform sacrificial rituals that please the gods. In this sense the Vedic rituals are believed to be efficacious because they provide humans with control over nature via deities.

Additionally, Hindu theologians developed ethical prescriptions based on the concepts outlined in the Rig Veda cosmogony. With the emergence of such texts as *Dharma-sastras* (commentaries on "sacred laws"), the loose class distinctions of ancient and medieval India became codified into specific social prescriptions defined by one's "caste" (*varna*). By fulfilling the personal duties (*sva-dharma*) required by one's caste, the part, the social world, and the whole would remain in order. Thus the primordial sacrifice of Purusha established the relationship between the gods and creation, and between humans themselves.

How does this conceptual scheme achieve coherence? The central concept that explains why rituals and social ethics work is the concept of *karma* ("actions and consequences"). According to the doctrine of karma, all thoughts and deeds produce effects. Good deeds like proper rituals and social acts produce good effects. Bad deeds produce bad effects. This concept not only provides a prosocial ethical incentive but also an explanation for human fate. Importantly, since the effects of human actions are cumulative and interconnected, my actions affect not just my fate but also the fates of other people. The world is therefore a web of karmic interconnection where no suffering is karmically innocent.

As in Christianity and Islam, Hindu theology possesses a deep tension. In the scheme of karmic interconnection, who causes what? If I am robbed by a thief, is it my fault for a previous misdeed? Is this a punishment from a deity? Is it the fault of the thief? Further, if it is my fault, then what caused me to do the misdeed in the first place—was that behavior a result of previous misdeeds, by me, by others, or by both? Does the doctrine of karma lead all the way back to the primordial sacrifice of Purusha?

Classically, Hindu theologians have generated three positions in response to this free-will problem. In one view, events are predetermined by karma, but our ability to react to them is not. According to A. Sharma, "everything is predetermined . . . however, we have freedom in the manner in which we react to these events, which then determines our future" (Sharma 2000, 99). At the other end of the conceptual spectrum is the view that everything is open to one's free will. By this account, "what appears as destiny is really disguised free will" (Sharma 2000, 100). Other Hindu theologians still have adopted a combinatorial position (a la Arminianism in Christianity and Mu'-tazila in Islam) that somehow humans are both free to act by their own will and yet determined by the karmic consequences of previous acts (Hiriyanna 1948). The notable S. Radhakrishnan has stated this position well: "The cards in the game of life are given to us. We do not select them. They are traced to our past karma, but we can call as we please, lead what suit we will, and as we play, we gain or lose. And there is freedom" (Radhakrishnan 1927, 54).

Buddhism

The conceptual tensions over agency in Hindu theology did not dissolve with the schismatic development of Buddhism in ancient India around 500 BCE. Though the historical Buddha (*nirmana-kaya*) Shakyamuni is said to have achieved enlightenment by his own efforts, the religious system nonetheless absorbed most of the conceptual scheme of Hinduism including the doctrine of karma. As such, Buddhism has a long history of theological debate over human agency.

The clearest example of the theological tension regarding human agency exists in the Pure Land traditions of Mahayana Buddhism. In general, Mahayana theology posits the existence of three forms of the Buddha (Sanskrit: *trikaya*): the historical Buddha (*nirmana-kaya*), the cosmic Buddha (*dharma-kaya*), and various celestial Buddhas (*sambhoga-kaya*). Among the celestial Buddhas revered in the Mahayana tradition is Amitabha, the Buddha of the Western Pure Land (*sukhavati*). According to Pure Land doctrine, rebirth in *sukhavati* ensures bliss because the lack of evil and suffering in this land means there are no impediments to enlightenment. Not surprisingly, Pure Land is one of the largest sects in all of Buddhism (Amstutz 1997; Robinson and Johnson 1997).

Of central concern in the Pure Land traditions, however, is how to ensure rebirth in *sukhavati* (Becker 1993, 46–68). Two of the greatest Pure Land theologians to reflect on this matter were the Japanese monks Honen (1133–1212), founder of the *Jodo-shu* sect (Pure Land), and his disciple Shinran (1173–1262), founder of the *Jodo-shin-shu* sect (True Pure Land). After years of training in various Mahayana practices, Honen became convinced that the world had fallen into deep moral disrepair (Japanese: *mappo*), that enlightenment through self-effort was a practical impossibility. Instead, the only thing that could save human beings was reliance on *Amida-butsu* (Sanskrit: *Amitabha*) for rebirth in the Pure Land. For Honen, the means by which humans could ensure rebirth in the Pure Land was to place one's faith in Amida, an act manifested in the chanting of the *nembutsu* ("*Namu Amida Butsu*": "I place my faith in Amida Butsu").

Shinran, however, reasoned that there was no way of ensuring rebirth in the Pure Land through human effort. For Shinran, emphasizing the efficacy of chanting the *nembutsu* implied that we have power over Amida. Indeed, how could the act of chanting itself engender rebirth into the Pure Land? Human power (*ji-riki*), he concluded, cannot supersede the "Other power" (*ta-riki*) of Amida. Like some theologians in Christianity, Islam, and Hinduism, Shinran concluded that humans are born in the Pure Land *only* through the grace of Amida (Unno 1996, 1998).

COGNITIVE CONSTRAINTS AND RELIGIOUS THOUGHT

How do we account for the recurrence of such similar theological concepts, all variations on the free will problem, in such seemingly disparate religious systems as Christianity, Islam, Hinduism, and Buddhism? A fruitful place to start is the rule of thumb that if a cluster of concepts recurs across cultures and eras, then explanations of that concept cluster's recurrence lie in universal generic cognitive architecture. Such phenomena are not, as postmodernist social constructionists have asserted, merely a "cultural" product (whatever that might mean). As such, the cognitive science of religion is best able to account for the phenomenon in question. So how might the cognitive sciences explain the recurrence of the free-will problem?

The cognitive science of religion is now in the midst of a second period of scholarship. The first period occurred in the 1990s and included the publication of five seminal books by six pioneering scholars in the field (Boyer 1994; Guthrie 1993; Lawson and McCauley 1990; Mithen 1996; Whitehouse 1995). Since 2000, however, a significant number of new books have emerged (e.g., Andresen 2000; Antonnen and Pyysiäinen 2002; Atran 2002; Barrett 2004; Boyer 2001; McCauley and Lawson 2002; Malley 2004; Pyysiäinen 2001, 2004; Pyysiäinen and Antonnen 2002; Rosengren, Johnson, and Harris 2000; Slone 2004; Whitehouse 2000, 2004; Whitehouse and Laidlaw 2004; Whitehouse and Martin 2004; Whitehouse and McCauley 2005). This is an important development because with a basic theoretical framework in place, scholars can now go about the important business of testing and refining foundational claims of the research program.

Two central principles established in the first period characterize the cognitive science of religion's research program. First, it is assumed for the sake of theorizing that what makes "religion" religion is the culturally recurrent postulation of MoCA. Second, representations of MoCA adhere to our ordinary natural-kind concepts of agents. In other words, though postulated as supernatural, MoCA concepts actually assume a great deal of tacit semantic knowledge about ordinary agents in general (Boyer 1994; Guthrie 1993; Lawson and McCauley 1990; McCauley and Lawson 2002). Therefore explaining religion requires connecting it with domain specificity (Hirschfeld and Gelman 1994).

One startling discovery of cognitive psychology is that humans, in fact infants, possess a great deal of knowledge about the world and its workings that they've *not* learned from culture (and so, the theory goes, some knowledge must be "innate"). For example, early in development infants are not only naturally able to distinguish agents (e.g., humans, animals) from objects (e.g., rocks, chairs), but they can also generate relatively accurate inferences about the ontological properties of those kinds. Infants know intuitively that agents possess goal-driven intentionality, that agents have goal-driven causal powers, and that agents can be manipulated by other agents (infants exploit this ability by crying). On the other hand, infants know that objects do not possess intentionality and that their causal powers are not intentional but rather are merely mechanical (e.g., to move, balls must be launched by being struck by some other moving object) (Baillargeon 1999; Gopnik, Meltzoff, and Kuhl 1999; Rochat 2001; Sperber, Premack, and Premack 1995; Wellman 1990).

While arguably ecologically rational (Gigerenzer 2000; Gigerenzer and Selten 2001), the outputs of cognition do not always accurately describe and predict the behavior of the world around us. Given that people must think and act in conditions of uncertainty, a good deal of human thought involves efficient inferential-reasoning strategies like intuitive judgments that rely on heuristics and biases. This means that human minds represent a useful but not entirely accurate intuitive ontology of the actual world and its workings. Intuition is fairly reliable for many tasks, but not all (Gilovich 1991; Gilovich, Griffin, and Kahneman 2002; Kahneman and Tversky 2000; Kahneman, Slovic, and Tversky 1982). Of course from a gene's point of view, cognition doesn't have to be perfect. Cognition needs only to be good enough for survival and reproduction, and our basic intuitive ontology is perhaps good enough in this sense.

That we represent the world according to natural kinds with different causal properties makes us susceptible to various types of ambiguities of agency. Events often involve the convergence of multiple sources of causality, and we have no good way of deciding on an actual cause. Consider the causal agency involved in a seemingly simple event: throwing a ball through a window. People know that we can break windows by throwing balls through them. Both the scientific physics and the psychology behind this event are actually quite complicated. Yet most of us would not find it too difficult to explain the cause of the event: the thrower did it. Of course physical laws were involved—indeed they are what made the event possible—but we are likely to think that the "true" cause was the thrower's intention.

Two features of this example are noteworthy. First, two causal stances—an intentional stance and a mechanical stance—can be assumed in the explanation of why this event happened (Dennett 1987). A human is the actor, but the act itself involves mechanical causality as well: the ball's force against the structural integrity of the glass. Interpreting this event therefore requires engagement with multiple domains of causal reasoning. However, despite there being multiple domains of causality actually involved, humans tend to prefer the intentional explanation over the mechanical one. The designs of the rock and of the window are such that when the two objects collide at a high enough velocity, the window's structural integrity will be compromised. Yet rocks don't fly through windows by their own volition; they must be launched (in this case, by being thrown). A rock breaking through a window is both a "happening" involving mechanical processes and an "event" caused by an agent. But we represent it as an event.

We not only distinguish between agents and objects, but we also make a very important distinction between other agents and ourselves. Although developmental psychologists have not reached a consensus on when babies begin to understand self-agency, it is safe to say that such knowledge is in place very early on (importantly, prior to the acquisition of higher-level cultural concepts like religious ideas). Tomasello (1999) argues that it develops as early as 9 months, but most psychologists agree that it is normally established by around 24 months (possibly the origins of the boundary-testing tactics of the "terrible twos") (Rochat 2001). Regardless, for the purpose here the point is that knowledge of self-agency, of our own causal powers, develops before religious indoctrination begins to take hold. So by the time children begin to engage religious ideas in meaningful ways, they have in place a robust intuitive ontology that governs their understanding of how agents and objects work. They possess causal knowledge of at least three domains: mechanical causality in objects, agency in other humans (and animals), and self-agency.

It is worth restating that humans tend to prefer intentional explanations for occurrences that are represented as events. In fact, it has been argued that humans might even possess a "hyperactive agency-detection device" (HADD) that predisposes us to misrepresent happenings as intentional events caused by agents (Barrett 2000). Obviously the presence of such a device is advantageous to our species because representing agency "promiscuously," to use D. Kelemen's term (Kelemen 1999), confers great benefits at relatively small costs. Mistaking rocks for bears is preferable to mistaking bears for rocks, because the former might be scary (and maybe a bit embarrassing), but the latter could be deadly (Atran 2002; Guthrie 1993).

Furthermore, representing occurrences as events provides us with a sense of control by triggering the inference that agents can be coerced (Vyse 1997). Having minds means that intentional events are caused by agents' mental forces such as beliefs, desires, and the like, and therefore the capacity to understand the mental activities of other agents (a.k.a., "theory of mind" [ToM]) means that intentional events are represented as having mental causes (Hirschfeld and Gelman 1994; Leslie 1982; Premack and Premack 1995). As such, humans can change the world by changing other agents' minds. This is good news, at least selfishly, because it means that we can influence others to act in ways that benefit us. Our capacity for ToM enables us to control the actions of other agents via communication, reciprocity, deception, and so forth.[4]

This intuitive ontological system constrains the way cultural concepts like MoCA are acquired, processed, employed, and transmitted. For example, that gods, goddesses, ghosts, ghouls, and the like exist is relatively easy to believe because, despite their counterintuitive properties (e.g., invisibility, omniscience, etc.), these types of agents generally conform to our expectations about what agents are like (Boyer 1994). Though invisible and omniscient, MoCA still take up space in the world and like us to tell them what we're thinking. So not only are humans naturally able to represent MoCA, as a result of the default assumptions in their intuitive ontology, but in turn are able to infer that we should take them seriously (e.g., attend to them in ritual) because of their postulated ability to cause things to happen to us. In this way, MoCA concepts enjoy a selection advantage in the pool of potential and actual cultural concepts humans engage.

Yet, a problem remains in the cognitive study of religion. The belief in MoCA results in a cognitive tension because the representations of MoCA that theologians construct (e.g., God is omnipotent and omniscient) are radically counterintuitive and therefore cognitively burdensome (Whitehouse 2004). As highlighted above, theologians make claims like God knows and controls everything, but our intuitions about agents tell us that He has limited power (e.g., He doesn't make both teams win the same football game) and limited knowledge (e.g., I should confess my thoughts to Him), and that we can control things (e.g., my computer starts when *I* hit the power switch). As such, there exists a natural free-will problem in religion that results from the theological postulation of extremely counterintuitive MoCA concepts like omnipotence colliding with the intuitive sense of human agency. Religion and theology thus speak with two different cognitive voices.

COGNITIVE CONSTRAINTS AND THEOLOGICAL DEVELOPMENT

The capacity to represent events as caused by other agents is, obviously, necessary for belief in MoCA, and representations of MoCA (with minds) exploit default expectations about ordinary external agency and so grab our attention. However, though salient and easy to acquire, MoCA concepts are not necessarily easy to employ online—at least not those in theologically postulated forms. Experimental studies by Barrett (1999) and Barrett and Keil (1996) show that the gods of theology are often so counterintuitive (e.g., God can perform an infinite number of functions at the same time) that it is difficult for individuals not to anthropomorphize them in online reasoning. This suggests, not surprisingly, that memorized theological creeds do not override noncultural conceptual schemata. In other words, learned theological conceptual schemes provide only one among many "multiple sufficient schemata" (Kelly 1972) for making sense of the world (Slone 2004). Likewise, theological concepts that postulate that the gods have agency that is greater than what humans possess do not override human bias toward self-agency. Experimental research by Lupfer and Spilka and their colleagues revealed that even individuals who sincerely believe in the omnipotence of God often still reveal a strong "internal locus of control" (Lupfer, Brock, and DePaola 1992; Lupfer, DePaola, Brock, and Clement 1994; Lupfer, Tolliver, and Jackson 1996; Spilka and Schmidt 1983; Spilka, Shaver, and Kirkpatrick 1985). This phenomenon is similar, of course, to research in the cognitive science of science, which shows that the acquisition of scientific physics does not necessarily override reliance on folk physics in online thought (Tweney, Doherty, and Mynatt 1981; McCauley 2000).

So, again, how do we account for the recurrence of the same types of problems in these different religious systems? If religion is more natural than theology, why does theology emerge in religious systems at all? The most likely hypothesis, offered by anthropologists, is that theologies emerge in religious systems in complex states where literacy allows for the development of religious guilds. In contrast, religious systems of small-scale oral societies typically do not develop theologies (Boyer 2001; Goody 1986, 2004; Malinowski 1925).[5]

As such, religious systems typically operate in one of two "modes of religiosity," according to a typology offered by Whitehouse, either a "doctrinal" or an "imagistic" mode, each of which is governed by thirteen different variables that govern transmission. (See table 10.1.)

Those religious systems that grow in scale and structure develop into a doctrinal mode of religiosity because of the need for standardized universalistic doctrines that can be transmitted as generalized schemata. The ideas found in these types of theological conceptual schemes are linked by implicational logic because of the need for doctrines in large-scale religious systems to be intellectually coherent (in order to persuade a wide range of members). It seems to follow, then, that given the need for intellectual coherence over time, theologians will reason, using "if-then" rules of inference, to the position that MoCA have absolute power. As religions grow and spread across diverse populations, the MoCA concepts that populate those systems must expand in postulated ability to be represented as having the ability to do many things in many places to many people. Moving from "God caused this to happen to us" to "God caused that to happen to them also" is likely to result in "God can cause many things to happen" and then "God can cause anything to happen." This, presumably, is the logical set of inferences

Table 10.1   Modes of Religiosity Contrasted (from Whitehouse 2004: 74)

Variable	Doctrinal	Imagistic
Psychological Features		
1. Transmissive frequency	High	Low
2. Level of arousal	Low	High
3. Principal memory system	Semantic schemas & implicit scripts	Episodic/ flashbulb memory
4. Ritual meaning	Learned/acquired	Internally generated
5. Techniques of revelation	Rhetoric, logical integration, narrative	Iconicity, multivocality, and multivalence
Sociopolitical Features		
6. Social cohesion	Diffuse	Intense
7. Leadership	Dynamic	Passive/absent
8. Inclusivity/exclusivity	Inclusive	Exclusive
9. Spread	Rapid, efficient	Slow, inefficient
10. Scale	Large-scale	Small-scale
11. Degree of uniformity	High	Low
12. Structure	Centralized	Non-centralized

a priest is likely to make along a single problem-solving path. Therefore certain theological concepts might be arrived at not because of the unique contents of religious conceptual schemes per se but rather because of basic problem-solving reasoning processes upon which theological thought relies.

However, as noted above, such deterministic theological positions rarely come to dominate the thought of adherents in a given system. While some theologians will reason to this conclusion, most people will maintain something like "combinatorial" positions in their online thought and behavior. That is, most people are most comfortable believing that the gods have absolute power but also that humans have free will. Why?

One likely answer is that MoCA concepts involving absolute divine sovereignty, although theologically necessary, are too cognitively burdensome to be employed online, given our strong sense of self-agency. For the same reasons that humans have difficulty using quantum physics when reasoning about how certain objects fall to the ground, religious people have difficulty in thinking that they have no self-agency. Hence the sense of needing to pray, worship, do rituals, evangelize, and the like even in religious systems whose conceptual schemes postulate absolute divine sovereignty (Slone 2004, chap. 5).

So what cognitive capacities are likely involved in the development of free-will problems? For one, obviously, humans must be able to know that agents, even invisible ones, can intentionally cause events to happen. Our basic intuitive ontology allows us to make such representations naturally. Second, we need to differentiate between the agency of others and ourselves. Our development of self-awareness enables us to know that others can cause events to happen to us and we to them (not to mention our knowledge that sometimes things just happen). Third, we must be able to reason inferentially in order to solve conceptual problems. According to Newell and Simon's (1972) general model of problem solving, humans rely on a fairly small number of general heuristics and strategies, such as simple "if-then" rules for finding a solution path to a problem in a given problem space (Mayer 1992; Newell and Simon 1972). Fourth, human cognition is aided by instruments of cognition outside the head (Goody 1986; Norman 1993; Simon 1996). Texts, seminars, creeds, routinization of rituals, and so on not only stabilize certain concepts for aid in transmission but also allow for evolution of the concepts by later generations of theologians by fixing concepts (Goody 2004). Theologies give priests thoughts to think with (Day 2004). Thus, as religious systems diverge into the doctrinal mode of religiosity, the processes of theological reasoning seem to coalesce around certain attractor positions, among them the two contradictory concepts that result in the free-will problem: absolute divine sovereignty and human agency. In this way, religions, at least those that operate in the doctrinal mode, develop free-will problems because of how the mind works.

NOTES

1. I agree with Bob McCauley who noted in personal communication to me that "modestly" counterintuitive is more accurate than the term "minimally" counterintuitive that cognitive scientists of religion typically use because in quantitative terms god concepts do not *minimally* (implying only one violation) violate natural kinds. God concepts *modestly* violate natural-kind concepts; they typically have a few violations, not just one. For example, in the Abrahamic theological traditions, God is omnipotent, omnipresent, omnibenevolent, and so on, and in the "online" manifestations of these religions God does not eat, does not go to the bathroom, can move places very quickly, and so on.

2. While acute, the problem of free will is not restricted to theology. It is also a problem in philosophy more generally and in the philosophies of science and of mind in particular. See Honderich (2002) for an introduction to the philosophy of free will.

3. I would argue that no religious system is or is ever likely to be exclusively monotheistic, especially in the online thought of its participants (cf. Barrett 2004). Two pieces of evidence support this claim. First, members of the major monotheistic religious systems of the world—Judaism, Christianity, and Islam—also believe in many other MoCA like angels, saints, demons, and ghosts. Second, the repeated theological emphasis by clergy on commitment to a single absolute deity—especially in the Jewish and Islamic traditions (note that commandments to monotheism are first in the Mosaic law and the Five Pillars of Islam), but also in the Christian Trinity—suggests that this has been an ongoing problem in these religions. Prohibitive creeds

do not emerge where no problems exist. Were people naturally and faithfully monotheistic, neither emphasis nor rule would be necessary.

    4. Of course, the downside to ToM is that we can be duped by others as well.

    5. Arguing that people of small-scale societies don't have theology is not the same thing as saying that they don't have reasons to support their beliefs, nor is it saying that they don't have the cognitive capacity to develop theology.

REFERENCES

Amstutz, G. D. 1997. *Interpreting Amida: History and Orientalism in the Study of Pure Land Buddhism.* Albany, NY: SUNY Press.

Andresen, J., ed. 2000. *Religion in Mind: Cognitive Perspectives on Religious Belief, Ritual and Experience.* Cambridge: Cambridge University Press.

Antonnen, V., and I. Pyysiäinen, eds. 2002. *Cognition and Religion: Cross-Disciplinary Perspectives.* London: Continuum Press.

Atran, S. 2002. *In Gods We Trust: The Evolutionary Landscape of Religion.* New York: Oxford University Press.

Baillargeon, R. 1999. The Object Concept Revisited: New Directions in the Investigation of Infants' Physical Knowledge. In *Concepts: Core Readings,* ed. E. Margolis and S. Laurence. Cambridge, MA: MIT Press.

Barkow, J., L. Cosmides, and J. Tooby, eds. 1992. *The Adapted Mind: Evolutionary Psychology and the Generation of Culture.* New York: Oxford University Press.

Barrett, J. L. 1999. Theological Correctness: Cognitive Constraint and the Study of Religion. *Method & Theory in the Study of Religion* 11(4): 325–39.

Barrett, J. L. 2000. Exploring the Naturalness of Religious Ideas. *Trends in Cognitive Science* 4: 29–34.

———. 2004. *Why Would Anyone Believe in God?* Walnut Creek, CA: AltaMira Press.

Barrett, J. L., and F. C. Keil. 1996. Anthropomorphism and God Concepts: Conceptualizing a Nonnatural Entity. *Cognitive Psychology* 3: 219–47.

Barrett, J. L., and M. A. Nyhof. 2001. Spreading Non-natural Concepts: The Role of Intuitive Conceptual Structures in Memory and Transmissions of Cultural Materials. *Journal of Cognition & Culture* 1: 69–100.

Bartlett, F. C. 1932. *Remembering: A Study in Experimental and Social Psychology.* Cambridge: Cambridge University Press.

Becker, C. B. 1993. *Breaking the Circle: Death and Afterlife in Buddhism.* Carbondale: Southern Illinois University Press.

Boyer, P. 1994. *The Naturalness of Religious Ideas: A Cognitive Theory of Religion.* Berkeley: University of California Press.

———. 2001. *Religion Explained: The Evolutionary Origins of Religious Thought.* New York: Basic Books.

Boyer, P., and C. Ramble. 2001. Cognitive Templates for Religious Concepts: Cross-Cultural Evidence for Recall of Counter-Intuitive Representations. *Cognitive Science* 25: 535–64.

Day, M. 2004. Religion, Off-Line Cognition, and the Virtues of Embeddedness. *Journal of Cognition and Culture* 14.

Dennett, D. 1987. *The Intentional Stance.* Cambridge, MA: MIT Press.

Elias, J. J. 1993. *Islam.* Religions of the World Series. Upper Saddle River, NJ: Prentice-Hall.

Embree, A. T., ed. 1988. *Sources of Indian Tradition, Volume One: From the Beginning to 1800.* New York: Columbia University Press.

Esposito, J. 1988. *Islam: The Straight Path.* New York: Oxford University Press.

Gigerenzer, G. 2000. *Adaptive Thinking: Rationality in the Real World.* Oxford: Oxford University Press.

Gigerenzer, G., and R. Selten, eds. 2001. *Bounded Rationality: The Adaptive Toolbox.* Cambridge, MA: MIT Press.

Gilovich, T. 1991. *How We Know What Isn't So: The Fallibility of Human Reason in Everyday Life.* New York: The Free Press.

Gilovich, T., D. Griffin, and D. Kahneman., eds. 2002. *Heuristics and Biases: The Psychology of Intuitive Judgment.* Cambridge: Cambridge University Press.

Gladwell, M. 2000. *The Tipping Point: How Little Things Can Make a Big Difference.* New York: Little, Brown and Company.

Goody, J. 1986. *The Logic of Writing and the Organization of Society.* Cambridge: Cambridge University Press.

———. 2004. Is Image to Doctrine as Speech to Writing? Modes of Communication and the Origins of Religion. In *Ritual and Memory: Toward a Comparative Anthropology of Religion,* ed. H. Whitehouse and J. Laidlaw. Walnut Creek, CA: AltaMira Press.

Gopnik, A., A. Meltzoff, and P. Kuhl. 1999. *The Scientist in the Crib: What Early Learning Tells Us About the Mind.* New York: Perennial Books.

Guthrie, S. 1993. *Faces in the Clouds: A New Theory of Religion.* New York: Oxford University Press.

Hick, J. 1963. *Philosophy of Religion.* Englewood Cliffs, NJ: Prentice-Hall.

Hiriyanna, M. 1948. *The Essentials of Indian Philosophy.* London: George Allen & Unwin.

Hirschfeld, L., and S. Gelman, eds. 1994. *Mapping the Mind: Domain Specificity in Cognition and Culture.* Cambridge: Cambridge University Press.

Honderich, T. 2002. *How Free Are You? The Determinism Problem.* Oxford: Oxford University Press.

Hourani, G. 1985. *Reason and Tradition in Islamic Ethics.* Cambridge: Cambridge University Press.

James, W. 1902. *The Varieties of Religious Experience: A Study in Human Nature.* London: Longmans, Green.

Kahneman, D., and A. Tversky. 2000. *Choices, Values, and Frames.* Cambridge: Cambridge University Press.

Kahneman, D., P. Slovic, and A. Tversky, eds. 1982. *Judgment under Uncertainty: Heuristics and Biases.* Cambridge: Cambridge University Press.

Kelemen, D. 1999. Beliefs about Purpose: On the Origins of Teleological Thought. In *The Descent of Mind: Psychological Perspectives on Hominid Evolution,* ed. M. Corballis and S. Lea. Oxford: Oxford University Press.

Kelly, H. H. 1972. *Causal Schemata and the Attribution Process.* Morristown, NJ: General Learning Press.

Lawson, E. T., and R. N. McCauley. 1990. *Rethinking Religion: Connecting Cognition and Culture*. New York: Cambridge University Press.

Leslie, A. 1982. The Perception of Causality in Infants. *Perception* 11: 173–86.

Lupfer, M. B., K. F. Brock, and S. J. DePaola. 1992. The Use of Secular and Religious Attributions to Explain Everyday Behavior. *Journal for the Scientific Study of Religion* 31: 486–503.

Lupfer, M. B., S. J. DePaola, K. F. Brock, and L. Clement. 1994. Making Secular and Religious Attributions: The Availability Hypothesis Revisited. *Journal for the Scientific Study of Religion* 33: 162–71.

Lupfer, M. B., D. Tolliver, and M. Jackson. 1996. Explaining Life-Altering Occurrences: A Test of the "God-of-the-Gaps" Hypothesis. *Journal for the Scientific Study of Religion* 35: 379–91.

Malinowski, B. 1925. Magic, Science and Religion. In *Science, Religion and Reality*, ed. J. Needham. New York: MacMillan Company.

Malley, B. 2004. *How the Bible Works: An Anthropological Study of Evangelical Biblicism*. Walnut Creek, CA: AltaMira Press.

Marmurra, M., ed. 1984. *Islamic Theology and Philosophy*. Albany: SUNY Press.

Mayer, R. E. 1992. *Thinking, Problem Solving, Cognition*, 2nd ed. New York: W. H. Freeman.

McCauley, R. N. 2000. The Naturalness of Religion and the Unnaturalness of Science. In *Explanation and Cognition*, ed. F. Keil and R. A. Wilson. Cambridge, MA: MIT Press.

———. 2003. Evaluating the Ritual Form Hypothesis. Paper delivered at the North American Association for the Study of Religion, Atlanta, GA, 20 November.

McCauley, R. N., and E. T. Lawson. 2002. *Bringing Ritual to Mind: Psychological Foundations of Cultural Forms*. Cambridge: Cambridge University Press.

Mithen, S. 1996. *The Prehistory of the Mind: The Cognitive Origins of Art and Science*. New York: Thames and Hudson.

Morewedge, P., ed. 1979. *Islamic Philosophical Theology*. Albany, NY: SUNY Press.

Newell, A., and H. A. Simon. 1972. *Human Problem Solving*. Englewood Cliffs, NJ: Prentice-Hall.

Nisbett, R., and L. Ross. 1980. *Human Inference: Strategies and Shortcomings of Social Judgment*. Englewood Cliffs, NJ: Prentice-Hall.

Norman, D. A. 1993. *Things That Make Us Smart: Defending Human Attributes in the Age of the Machine*. New York: Addison-Wesley Publishing Company.

Paley, W. 1838. *Natural Theology*. London: Longmans, Green & Co.

Pinker, S. 1997. *How the Mind Works*. New York: W. W. Norton & Company.

———. 2002. *The Blank Slate: The Modern Denial of Human Nature*. New York: Viking Press.

Premack, D., and A. J. Premack. 1995. Intention as Psychological Cause. In *Causal Cognition: A Multidisciplinary Debate*, ed. D. Sperber, D. Premack, and A. J. Premack. Oxford: Oxford University Press.

Pyysiäinen, I. 2001. *How Religion Works: Towards a New Cognitive Science of Religion*. Leiden: Brill.

———. 2004. *Magic, Miracles, and Religion: A Scientist's Perspective*. Walnut Creek, CA: AltaMira Press.

Pyysiäinen, I., and V. Antonnen, eds. 2002. *Current Approaches in the Cognitive Science of Religion*. London: Continuum Press.

Radhakrishnan, S. 1927. *The Hindu View of Life*. New York: MacMillan.

Robinson, R. H., and W. L. Johnson. 1997. *The Buddhist Religion: A Historical Introduction*, 2nd ed. Belmont, CA: Wadsworth Publishing Company.

Rochat, P., ed. 2001. *The Infant's World (The Developing Child)*. Cambridge, MA: Harvard University Press.

Rosengren, K., C. Johnson, and P. Harris, eds. 2000. *Imagining the Impossible: Magical, Scientific, and Religious Thinking in Children*. Cambridge: Cambridge University Press.

Sharma, A. 2000. *Classical Hindu Thought: An Introduction*. New York: Oxford University Press.

Simon, H. 1996. *The Sciences of the Artificial*, 3rd ed. Cambridge, MA: MIT Press.

Slone, D. J. 2004. *Theological Incorrectness: Why Religious People Believe What They Shouldn't*. New York: Oxford University Press.

Sperber, D. 1996. *Explaining Culture: A Naturalistic Approach*. Oxford: Blackwell Publishers.

Sperber, D., D. Premack, and A. J. Premack, eds. 1995. *Causal Cognition: A Multidisciplinary Debate*. Oxford: Oxford University Press.

Spilka, B., and G. Schmidt. 1983. General Attribution Theory for the Psychology of Religion: The Influence of Event-Character on Attributions to God. *Journal for the Scientific Study of Religion* 22: 326–39.

Spilka, B., P. Shaver, and L. A. Kirkpatrick. 1985. General Attribution Theory for the Psychology of Religion. *Journal for the Scientific Study of Religion* 24: 1–118.

Tomasello, M. 1999. *The Cultural Origins of Human Cognition*. New York: Oxford University Press.

Tweney, R., M. Doherty, and C. R. Mynatt, eds. 1981. *On Scientific Thinking*. New York: Columbia University Press.

Unno, T. 1996. *Tannisho: A Shin Buddhist Classic*. Honolulu, HI: Buddhist Study Center Press.

———. 1998. *River of Fire, River of Water: An Introduction to the Pure Land Tradition of Shin Buddhism*. New York: Doubleday Press.

Vyse, S. 1997. *Believing in Magic: The Psychology of Superstition*. New York: Oxford University Press.

Waines, D. 1995. *An Introduction to Islam*. Cambridge: Cambridge University Press.

Watt, W. M. 1973. *The Formative Period of Islamic Thought*. Edinburgh: Edinburgh University Press.

Wellman, H. 1990. *The Child's Theory of Mind*. Cambridge, MA: MIT Press.

Whitehouse, H. 1995. *Inside the Cult: Religious Innovation and Transmission in Papua New Guinea*. Oxford: Clarendon Press.

———. 2000. *Arguments and Icons: Divergent Modes of Religiosity*. Oxford: Oxford University Press.

———. 2004. *Modes of Religiosity: A Cognitive Theory of Religious Transmission*. Walnut Creek, CA: AltaMira Press.

Whitehouse, H., and J. Laidlaw, eds. 2004. *Ritual and Memory: Toward a Comparative Anthropology of Religion*. Walnut Creek, CA: AltaMira Press.

Whitehouse, H., and L. Martin, eds. 2004. *Theorizing Religions Past: History, Archaeology, and Cognition*. Walnut Creek, CA: AltaMira Press.

Whitehouse, H., and R. N. McCauley, eds. 2005. *Mind and Religion: Psychological and Cognitive Foundations of Religion*. Walnut Creek, CA: AltaMira Press.

Wolfson, H. A. (1976). *The Philosophy of the Kalam*. Cambridge, MA: Harvard University Press.

11

The Cognitive Foundations of Religiosity

Harvey Whitehouse

In the cognitive science of religion, the challenge confronting us is to show that significant features of the content, organization, and spread of religious phenomena can be explained in terms of the ways in which panhuman, evolved psychological mechanisms are activated. This is not a simple task, however. We all know that one cannot explain variables in terms of constants, so how can theories about a universal mind help to explain variable religious outputs? Part of the answer is that religion is not as variable as all that: much of what we have learned from ethnography, historiography, and archaeology (for instance) points to a massive amount of cross-cultural recurrence not only in the forms that religious systems take but even in relation to some aspects of doctrinal content. Another part of the answer is that universal cognitive mechanisms can be activated in different ways, with predictably variable consequences for the way religions are organized and their concepts are formed and transmitted.

OPEN AND CLOSED BEHAVIOR PROGRAMS IN THE TRANSMISSION OF RELIGION

Most cognitive scientists agree that the outputs of specialized mechanisms in the human mind are not equally malleable. More than twenty years ago, it was suggested that we should at the very least distinguish between "open" and "closed" behavior programs.[1] Closed behavior programs are ones that generate the same outputs in all known human environments, because those environments do not deliver inputs that vary in ways that the mechanisms in question would be sensitive to. Obvious examples would include the behavior programs responsible for relatively involuntary reactions—like flinching, laughing, crying, and so on. True, we can try to exercise conscious control over these programs (by keeping a straight face or holding back the tears) and with some effort and practice we can even fake expressive behaviors like these so that it is hard or even possible to spot the difference between real weeping and crocodile tears. But the spontaneous outputs of these kinds of behavior programs do not vary all that much from one society to the next. Language, by contrast, is a somewhat more open program.[2] Although the processes by which children learn a mother tongue exhibit a wide range of fascinating regularities the world over, they do of course end up speaking different languages. But when we consider a wide range of cultural competences, it's clear that the behavior programs they require are not simply closed or open, but involve *varying degrees of openness*. Religion provides a good testing ground for this argument because it constitutes a domain of culture in which there is exceptionally broad variation across space and time, at least with regard to conceptual frameworks and beliefs.

Despite the great diversity in religious traditions, past and present, many simple religious concepts depend on what we might describe as relatively closed behavior programs. For instance, in the course of normal development, all humans come to display concerns about contamination from pollutants. These displays have been plausibly linked to evolved neural mechanisms dedicated to preventing the spread of disease (see Boyer, this volume). Although these contamination-avoidance programs do not rigidly determine which exact substances will be treated with special care and attention (although the handling of feces, blood, rotting flesh, and other potentially hazardous materials seems to be subjected to more or less stringent taboos in most societies), they do seem to specify a set of protocols for how to proceed. A typical list of behavioral outputs might include the following: attention to threshold or entrance, washing or grooming, touching, tapping, or rubbing, concern about symmetry or exactness, cleaning things, fear of harming others if insufficiently careful.[3] These sorts of behaviors are found in all human populations, and they are particularly prominent in ritualized behaviors. Moreover, there are other relatively closed behavior programs that seem to be activated in ritual settings. In this volume, Tom Lawson engagingly sets out a number of key features of the structure of religious rituals that derive from cognitive mechanisms specialized for processing the attributes of action and agency. Without necessarily being aware of it, we all make sense of actions in terms of the relationships between basic formal categories: agent (the one performing the action), patient (the one on the receiving end), action (whatever it is the agent does), and instrument (the artifacts, if any, that are used in the action). Religious rituals also activate these categories, but in ways that postulate the involvement of supernatural beings by associating them with the patient, instrument, or agent roles in the ritual sequence. Over a number of years, Lawson and his coauthor McCauley have pioneered our understanding of the role of this kind of intuitive thinking in people's judgments of the efficacy and appropriateness of ritual behavior.[4] They have shown that many of these judgments are, like the concern with contaminants, largely unconscious, involuntary, fixed, and universal. These are therefore good examples of behavior programs whose outputs are somewhat closed.

Pascal Boyer has meanwhile shown that basic concepts of supernatural agency also arise from somewhat closed behavior programs, although they are not quite as closed as contamination-avoidance mechanisms. Supernatural agent concepts are based on perfectly ordinary agent concepts that emerge quite predictably in the course of normal development, regardless of cultural variation, but they also incorporate one or more added twists: in supernatural beings some standard property of the agent is missing or altered (e.g., the agent has no body), or some property from the intuitive categories normally appropriate to thinking about agents has somehow been exchanged for a property of an inappropriate category (e.g., a statue that can drink milk or hear people's prayers). Boyer refers to these as "minimally counterintuitive" concepts (also described by Slone in this volume as "modestly counterintuitive" concepts).

When we look at the range of minimally counterintuitive concepts across human societies, we find a certain amount of variability. Some populations devote a lot of energy and time to dealing with threats of witchcraft and sorcery, whereas others worry more about offending ancestral spirits, or propitiating deities. But even though there is quite significant variation in the kinds of concepts that can be labeled minimally counterintuitive, this category of concepts is not as rich and malleable as one might think. Some such concepts recur in lots of different societies, following patterns of cross-cultural recurrence that could not possibly be explained in terms of contact and diffusion. The range of all possible concepts of this kind may be sorted into a "catalog of supernatural templates,"[5] but the catalog is finite—indeed, somewhat limited. So we have a degree of openness—but the behavior programs are not as open as all that, because the range of possible breaches and cross-domain transfers of intuitive expectations is not very great. Some of us now refer to these sorts of limited open programs as "cognitively optimal" concepts.[6]

We now have a lot of evidence that religious traditions composed largely of cognitively optimal concepts should be quite widespread, because they deploy basic mechanisms in the human psyche that are both universal and ancient. But there is more to religion than that. Cognitively optimal concepts are, in a great many of the world's religions, *differentiated* from teachings and revelations that carry a heavier conceptual load (and thus require special mnemonic support in order to be transmitted). Some authors refer to this as the difference between (a) relatively intuitive (or minimally counterintuitive) religious thinking and (b) more drastically counterintuitive and abstract theologizing (see Slone, Tremlin, Boyer, and others in this volume). And it is not simply a matter of difference. The "heavier" concepts are often the more highly valued ones. Since these heavy concepts tend to be especially variable cross-culturally, they would seem to be the outputs of even more open behavior programs than those involved in cognitively optimal transmission. But what kinds of programs are these, and how are they activated?

One way of tackling this problem is to look at ethnographic and historical variation in religious traditions and try to identify cross-culturally recurrent patterns in the way complex religious concepts come to be transmitted. Two patterns immediately stand out. One is *repetition*: many religious traditions are founded upon extremely frequent transmission of core concepts—indeed involving regimes of routinized verbal transmission that are markedly more intense and prolonged over the life cycle than in most other kinds of information exchange. The second is the use of *shock tactics*: some religious traditions, ancient and modern, place great store on rarely performed rituals that, almost without exception, involve exceedingly high levels of emotional arousal and (at least for those undergoing them for the first time) a marked element of surprise. Both patterns of transmission involve the reproduction of extraordinarily complex, cognitively challenging religious concepts. In the case of the routinized traditions, we generally find some sort of doctrinal orthodoxy at the core—typically controlled by recognized experts operating within a centralized priestly hierarchy. In the case of the more shocking rituals, by contrast, we find a far greater emphasis on the mystical revelations of individual participants. Instead of teachings being transmitted by word of mouth, from experts to laity, the pattern is more like a private esoteric journey—often a slow journey taking many years to complete—whereby adherents try to investigate religious riddles independently through personal contemplation. More often than not, we find complex interactions between these two patterns.

The bifurcation noted here is not in itself a new discovery. Over the course of several hundred years, but particularly since the seminal work of Emile Durkheim and Max Weber, it has been appreciated that religious traditions tend toward two major poles, subsequently described in a series of major dichotomous theories from such anthropological luminaries as Ruth Benedict, Ernest Gellner, Jack Goody, Victor Turner, Ioan Lewis, Richard Werbner, Robin Horton, and Fredrik Barth.[7] In this pioneering scholarship, many fine-grained details of patterns of religious transmission have been noted, but it remained necessary to draw all these details together into a single theory of religion and to provide a scientifically grounded explanation for their coalescence. What we needed was a theory that could anchor these patterns of religious behavior in the biological and cognitive theories introduced above.

From the viewpoint of evolutionary psychology and the neurosciences, the presence of two major strategies of religious transmission made immediate sense. Not only in humans but in a wide range of other species with complex nervous systems, learning and memory (the building blocks of behavioral flexibility) depend upon the twin strategies of *rehearsal* (that is, repeating particular behaviors) and *arousal* (that is, being able to recall exceptional events associated with strong emotional valence). In the case of humans, these strategies are expressed in enormously complex cognitive systems that handle explicit knowledge—sometimes conveniently distinguished by the terms "semantic" and "episodic" memory.[8] Semantic memory is built around patterns of repeated rehearsal: it consists of general knowledge we have acquired about the world, based on experiences so varied and numerous we can seldom recall when or how we first learned any of it. By contrast, episodic memory consists of our recollections of distinct moments in our life experience, that stand out as somewhat unique. Experiences that are especially surprising, arousing, and personally consequential typically give rise to vivid and enduring episodic memories. To put it crudely, semantic and episodic memory are psychologically complex expressions of biologically ancient strategies of learning through repetition and arousal. Religious traditions clearly make use of these learning strategies in various ways, but the challenge was to explain how.

In a series of recent books, I developed a distinction between two contrasting "modes of religiosity": doctrinal and imagistic.[9] The doctrinal mode is based around frequently repeated teachings and rituals. Religious knowledge is codified in language and transmitted primarily via recognized leaders and authoritative texts. Routinized transmission allows cognitively challenging ideas, even maximally counterintuitive concepts, to be learned and stored in semantic memory. But heavy repetition also makes it possible for theological or cosmological ideas to become rather rigidly systematized and standardized in a population. If the religious concepts, and the authoritative logical and interpretive connections that bind them together, are frequently reiterated, then it becomes easier to spot deviations from the standard account. At the same time, as ritual behavior in general becomes habituated, much of the procedural knowledge is activated implicitly—rather like the way competent cyclists know how to peddle and steer around obstacles without necessarily being able to express or communicate those skills at a verbal level. The ability to carry out procedures without conscious reflection—that is, without "knowing how" you do it—has consequences for the way people reflect on why they perform the actions in question. In particular, it appears that routinized participation in rituals tends to suppress certain kinds of creative thinking about the *meanings* of the acts, and also makes people more receptive to authoritative, verbally transmitted meanings.

The theory of the doctrinal mode of religiosity maintains that all these cognitive features are causally linked to a set of sociopolitical arrangements. The emphasis on verbal transmission facilitates highly efficient spread of such traditions, so *routinized* religions are generally also relatively *large-scale* traditions. With only a little tweaking from other relevant variables, religions operating in this way can expand rapidly, through processes of evangelism and missionization. The doctrinal modality of codification and transmission emphasizes oratory and learning, and so it facilitates the emergence of venerable leaders and teachers: gurus, prophets, priests, messiahs, and so on. At the same time, it opens up the possibility for standardized creeds, and thus the emergence of religious orthodoxies over which leaders can exercise control. So the doctrinal mode tends to establish centralized ecclesiastic hierarchies, exerting influence over the content and organization of authoritative religious knowledge.

By contrast, the imagistic mode of religiosity is based on rare, climactic rituals—for instance, the hair-raising ordeals of initiation cults, millenarian sects, vision quests, and so on—typically involving extreme forms of deprivation, bodily mutilation and flagellation, and psychological trauma based around participation in shocking acts (such as ritualized cannibalism or murder). The imagistic mode figures especially in the religions of the ancient world and, until recently, in many small-scale societies and cults. Its practices trigger enduring and vivid episodic memories for ritual ordeals, encouraging long-term reflection on the mystical significance of the acts and artifacts involved. We know from detailed ethnographic research on these practices (for instance in aboriginal Australia, New Guinea, Africa, Amazonia, and many parts of Asia) that the esoteric revelations induced by the imagistic mode are seldom communicated verbally as a set of explicit teachings. It is not just that the practices are too infrequent to allow this kind of transmission but that their persuasiveness derives from the fact that they originate in internal mental processes of personal rumination. Such processes tend to be slow; indeed they may take many years to unfold, with the result that religious expertise tends to be concentrated in the hands of elders, who can only transmit the tradition by forcing others to go through similarly protracted processes of ritual participation and private reflection.

Imagistic practices are associated with very different sociopolitical arrangements from those found in the doctrinal mode. The revelatory knowledge is much harder to spread, for it emerges out of collective participation rather than being codified in speech or text. Its traumatic rituals create intense solidarity among those who experience them together, establishing in people's episodic memories who was present when a particular cycle of rituals took place. The tendency is toward localized social cohesion, based on patterns of following by example, and so we never find the same kind of scale, uniformity, centralization, or hierarchical structure that typifies the doctrinal mode.

Like many other models in the cognitive science of religion, the modes theory couches its hypotheses in terms of principles of *selection*. Doctrinal and imagistic modes are best understood as *attractor positions* around which ritual actions and associated religious beliefs *cumulatively* tend to congregate. New rituals and beliefs that fail the meet the requirements of memory and motivation proposed by the theory are simply selected out. Within these constraints, however, a very broad range of religious behaviors becomes possible. And this brings us back to the question of closed versus open behavior programs.

We have noted that some aspects of religious thinking depend on relatively closed programs—those concepts and other behavioral outputs that are much the same in human populations everywhere. In addition, we find that religious concepts may involve some small but cognitively salient violations of the inferences delivered by closed behavior programs. Such concepts may be described as "cognitively optimal" (in the sense of being especially easy to recall and pass on, all else being equal). Then again, we also seem to have religious concepts that are *exceedingly remote* from anything our evolved cognitive systems could anticipate. These hard-to-learn concepts can only be acquired if special mnemonic techniques are available, and at least two broadly contrasting kinds of techniques have been identified, built around the manipulation of performance frequency and arousal. When we look at the kind of concepts arising from our two modes of religiosity, it is clear that we are entering the realm of extremely open programs, and the constraints of biology seem to be somewhat distant. The situation, though, is more complicated (and moreover far more interesting) even than that.

Some particularly illuminating perspectives on the contrasts between elaborate, explicit religious knowledge (as generated by the relatively open behavior programs postulated by the modes theory) and more cognitively optimal religious thinking (as generated by relatively closed behavior programs founded on tacit, generic mechanisms) are presented in this volume by Todd Tremlin and Jason Slone. Although Tremlin does not specifically couch the distinction in terms of the relative openness of behavior programs, he nevertheless identifies a wide range of ways in which much the same basic distinction has been developed in the cognitive sciences. The open–closed dichotomy overlaps, for instance, with distinctions between analytical and intuitive thinking, between abstract and inferentially rich representations, between slow and fast, reflective and reflexive, conscious and unconscious/automatic types of computation (Tremlin, 70–71). Further, Tremlin links these distinctions to the evolution of consciousness via a series of contrasts between rational/analytical thought and automatic/rapid/ effortless processing, envisaging the former as language-based, relatively affect-free, highly abstract, propositional, and recently evolved, and the latter as essentially nonverbal, affective, concrete, experiential, and biologically more ancient. The point is succinctly and powerfully made with reference to a wide body of literature in the cognitive sciences, although arguably some of the dichotomies that are piled on are more controversial than others. I have doubts, for instance, that levels of affectivity can be mapped onto the sequence of binary oppositions adumbrated by Tremlin—indeed, recent developments in the neurosciences suggest that even the most rational and abstract "higher-level" forms of cognition are necessarily emotion laden.[10] Nor do I agree with Tremlin that the outputs of implicit systems are more plausible or relevant than the outputs of explicit systems.[11] But Tremlin's general argument fits well with the view, to which I also subscribe, that religious thinking derives from *both* relatively closed behavior programs (taking the form of online, intuitive, largely tacit operations, associated with the transmission of cognitively optimal representations), *and* much more open behavior programs (resulting in abstract, computationally challenging, counterintuitive, explicit discourse and offline rumination). Following Justin Barrett (1999), many of us now refer to religious thinking and behavior of the latter kind as "theologically correct," and have noted how this contrasts with more intuitive kinds of religiosity.

Jason Slone, author of the recent book *Theological Incorrectness: Why Religious People Believe What They Shouldn't*, argues in his contribution to the present volume that "concepts within religious systems typically lie on a *continuum of complexity* from explicit offline theology to intuitive online religion" (187, emphasis added), a view that clearly accords well with the notion of varying degrees of openness of behavior programs. What seems to happen in religious traditions, when observed on the ground through ethnographic studies or over time through historiographical and archaeological research, is that different kinds of behavior programs of varying degrees of openness are continually activated, resulting in an array of different patterns of interaction, cultural transmission, and historical transformation. To my mind, this is one of the most fascinating areas in which the cognitive science of religion has made progress in recent years, and it is one in which particularly large-scale interdisciplinary collaboration has fruitfully unfolded (see Whitehouse and Laidlaw 2004; Whitehouse and Martin 2004; Martin and Whitehouse, 2006). What is becoming increasingly clear is that some religious activities draw heavily on cognitively optimal concepts and practices while others place great store on more elaborate, theoretically correct forms of knowledge. Indeed, these differences of emphasis can sometimes be apparent across entire religious traditions. There are some religions, for instance, that eschew theologizing more or less across the board and seem, instead, to be preoccupied with the minimally counterintuitive properties of certain kinds of events, such as the nefarious activities of witches and sorcerers (as in some traditional African societies), or spirit possession and magico-medical rituals (as in some contemporary Afro-Brazilian cults). There are also religious systems that are internally stratified, such that "highbrow" theological discourse is carried on mainly by educated elites, and cognitively optimal variants are the province of lay adherents (a pattern that has been noted, for instance, in medieval Christianity and many contemporary Asian religions[12]). At the other end of the spectrum, we find religious systems dominated at all levels by one or the other (or both) of our two modes of religiosity, placing great emphasis on the uniform dissemination of elaborate doctrinal knowledge codified in language (e.g., most fundamentalist varieties of the Abrahamic religions) and/or being greatly concerned with esoteric revelations arising from personal rumination (e.g., evangelical traditions that emphasize epiphanic episodes and conversion experiences, as well as imagistic practices in cultic organizations of various kinds). Matters are further complicated by the fact that individual worshippers can move almost seamlessly between these different types of religious thinking: drawing on doctrinal testimony in one context and personal revelation in another, and then falling back on tacit, theologically incorrect reasoning for certain other tasks and purposes. So the extent to which these different facets of religious experience exercise dominance in people's religious experience varies at an individual level as well as across entire traditions.

A crucially important question is to what extent we can formulate generalizing theories about the *causes* and *consequences* of these different "layers" of religious thinking and behavior. In this volume, broadly two theoretical positions are taken up, differentiated by the degree of emphasis placed on cognitively optimal versus theologically correct religious transmission (and, correspondingly, by the relative importance attached to more closed behavior programs versus more open ones). On the one hand, there are those who argue that theologically correct religious discourse and revelatory experience are largely epiphenomenal. According to this view, the establishment of elaborate and explicit religious concepts may well result from particularly open behavior programs (e.g., explicit memory systems and mechanisms for high-level analogical thinking), but what makes these cognitively complex and somewhat indigestible outputs *widespread* is best explained by a combination of historical particularity (e.g., opportunities for establishment of religious guilds) and the way these environmental factors interact with tacit, intuitive (relatively closed) behavior programs (e.g., evolved mechanisms dedicated to coalitional thinking). One of the hallmarks of this perspective, which I shall call the "tacit religion hypothesis,[13] is that it upholds largely unconscious, intuitive mechanisms as the real causes of most (if not all) behavior, including religious behavior. We do what we do without knowing why, and our more elaborate religious beliefs and actions are mostly post-hoc rationalizations for things we would say or do regardless of what our doctrinal systems or personal theologies might stipulate or prescribe.

On the other hand, there are those who argue that our religious commitments are shaped by a *combination* of implicit inferences and explicit reasoning and that certain modes of transmission (e.g., doctrinal and imagistic) foster the emergence of especially elaborate religious belief systems that vie with our implicit cognitive mechanisms for control over our behavior. The extent to which they succeed depends on processes of cognition that are embedded in socially regulated contexts, and is apt to change over time in ways that may be increasingly predictable. This perspective, which I shall call the "layered religion hypothesis," accords considerable weight to tacit, evolved cognition but does not regard this as the be-all and end-all of explanatory theory. Let us consider each of these perspectives in turn.

TACIT COGNITION AND THE STUDY OF RELIGION

Undoubtedly the most persuasive champion of the tacit religion hypothesis is the justly renowned cognitive theorist, Pascal Boyer. In his chapter for this volume, Boyer argues that tacit, intuitive mechanisms and their cognitively optimal outputs constitute the *key* to explanation in the cognitive science of religion. To the extent that people's actual religious concepts may vary somewhat from one community to the next, Boyer argues that the reasons for this must lie in the interaction between specialized cognitive mechanisms and historically particular circumstances. The challenge, accordingly, is to show how specific variations in historical circumstances affect the outcomes of fixed, generic cognitive mechanisms. Boyer contrasts this approach with my own, which (as we have seen) treats only some aspects of cognition (and their outputs) as relatively fixed and implicit and others as inherently more flexible, conscious, and context sensitive.

Boyer goes on to draw a sharp but illuminating contrast between "religion in general" (properties that all religions have, at least beneath the surface, by virtue of generic evolved cognitive mechanisms) and "specific religious systems" (properties that religions overtly exhibit, such as particular beliefs, rituals, myths, and so on). Specific religious concepts vary somewhat, but in a way that is quite tightly constrained by the intuitive properties of religion in general. Boyer refers to the range of all possible minimally counterintuitive concepts, for instance, as a "catalog of the supernatural," but the catalog is finite—indeed, somewhat limited. Minimally counterintuitive concepts, like other cognitively optimal aspects of religion, might be compared to common weeds: they spread and take root easily, unless efforts are made to control them. By contrast, official (theologically correct) religious concepts are more variable and distinctive, more like expensive plants with exotic-sounding names: they require much care and attention (e.g., special mnemonic and pedagogic support) if they are to survive. Religious authorities are like gardeners who live in constant dread of weed infestation.

As far as cognitively optimal concepts are concerned, the gap between religion in general and specific religious systems is not all that great. Indeed, the fact that one group believes in statues that hear prayers, and another in carved masks that crave sacrificial offerings, is arguably trivial. Both groups share the same basic psychological mechanisms that made these minimally counterintuitive concepts appealing and memorable, and, according to Boyer, the fact that the surface-level concepts take slightly different forms in different places can be put down to historically contingent factors (including mere chance) that need not concern us too much. But what about the official, theologically correct concepts? Their diversity presents a bigger problem, opening a gulf between religion in general as postulated by cognitive science and specific religious systems as found on the ground. This is really the nub of the problem, and it is also where Boyer's and my intuitions about how to proceed start to look more radically different.

Boyer's argument is that we should stick with our conception of religion in general as a set of universal, largely unconscious cognitive constraints and turn to factors outside cognitive science (for instance, what he refers to as "cultural or historical factors" and "political conditions") to explain the emergence of theological concepts and other diverse outputs of religious experts. If we identify these "outside factors" correctly, then all that remains, according to Boyer, is to predict accurately how our generic, tacit cognitive mechanisms will respond to those factors, giving rise to well-known patterns in religious organization (e.g., as identified by the theory of doctrinal and imagistic modes of religiosity and/or by other theories that might augment or eclipse it). If, for instance, archaeologists and social theorists can tell us how centralized states and technologies of inscription emerge, then cognitive science can fill various remaining parts of the picture, by explaining how our cognitive capacities for managing coalitions and intergroup competition or for utilizing possibilities afforded by literacy for storing and organizing information, are going to drive us toward the formation of religious guilds with standardized theological products. According to Boyer, this would account for most (if not all) the features of the doctrinal mode, with reference to only a small number of cognitive mechanisms. Or, alternatively, if there are experts out there who can tell us why certain populations form themselves into warring factions or end up developing methods of hunting that are especially dangerous, then we can fall back on tacit, generic cognitive mechanisms specialized for coalitional thinking to explain why such populations tend to go in for initiation rituals (the answer would be that these rituals prove the loyalty and trustworthiness of those who undergo them). Boyer argues that this strategy will deliver a theoretically economical explanation for features of the imagistic mode.

Much as I can see the appeals of reduction to tacit, generic mechanisms—not least the neatness and simplicity of Boyer's arguments—the strategy ultimately depends on the presence of sociological and historical theories that really can deliver the premises we require. This is not, in my view, the case. The modes theory does not take centralized states or writing technologies as given (as "already explained") for the purposes of the emergence of the doctrinal mode. It proceeds from the assumption that these are things that *still require an explanation*. The theory maintains that the emergence of the doctrinal mode, via intricate mechanisms of reinforcement among its component elements, provides some plausible starting points for a thoroughgoing explanation for the first appearance of states *and* literacy practices.[14] The environmental triggers required to kick-start this process[15] are far more parsimonious than Boyer's theory requires, depending on variables that archaeologists and other relevant specialists are well placed to account for (such as the developing impact of environmental and technological factors on increasing population densities and frequencies of productive and ritual activities). To take as our starting point, as Boyer suggests, immensely complex processes of state formation, including increasingly centralized and hierarchical patterns of social interaction and the emergence of increasingly homogeneous regional cultural systems, is to put the cart before the horse and to limit the relevance and explanatory scope of cognitive theories.

Similar problems are raised by Boyer's explanation for core features of the imagistic mode. Here too he takes as given something for which an explanation is urgently required: namely the presence of cohesive coalitions set against each other in relations of covert tension or outright conflict, for instance in conditions of chronic warfare. Universal mechanisms of coalitional thinking cannot account for such arrangements (recall the point that variables cannot be explained by constants). Nor do I think they could explain, as Boyer suggests, the presence of traumatic initiation rites in such coalitions. Boyer's argument on that front is based on the idea that participation in rites of terror, in the role of novice or victim, provides a public demonstration of one's loyalty to the group and thus one's trustworthiness in future situations of danger (e.g., on the battlefield or hunting ground). But in the vast majority (if not all) of ritual systems of this kind, novices are literally forced to undergo the tortures and privations of initiation, and the price of defection (usually a horrible death) is far greater than of compliance (temporary trauma). Not only do people *not choose* to be initiated, but, having been coerced into it, everyone knows it is more or less a forgone conclusion that they will pass the "test" (accidents notwithstanding). Even at the most implicit intuitive level, this is no demonstration of loyalty, though it may (as I have often argued) give rise to intense group cohesion and patterns of loyalty to the group that this entails. And that brings us to another set of thorny issues in relation to which Boyer's and my understandings diverge. These issues concern the origins and nature of motivational states in religious transmission.

Much of my work on modes of religiosity is geared to showing that the complex, explicit religious knowledge that arises from doctrinal and imagistic forms of transmission has considerable motivating force. By contrast, Boyer would argue that what people think they believe, and what they say they believe, has little direct impact on what they do. In other words, according to Boyer the real motivations behind apparently religious behavior operate outside conscious awareness, at the level of tacit, intuitive thinking. Where I have argued, for instance, that imagistic practices gradually give rise to esoteric exegesis of an intensely revelatory kind which in turn drives the guardians of this sort of religious knowledge to pass on the tradition, Boyer argues that in fact the transmission of imagistic practices is explained by evolved contamination-avoidance mechanisms, operating largely below the level of conscious awareness.

Boyer maintains that ethnographic research has failed to deliver convincing evidence of revelatory knowledge generated by traumatic initiations and other rituals operating in the imagistic mode. As Hinde (this volume) points out, the claim that ritual exegesis is *secret* understandably arouses doubts about its existence and places the burden of proof on those who assert that it is really there. The point is well taken. Clearly we require more sophisticated methodological techniques to investigate the topic with greater precision and depth. Nevertheless, most ethnographers who (like me) have worked closely with ritual experts in cults of initiation are in little doubt that elaborate revelatory knowledge informs and shapes their activities. Given the general reluctance of participants to present esoteric exegesis as connected narrative, much of the work devoted to reconstructing these bodies of knowledge does so in a piecemeal fashion, putting together pieces of evidence gathered over lengthy periods of time in conversation with ritual experts and through direct observation of their activities. More recently, several of us have been trying to devise new techniques of investigating the nature (e.g., elaborateness and coherence) and developmental characteristics (emergence over time, including impact of age) of spontaneous exegetical reflection associated with high-arousal rituals. These techniques would seek to overcome the limitations of methods based on interview and anecdote. Moreover, we are designing experimental techniques of establishing the effects of low-frequency, high-arousal rituals on spontaneous exegetical reflection (see Whitehouse, Richert, and Stewart, this volume), so it is hoped that some of the empirical issues will be resolved satisfactorily in due course. In the meantime, there is still a broader theoretical issue to address, namely whether it is safe to assume that statable beliefs, religious or otherwise, have little or no role in motivating behavior.

In relation to this question, Boyer seems to regard the matter as some-thing of a zero-sum game: if tacit, intuitive processing influences behavior, then explicit religious beliefs motivate nothing. But surely the reality is that both kinds of knowledge, implicit and explicit, can be implicated (perhaps to different degrees) in various kinds of religiously motivated behavior (see also Hinde, this volume). A major problem with the argument that contam-ination-avoidance mechanisms explain "the urgency of repetition for ritu-als" (Boyer, 25), at least as applied to imagistic practices, is precisely that there is little sense of urgency (in the sense of continual nagging) to repeat them. On the contrary, these are among the most *infrequently performed* rituals we know about. We could concede the point that all rituals tacitly ac-tivate contamination-avoidance systems to some extent some of the time, but that does not explain any of the peculiar properties of religious rituals in traditions dominated by modes dynamics. A prominent feature of our two modes of religiosity is the presence of elaborate exegesis, whether codified in language (doctrinal mode) or guardedly elaborated through private ru-mination (imagistic mode). Now, a striking feature of rituals in doctrinal and imagistic traditions, unlike those that genuinely lack elaborate exegesis (and which presumably must, as Boyer suggests, incorporate cognitively optimal traits in order to survive), is that people are willing to make massive sacrifices to defend them. Some of those sacrifices are made in isolated in-dividual acts ("turning the other cheek," resisting temptation, etc.), and oth-ers in more collective settings (organized sectarian violence, religiously mo-tivated crusades, etc.) While one could in principle argue that the explicit religious convictions that people claim to motivate such behavior are purely illusory, I can see little reason to take that view and plenty of good reasons to take people's statements on the matter seriously: not least the fact that many explicit religious commitments and the behaviors they are said to mo-tivate often run directly against normal drives, calculations of self-interest, intuitive knowledge, and so on. To say that explicit religious ideas influence behavior is not to say anything radically implausible, either intuitively or sci-entifically, but it does raise the question of how such ideas come into being. The modes theory tries to answer that question, but it does not assume that these explicit ideas are *solely* responsible for the behavior of religious peo-ple. The tacit, generic mechanisms that Boyer identifies (and that may be relevant to understanding *all* kinds of behavior) must also be taken into ac-count. Part of the challenge is to see how these various kinds of cognitive mechanisms (of varying degrees of explicitness) and their outputs (ranging from the intuitive to the massively counterintuitive) vie for control of our in-dividual behavior and, at a collective or institutional level, help to shape the sociopolitical conditions in which religious behavior is embedded.

The tacit religion hypothesis surrenders a great deal of explanatory po-tential to noncognitive (and rather vaguely delimited) factors, such as "historical contingency" and "sociopolitical arrangements." Although this implies a division of intellectual labor generous to historians, anthropologists, and other kinds of social theorists, it does not really help them to get on with their part of the job. Historians and anthropologists (and I count myself among the latter) want well-founded theories to explain variations and transformations in explicit cultural (including religious) thought and behavior, since that is primarily what we study. We want to know not only what causes this diversity and change but also what effects it then has on the world around us. We know that these processes must involve complex interactions between cognition "in the head" and events in the environment, but we need theories that address both sides of the equation with equal resolve.

LAYERED COGNITION AND THE STUDY OF RELIGION

In responding to the above debates, Robert Hinde cautions that some of the variables influencing religious transmission and transformation may always lie beyond the compass of cognitive explanations. He writes,

> Human activities involve a number of levels of complexity—intraindividual (e.g., cognitive) processes, individual actions, short-term interactions between individuals, relationships between individuals, groups and societies. . . . Each of these affects, and is affected by, others. For instance, cognitive processes affect individual behavior, and how an individual behaves affects how he thinks; what goes on in an interaction influences, and is influenced by, the relationship in which it is embedded; and so on. Furthermore, each of these levels affects and is affected by the physical environment and by the sociocultural structure, including the morals and beliefs shared with others in the group. (44)

Much depends, however, on what qualifies as "cognitive" phenomena rather than as "sociocultural structure" or "the physical environment." The latter, I would argue, only impact human behavior insofar as their effects are mediated through cognitive processes. Environments and sociocultural systems do not affect people's thoughts and actions unless they are somehow registered by their perceptual systems, resulting in responses generated by intricate and flexible processes of mentation. Designating some cognitive mechanisms relatively open and others relatively closed (see above) acknowledges that environmental variables, and perhaps most importantly socially regulated environments, are part and parcel of a great deal of cognitive development, processing, and resulting behavior, all the more so as the behavior programs in question become progressively more open. Rather than thinking of cognition as something that takes place exclusively in the mind/brain, it makes sense to think of it as "extended" and thus to talk about "cognitive environments" rather than purely interior cognition.[16]

Matthew Day attends to this point rather more directly than other contributors to the present volume. He observes that the tendency (following Boyer, Barrett, and others) to emphasize the naturalness of both language and religion masks the fact that not all aspects of religion are expressions of fixed, generic cognitive architecture. Spoken languages are certainly "natural" to humans in the sense that they exhibit many general properties that are more or less invariable, regardless of local or historical particularities. For instance, natural languages display similar levels of complexity regardless of the strikingly differing levels of technological development among the populations that sustain them. But religious systems vary much more strikingly in terms of levels of complexity, both in terms of theological content and social morphology. A more compelling analogy, Day suggests, might be drawn between religion and mathematical knowledge. To be sure, we require many standard evolved mental capacities to think with numbers, just as we do to think about gods and spirits, but to acquire an understanding of advanced mathematics requires elaborate cultural tools that are, quite literally, outside the brains of individual mathematicians. We need not only material tools of the trade (e.g., technologies of inscription and information storage) but regimes of institutional training through which would-be mathematicians are able to hone their skills under competent supervision. So, in turn, a great deal of religious innovation and transmission depends on forms of extended cognition, of the sort proposed by the theory of modes of religiosity.

Seen in this light, the gap postulated (in admittedly rather different ways) by both Boyer and Hinde, between historical contingency and cognitive causes, begins to narrow and we can imagine instead the possibility of a "cognitive historiography" (Whitehouse 2005) as well as a more comprehensive cognitive anthropology. The manner in which such projects might proceed is suggested by contributions to this volume that focus on the *layered* nature of religious experience and behavior.

Todd Tremlin observes that patterns of historical transformation in religious systems are likely to be influenced not only by modes dynamics (e.g., the tedium effect in the doctrinal mode or the strengths and weaknesses of imagistic coalitions in the face of larger-scale, routinized orthodoxies) but *also* by the pervasive allure of cognitively optimal concepts. This serves to underline the point, already noted, that the choice between tacit/intuitive and explicit/counterintuitive religious thinking should not be construed in zero-sum terms. Both kinds of thinking, and the patterns of religious transmission to which they give rise, are usually present simultaneously. What can change is their relative influence over religious transmission in the round, and thus their impact on the stability of religious systems over time. Further examples of this line of argument are suggested in this volume by both Jesper Sørensen and Jason Slone.

In an exceptionally wide-ranging discussion of the cognitive underpinnings of ritual behavior and its interpretation, Sørensen draws a series of fruitful contrasts between assessments of ritual acts that emphasize *magical efficacy*, on the one hand, and those that focus on *exegetical meaning*, on the other. Concerns with magical efficacy would appear to be driven by highly intuitive, largely tacit cognitive mechanisms concerned with attributions of agentive force, basic-level action representation concepts, and intuitive ontological knowledge. In an intriguing discussion of how these sorts of mechanisms are implicated in the formation of notions of charismatic authority and supernatural agency, Sørensen provides compelling grounds for supposing that evaluations of magicial efficacy form part of our repertoire of *cognitively optimal* responses to ritual behavior. At the same time, however, rituals may trigger a quest for explicit exegetical meaning capable of hardening into routinized and doctrinally elaborated orthodoxies. Drawing on both my own work and that of Max Weber, Sørensen suggests that although concerns with efficacy and exegesis may seem to be mutually exclusive (and in practice, emphasis on one implies deemphasis of the other), they are in fact dialectically connected in the development of religious traditions. Thus, explicit exegetical and doctrinal knowledge, generated and transmitted through relatively open behavior programs, is always constrained and influenced by the ubiquitous presence of intuitive judgments of magical efficacy that are generated by rather more closed behavior programs. Religious history is, much as Weber originally envisaged, a ceaseless oscillation between institutional arrangements dominated by one or other of these "layers" of cognitive processing.

In a comparable fashion, Slone considers the question of why many theological traditions develop free-will problems. Such problems, he observes, arise from explicit reasoning of a kind that is broadly analogous to the logical operations entailed in a scientific or philosophical argumentation. But because some of the crucial premises of this reasoning are delivered by relatively closed behavior programs (especially those delivering inferences about the freedom of agents to choose how they act), the conclusions of theological rumination on questions of divine omnipotence (running as they do against our intuitions about individual responsibility and choice) are likely to be convergent. Thus, he postulates an *interaction* between the outputs of implicit/intuitive thinking, on the one hand, and explicit, highly abstract reasoning, on the other. Insofar as the conclusions of this sort of theological rumination result in bodies of fixed, authoritative religious knowledge, they depend on the mnemonic gimmicks of the doctrinal mode of religiosity to be reproduced intact (although Slone attaches importance to uses of literacy in this regard). But the "theologically correct" position on free-will problems never completely eclipses more intuitive ways of thinking about divine agency. Slone observes,

> memorized theological creeds do not override noncultural conceptual schemata. In other words, learned theological conceptual schemes provide only one among many "multiple sufficient schemata" (Kelly 1972) for making sense of the world (Slone 2004). Likewise, theological concepts that postulate that the gods have agency that is greater than what humans possess do not override human bias toward self-agency. (199)

Slone's example of the development of theologically correct solutions to free-will problems suggests one possible way in which the interaction of implicit and explicit cognitive systems can influence the direction of religious thought over time. But there are also a number of other ways in which a *layered* approach to cognition can shed light on the historical development and transformation of religious systems. Ilkka Pyysiäinen has made some particularly wide-ranging contributions in this area.

In a previous contribution to this book series, Pyysiäinen argued that the doctrinal mode of religiosity is vulnerable to broadly two kinds of motivational problems.[17] First, there are problems that result from excessive discipline and routinization. In some traditions, religious authorities insist on the observance of very frequent ritual obligations and patterns of doctrinal repetition, the appeals of which may be outweighed by the heavy demands they impose (in terms of time, energy, attention, etc.). Such a situation may be described as the "tedium effect."[18] Second, there are problems that arise from too liberal an approach to the maintenance of the orthodoxy, expressed in lowered frequency of doctrinal repetition (and other routinized forms of transmission), and a general reduction in the vigor with which unauthorized innovation is detected and punished. This situation allows more "cognitively optimal" versions of the orthodoxy to spread and to become entrenched. Pyysiäinen has suggested that these two kinds of problems may be associated with contrasting patterns of historical transformation:[19] "over-policing" (manifested as tedium and demoralization) may give rise to imagistic splintering[20] and "under-policing" (manifested as loss of doctrinal coherence and uniformity) may result in programs of reform, aimed at restoring the disciplines of the doctrinal mode.[21]

In his contribution to the present collection, Pyysiäinen explores more closely the hypothesis that the tedium effect gives rise to styles of religiosity that are somewhat imagistic in orientation. He argues that the imagistic mode, *contra* Boyer, delivers high levels of commitment through processes of revelation and spontaneous exegetical reflection, and that people will be especially susceptible to its effects in conditions of flagging commitment. And yet he also points out that the tedium effect can be effectively counteracted by just *some* features of imagistic transmission, without necessarily activating the entire nexus of features associated with the imagistic mode. Pyysiäinen observes that the phenomenon of "religious conversion" is an excellent case in point.

Typically, conversion experiences involve high levels of emotional arousal, giving rise to enduring episodic memory, and resulting in revelatory religious insights developing through internal rumination. Nevertheless, religious conversions take place mainly in religious traditions dominated by the doctrinal mode (for reasons that Pyysiäinen also discusses in some detail). As such, the revelatory ideas these experiences deliver are generated against a background of doctrinal knowledge and progressively integrated into it through the "schematization" of episodic encodings. For instance, conversion experiences can become somewhat stereotyped through subsequent narrative rehearsal, even if the motivational effects occasioned by high-arousal, epiphanic episodes are to some extent retained. Since these kinds of practices often serve to reinforce commitment to a widely distributed, already-established orthodoxy (and orthopraxy), they do not have the sociopolitical consequences that typify imagistic practices occurring in isolation from a doctrinal tradition. Although Pyysiäinen does not dwell on this point, it is also significant that religious conversions often take place in solitude, rather than involving sizeable ritual groupings (e.g., cohorts of initiates) as would be typical of *bona fide* imagistic traditions. And this too would help to explain why religious conversions do not produce cohesive ritual communities and other sociopolitical traits normally associated with the imagistic mode.

Pyysiäinen's arguments are persuasive.[22] If I have any quibble, however, it is that he may exaggerate the vulnerabilities of doctrinal transmission—a tendency that is apparent also in Tremlin's chapter. Both authors regard the theologically correct concepts of the doctrinal mode as lacking in motivational force, at least as compared with cognitively optimal concepts and imagistic revelations. As far as the latter comparison (doctrinal versus imagistic) is concerned, we are probably in agreement. Indeed, I have argued elsewhere at some length that religious commitments derived from internal rumination tend to exercise greater motivational force (at least on certain definable parameters) than commitments derived primarily from oral testimony.[23] What I find less convincing is the argument that theologically correct teachings are inherently less persuasive and motivationally salient than cognitively optimal religious ideas. Tremlin, for instance, talks about "the affect-free propositions of theological reasoning, whose abstract qualities both minimize their computational utility and reduce their psychological relevance" (71), all of which contrasts with the "inferential richness" of cognitively optimal concepts. And Pyysiäinen[24] describes theologically correct discourse as "an epiphenomenal overlay on natural religiosity" (160). There is little doubt that cognitively optimal religious ideas and practices are exceptionally robust (hence the analogy with prolific weeds, suggested earlier) and that complex doctrinal systems (like rare and delicate plants) require careful maintenance if they are to thrive. But, properly maintained, doctrinal teachings can thrive rather impressively in the sense of being well remembered by large numbers of people but also in the sense that they can exercise a powerful influence on behavior. Malley, for instance, explains how the relevance of theologically correct discourse can be enhanced through specifiable techniques of rhetoric and sermonizing.[25] And Thargard shows that such concepts can acquire emotional as well as intellectual coherence.[26] Moreover, the very act of repeating particular bodies of doctrine can have enduring salience effects that have yet to be fully investigated.[27] So it may be judicious to keep an open mind about the motivational properties of doctrinal transmission, at least until more evidence on the matter is available.

FUTURE DIRECTIONS IN EMPIRICAL RESEARCH

Barrett's concise overview of the evidential needs of the modes theory (this volume) presents us with some daunting challenges for future research. Some of the topics he identifies, however, are now beginning to be addressed. Barrett distinguishes between three major categories of empirical evidence needed to test the theory adequately: ethnographic, naturalistic, and experimental.

In talking about "ethnographic" evidence, Barrett means not merely the kinds of research, much prized by anthropologists like myself, that is based upon long-term participant observation in rather small locations but, rather, all types of descriptive information on religious beliefs and practices over time and space. Such evidence might come from historiography or archaeology rather than from ethnography more narrowly defined. Moreover, it would also include quantitative evidence pertaining to sociocultural phenomena, including statistical studies of naturally occurring distributions of concepts, rituals, and patterns of social interaction.

Coordinated attempts to test the modes theory ethnographically (in Barrett's sense) have so far pursued two major strategies. First, we have sought to draw on the existing knowledge of significant cross-sections of experienced anthropologists, historians, and archaeologists by asking them to subject the modes theory to critical scrutiny in light of the bodies of evidence they command. This work, resulting in a series of recent collections of essays,[28] has undoubtedly gone some way to refining the predictions of the modes theory. It has shown, for instance, that doctrinal and imagistic modes (at least as "bundles of features," as Boyer puts it) are indeed *globally distributed* and *ancient* features of religious systems, but *also* that their operation is influenced by *cognitively optimal* religious transmission in the sorts of ways briefly outlined above. We still do not know, however, if the samples of religious traditions covered by this research are representative of religious traditions everywhere. To assess accurately the extent to which modes of religiosity impact on patterns of religious transmission, past and present, we require a second type of ethnographic strategy, based on *surveys* of the ethnographic/historical/archaeological record and detailed *quantification* of the coalescence of doctrinal and imagistic features in all known religious traditions (or what might be suitably judged to be a representative sample of them). Work in this area is still in its infancy. To carry out surveys on the scale required is far from straightforward. We need, for instance, to establish methods of *codifying* the relevant features of doctrinal and imagistic modes and *measuring* degrees of coalescence in a reliable fashion, such that independent coders and measurers would make similar judgments. We also need to access reliable evidence from a sufficiently large (and representative) group of case studies. A potential problem here is that some variables of crucial importance, such as ritual frequency, are seldom recorded precisely in ethnographic and historiographical sources (and may simply be unavailable in the case of archaeological evidence[29]). One way of addressing these problems is to build new bodies of ethnographic evidence, rather than to rely on existing reports, and a start has been made on this attempting to establish a database on the Web (http://www.qub.ac.uk/fhum/banp) constructed around a 50-point questionnaire designed to elicit information essential to testing the modes theory's predictions.

Barrett's category of "naturalistic" studies is also an area in which, thanks in large part to his creative suggestions over a number of years, concrete research plans have begun to develop. A difficulty with this kind of research is, of course, that it requires naturally occurring "controls" on key variables of a kind that the modes theory predicts will not occur (or that if they occur, will rapidly become extinct). For instance, we know that there are many low-frequency, high-arousal rituals in religious traditions the world over, but it is extremely difficult (if not impossible) to find versions of these same rituals in which performative frequency is greatly increased or levels of arousal greatly reduced. Much as the theory predicts, we do not find situations of imagistic transmission in which the two main variables we are interested in are naturally controlled. We can, however, sometimes identify circumstances in which what are normally high-frequency, low-arousal rituals are experienced for the first time, and it is also clearly possible to find high-frequency rituals in which arousal levels vary. To take the first of these scenarios, studies have been designed (but not yet carried out) to compare levels of spontaneous exegetical reflection among (a) fresh converts (or newly ordained ministers) and (b) established members of the tradition (or experienced ministers).[30] If "first timers" prove to be more reflective than "old hands" (and assuming this finding could be widely replicated) then this would support the prediction that ritual frequency correlates inversely with spontaneous exegetical thinking. We might then consider whether elevated arousal amplifies these effects, through similar studies of naturally-occurring high- and low-arousal variants of high-frequency rituals (e.g., based on existing variations in emotional response among religious congregations). Of course, such studies do not enable us to compare bona fide imagistic practices (i.e., traumatic, one-off ritual episodes) with low-arousal and/or high-frequency versions of the same activities. But they do, arguably, approximate to that ideal.

Experimental research, as testified by the contribution to this volume by Richert and others, is also well under way. As Barrett notes, however, work of this kind must deal with the problem that real-world religious activities are typically embedded in highly motivating systems, whereas activities contrived in the laboratory (e.g., artificial rituals) are unlikely to elicit the same kinds and levels of motivation and meaning among participants (and if they did, this would raise thorny ethical problems). Earlier experiments designed to investigate levels of verbal repetition necessary for successful doctrinal transmission produced extraordinarily poor recall for a small volume of fictitious theology delivered twice a week over seven weeks (see Whitehouse 2004, 84). But it is possible that recall would have been better in a group of more highly motivated participants, as for instance we might expect to find in a genuine religious tradition. More promising have been pilot studies to assess levels of spontaneous exegetical reflection (SER) with respect to artificial rituals (based on the Catholic practice of self-crossing), which suggest that SER levels correlate inversely with the number of repetitions (rates of SER dropping off as the procedures become increasingly familiar) (see Whitehouse 2004, 83). In this case we might assume that even if high motivation in genuine religious settings reduces (or, for that matter, amplifies) the effects of repetition on SER, the underlying trend is likely to be the same in naturally occurring rituals.

These are just some of the areas in which research is under way but it remains embryonic, and, of course, Barrett has identified many more issues that urgently require further empirical investigation. Perhaps the most prominent of these is the need to establish the extent to which *explicit* religious thinking motivates and influences behavior. This topic has been a recurrent theme of the present volume (as noted at some length in this concluding chapter) and provides the launching point for Barrett's survey of empirical needs. Ethnographic research, as broadly construed by Barrett, can contribute to our understanding insofar as it delivers detailed descriptive information on people's explicit knowledge (based on texts, interviews, documentation of speech in natural settings, and so on) and on actual behavior (whether directly observed or recorded in secondary sources). What ethnography cannot provide, however, is direct evidence on how tacit motivations influence behavior, perhaps overriding explicitly expressed commitments.

Experimental designs do rather better in this regard but are often set up in such a way as to demonstrate the motivating force of unconscious processes, rather than to provide a balanced portrayal of the role of both explicit and implicit processes in behavior. Perhaps this is because it is more interesting (in the sense of titillating) to show that people sometimes fail to practice what they preach, but to set up experiments solely to make that point (albeit in fascinatingly myriad ways) carries the risk of self-fulfilling prophecy. We also need research designs that show when and why preaching determines practice. The possibilities for naturalistic research in this area are many and varied. As a starting point, one might imagine studies that examine decision-making processes and their outcomes in relation to dilemmas of a doctrinally significant kind based on comparisons between participants who espouse the relevant doctrines and those who do not. Basic research of that kind does not, as far as I am aware, already exist. But there are also many more subtle problems to investigate, such as the relative sway of beliefs based on testimony as compared with those based on internal rumination, the effects of implicit mechanisms (e.g., coalitional thinking) on theologically correct decision making, and so on. Clearly, there is much work to be done. But as many of the *mysteries* surrounding religious thought and behavior come to be converted into potentially solvable *problems*,[31] there is increasing reason to believe that one day we shall justly be able to claim to have laid bare the cognitive foundations of religiosity.

NOTES

1. Mayr 1976; see also Hinde, this volume.
2. See Tooby and Cosmides 1992, 46.
3. Fiske and Haslam 1997, 218.
4. Lawson and McCauley 1990; McCauley and Lawson 2002.
5. Boyer 2001.
6. For a fuller explication of this term, see Whitehouse 2004a.
7. For a summary of this scholarship, see Whitehouse 1995, chap. 8.
8. This distinction was first advanced in detail by Tulving 1972.
9. Whitehouse 1995, 2000, 2004a.
10. See Thagard 2004; Barsalou et al. 2004; Livingston 2004; see also Pyysiäinen, this volume.
11. See Whitehouse 2004a; Malley 2004; Pyysiäinen, this volume.
12. See, for instance, Howe 2004; Vial 2004.
13. It is tempting to call it the "Dumb Religion Hypothesis," partly because it downplays the role of conscious, intelligent thought in religious discourse, but also because it regards the "real stuff" of religion as "dumb" in the English sense of being mute (in this case, unavailable to verbal report). But I have resisted that temptation since it might, very misleadingly, suggest a lack of respect for religious sensibilities.

14. Whitehouse 2000, 2004a.
15. See Whitehouse 2004b in response to Wiebe 2004.
16. See Sperber 1996.
17. Pyysiäinen 2004.
18. Whitehouse 2000.
19. Pyysiäinen 2004, 187.
20. See Whitehouse 1995.
21. See Whitehouse 2000; Whitehouse and Laidlaw 2004; and Whitehouse and Martin 2004.
22. See also Whitehouse 2004.
23. Whitehouse 2004a, chap. 7; though see also McCauley and Whitehouse 2004.
24. Following McCauley 2000.
25. Malley 2004.
26. Thargard 2004.
27. See Whitehouse 2004a.
28. Whitehouse and Laidlaw 2004; Whitehouse and Martin 2004; Martin and Whitehouse 2004a; Martin and Whitehouse 2006.
29. But note Johnson's (2004) helpful suggestions on this front.
30. The designs for these studies were inspired by Barrett and refined through collaboration between myself and Rebekah Richert.
31. This distinction, first made by Noam Chomsky, has already been aptly applied by Pascal Boyer to the cognitive science of religion (2001, 2).

REFERENCES

Barrett, J. L. 1999. Theolgical Correctness: Cognitive Constraint and the Study of Religion. *Method & Theory in the Study of Religion* 11: 325–39.
Barsalou, Lawrence W., Aron K. Barbey, W. Kyle Simmons, and Ava Santos. 2004. Embodiment in Religious Knowledge. In *The Psychological and Cognitive Foundations of Religiosity*, ed. Robert N. McCauley and Harvey Whitehouse. Special issue, *Journal of Cognition and Culture* 4, no. 3.
Boyer, Pascal. 2001. *Religion Explained: The Evolutionary Origins of Religious Thought.* New York: Basic Books.
Fiske, A. P., and N. Haslam. 1997. Is Obsessive-Compulsive Disorder a Pathology of the Human Disposition to Perform Socially Meaningful Rituals? Evidence of Similar Content. *Journal of Nervous and Mental Disease* 185: 211–22.
Howe. 2004. Late Medieval Christianity, Balinese Hinduism, and the Doctrinal Mode of Religiosity. In *Ritual and Memory: Toward a Comparative Anthropology of Religion*, ed. Harvey Whitehouse and James Laidlaw. Walnut Creek, CA: AltaMira Press.
Johnson, Karen. 2004. Primary Emergence of the Doctrinal Mode of Religiosity in Prehistoric Southwestern Iran. In *Theorizing Religions Past: History, Archaeology, and Cognition*, ed. Harvey Whitehouse and Luther H. Martin. Walnut Creek, CA: AltaMira Press.
Lawson, E. Thomas, and Robert N. McCauley. 1990. *Rethinking Religion.* New York: Cambridge University Press.

Livingston, Kenneth R. 2004. Religious Practice, Brain, and Belief. In *The Psychological and Cognitive Foundations of Religiosity*, ed. Robert N. McCauley and Harvey Whitehouse. Special issue, *Journal of Cognition and Culture* 4, no. 3.

Malley, B. 2004. *How the Bible Works: An Anthropological Study of Evangelical Biblicism*. Walnut Creek, CA: AltaMira Press.

Martin, Luther H., and Harvey Whitehouse, eds. 2004. *The Cognitive Science of Religion*. Special issue, *Method and Theory in the Study of Religion* 16, no. 3.

———. 2006. *History, Memory, and Cognition*. Special issue, *Historical Reflections/Reflexions Historiques* 32, no. 1.

Mayr, E. 1976. Behavior Programs and Evolutionary Strategies. In *Evolution and the Diversity of Life: Selected Essays*, ed. E. Mayr. Cambridge, MA: Harvard University Press.

McCauley, Robert N. 2000. The Naturalness of Religion and the Unnaturalness of Science. In *Explanation and Cognition*, ed. Frank C. Keil and Robert A. Wilson. Cambridge, MA: MIT Press.

McCauley, Robert N., and E. Thomas Lawson. 2002. *Bringing Ritual to Mind: Psychological Foundations of Cultural Forms*. Cambridge: Cambridge University Press.

McCauley, Robert N., and Harvey Whitehouse, eds. 2004. *The Psychological and Cognitive Foundations of Religiosity*. Special issue, *Journal of Cognition and Culture* 4, no. 3.

Pyysiäinen, Ilkka. 2004. Corrupt Doctrine and Doctrinal Revival: On the Nature and Limits of the Modes Theory. In *Theorizing Religions Past: Historical and Archaeological Perspectives on "Modes of Religiosity,"* ed. Harvey Whitehouse and Luther H. Martin. Walnut Creek, CA: AltaMira Press.

Sperber, Dan. 1996. *Explaining Culture: A Naturalistic Approach*. London: Blackwells.

Thargard, Paul. 2004. The Emotional Coherence of Religion. In *The Psychological and Cognitive Foundations of Religiosity*, ed. Robert N. McCauley and Harvey Whitehouse. Special issue of *Journal of Cognition and Culture* 4, no. 3.

Tooby, John, and Leda Cosmides. 1992. The Psychological Foundations of Culture. In *The Adapted Mind*, ed. Jerome Barkow, Leda Cosmides, and John Tooby. New York: Oxford University Press.

Tulving, E. 1972. Episodic and Semantic Memory. In *Organization of Memory*, ed. E. Tulving and W. Donaldson. New York: Academic Press.

Vial, Theodore. 2004. Modes of Religiosity and Popular Religious Practices at the Time of the Reformation. In *Theorizing Religions Past: Historical and Archaeological Perspectives on Modes of Religiosity*, ed. Harvey Whitehouse and Luther H. Martin. Walnut Creek, CA: AltaMira Press.

Whitehouse, H. 1995. *Inside the Cult: Religious Innovation and Transmission in Papua New Guinea*. Oxford: Clarendon Press.

———. 2000. *Arguments and Icons: Divergent Modes of Religiosity*. Oxford: Oxford University Press.

———. 2004a. *Modes of Religiosity: A Cognitive Theory of Religious Transmission*. Walnut Creek, CA: AltaMira Press.

———. 2004b. Modes of Religiosity and the Cognitive Science of Religion. In *The Cognitive Science of Religion*, ed. Luther H. Martin and Harvey Whitehouse. Special issue, *Method and Theory in the Study of Religion* 16, no. 3.

———. 2005. Cognitive Science and the Art of Historiography. In *History, Memory, and Cognition*, ed. Luther H. Martin and Harvey Whitehouse. Special issue, *Historical Reflections/Réflexions Historiques* 15, no. 4.

Whitehouse, H., and J. Laidlaw, eds. 2004. *Ritual and Memory: Toward a Comparative Anthropology of Religion*. Walnut Creek, CA: AltaMira Press.

Whitehouse, H., and L. Martin, eds. 2004. *Theorizing Religions Past: History, Archaeology, and Cognition*. Walnut Creek, CA: AltaMira Press.

Wiebe, Donald. 2004. Implications of the "Modes of Religiosity Theory" for the Scientific Study of Religion. In *The Cognitive Science of Religion*, ed. Luther H. Martin and Harvey Whitehouse. Special issue of *Method and Theory in the Study of Religion* 16, no. 3.

Index

Page numbers in italic type refer to tables or figures.

agency: actional, 173; ambiguity of, 189–90, 196; ascription of, 173, 175, 177, 179–80, 181; in behavioral programs, 208–9; causal, 196–98; force as defining characteristic of, 172–74; free-will problems in, 188–89, 189–95; HADD detecting, 197; Leslie's argument of, 172–73; magical, 172–77, 177, 178, 180–82, *181;* in other humans, 197; in ritual action, 171–77; in self, 197, 199–201, 224; superempirical, 169, 171, 177, 181, 183n2

agents, supernatural: cognitive template of, 90; as counterintuitive, 94–95; mindful, 90–93; MoCA as, 32–33, 40–41, 75, 94; as socially omniscient, 90–93; superhuman, 5–6, 7, 8, 34, 35, 90–93. *See also* modestly counterintuitive agents; supernatural concepts

altar ritual experiment: description of, 138–40; propagation experiment correcting, 138; results of, 140–43

analogical thinking: about rituals, 64–65; concrete v. abstract in, 133; depth in, 131–33; exegesis causing, 130, 131–33, 135–38, *137,* 140–44, *142;* in natural settings, 132; purpose of, 132; relational structures in, 131; SER caused by, 130, 131–33, 135–36; source analog of, 130, 132, *134;* target analog of, 130, 132; within-domain v. cross-domain in, 133. *See also* spontaneous exegetical reflection

anonymous religious communities, 117–18

anthropomorphic deities, 40, 41, 43, 49–50, 199

Arminius, Jacobus, 191

arousal: in behavioral programs, 213; charisma producing, 171; as conversion variable, 155, 162, 225; in learning and memory, 211

ascribed charisma, 169–71, 177, 181

Atran, Scott, 151–53

attachment-theoretical approach, 151

standard model

177; standard model of religious cognition neglecting, 103n7; theological knowledge and, *114,* 114–15
extended cognition, 221–22

flashbulb memory, 47, 119–20, 162
force dynamics, 172–73, 174
the four whys: definition of, 38–39; interrelation of, 39, 50–51; receptivity and consequences in, 39–40
free-will problems: in agency, 188–89, 189–95; in Buddhism, 194–95; in Christianity, 189–91; closed behavior programs and, 223; combinatorial positions on, 191–92, 194, 200; constraints and, 195–98; counterintuitive concepts and, 187, 189, 191, 192–93, 195, 198–99, 201n1; in Hinduism, 192–94; inferential reasoning causing, 199–201; in Islam, 191–92; MoCA and, 187, 189, 191, 192–93, 195, 198–99, 201n1; in rational powers, 190; recurrence of, 195, 199–201; the Reformation and, 190–91. *See also* agency; constraints
frequency-related biases, 24
functional autonomy, 46–47
functional why, 38–39

game theory, 92
god/goddess concepts: cognitive foundations of, 75–78; complexity of, 187–89, *188;* representation variables of, *78*
Great Awakenings, 162
guilds: brands created by, 20, 26; against imagist practices, 20–22; literacy and, 20–26, 199, 217; political influence of, 18–20; rituals in, 18–19, 182; supernatural concepts controlled by, 20–21, 22–23, 182

habituation, 61–63, 211
HADD. *See* hyperactivity agency-detection device (HADD)

Heyes, Cecilia, 95
Hinduism: creation story of, 192–93; free-will problems in, 192–94; karma's role in, 193; as polytheism, 192; Purusha's sacrifice in, 192–93; Rig Veda of, 192–93
historical contingency. *See* sociocultural context
historiography, 222
Honen, 194
hyperactivity agency-detection device (HADD), 197
hypothesis: of cognitive alarm, 65; of cognitive optimum, 94–98; of divergent religions, 79–80; of layered religion, 215–16, 222–26; of ritual form, 60–61, 65–66, 102n4; of ritual frequency, 58–60, 64, 102n4, 113–14, 116, 128–29, 132–33, 162, 220; of tacit religion, 216–21, 229n13

imagistic mode: as analytical distinction, 149–50; as attractor position, 213; compulsive rituals of, 12–14; contagion-avoidance systems in, 12–14, 25, 208, 218, 220; conversion in, 159–62; definition of, 9, 10–11, 12, 14, 33, 86; in dual-process terminology, 80; episodic memory in, 47, 86, 119–21, 155–57, 162, 178, 179, 211, 212; flashbulb memory in, 47, 119–20, 162; functional autonomy in, 46–47; guilds v., 20–22; habituation in, 61–62, 211; innovation and, 170; instability of, 46–47, 63; modal variables and, 154–62; in reductionist model of transmission, 10–11; revelation in, 10–11, 37–38, 212; ritual meaning generated in, 156–57; social organization supported by, 168; thought reform parallels with, 38; variables of, 149–50, 154–62, 199, *200. See also* modes of religiosity; transmission, cultural
inclusivity, in conversion, 158
individual development, 42

Contributors

Justin L. Barrett is international coordinator of experimental research programmes in the Institute of Cognition and Culture at Queen's University Belfast. He received his PhD in experimental psychology from Cornell University. He has served on the faculties of Calvin College and the University of Michigan, and as associate director of the International Culture and Cognition Consortium, and on the editorial board of the *Journal of Cognition and Culture*. Barrett's research explores religious thought and action using theoretical and empirical tools of the cognitive sciences. He is author of *Why Would Anyone Believe in God?* (2004) and currently serves as codirector of Young Life in Lawrence, Kansas.

Pascal Boyer is Henry Luce Professor of individual and collective memory in the Department of Psychology at Washington University, St. Louis. He originally studied philosophy and anthropology at Universities of Paris and Cambridge. His graduate work with Professor Jack Goody focused on memory constraints on the transmission of oral literature. He has carried out anthropological fieldwork in Cameroon on the transmission of Fang oral epics and on Fang traditional religion. Since then he has worked mostly on the experimental study of cognitive capacities underlying cultural transmission. This work focuses on the development of core domain concepts (such as "person," "animal," "artifact") in young children and on the representations associated with such core concepts in adults. The aim is to gather behavioral, developmental, and neurocognitive evidence for domain-specific capacities in human minds. Boyer taught in Cambridge, San Diego, Lyon, and Santa Barbara before moving to St. Louis. His previous books include *Tradition as Truth and Communication* (1990), *The Naturalness of Religious Ideas* (1994), and *Religion Explained* (2001).

Matthew Day is assistant professor of religion and science in the Department of Religion and the Program in the History and Philosophy of Science at Florida State University. His research focuses on the history of engagement between religion and the modern natural sciences in the West since the eighteenth century, with particular attention paid to the impact of Charles Darwin's evolutionary thought. This includes building empirically-grounded, evolutionary theories of religious belief and behavior that treat human beings as both artifacts of natural selection and culturally embedded and embodied cognitive agents. He is currently working on a book about the nineteenth-century "biologization" of mind, early neuroscientific debates about cerebral localization, and protocognitive theories of religion.

Robert A. Hinde, CBE, FRS, FBA, served as a pilot in RAF Coastal Command during the war before taking a degree in biology at Cambridge and a PhD at Oxford. He was later awarded a Royal Society Research Professorship and has worked at Cambridge on animal behavior and on the relationships between individuals in human families. He was Master of St. John's College, Cambridge, from 1989 to 1994, and since then has used a biological and social science approach to study the bases of religion and morality in human nature, and the causes of international war. He is chairman of the British Pugwash Group. His most recent books are *Why Gods Persist* (1999), *Why Good Is Good* (2002), and *War No More* (with J. Rotblat, 2003).

E. Thomas Lawson is emeritus professor of comparative religion at Western Michigan University. He is the author of *Religions of Africa: Traditions in Transformation* (1984) and, with Robert N. McCauley, *Rethinking Religion: Connecting Religion and Culture* (1990) and *Bringing Ritual to Mind: Psychological Foundations of Ritual Forms* (2002), and he has contributed chapters to many books, articles to a wide variety of journals, and a large number of entries to encyclopaedias. He is executive editor of the *Journal of Cognition and Culture* and distinguished international fellow at the Institute of Cognition and Culture at Queen's University Belfast.

Robert N. McCauley is professor of philosophy at Emory University in Atlanta. He is the author, with E. Thomas Lawson, of *Rethinking Religion: Connecting Cognition and Culture* (1990) and *Bringing Ritual to Mind: Psychological Foundations of Cultural Forms* (2002). He is also editor of *The Churchlands and Their Critics* (1996) and has contributed articles to a wide variety of journals, including *Philosophy of Science, Synthese, Philosophical Psychology, Consciousness and Cognition, Theory and Psychology, Method and Theory in the Study of Religion, Journal of the American Academy of Religion*, and *History of Religions*. He is currently writing a book comparing the cognitive foundations of science and religion.

Ilkka Pyysiäinen works at the Helsinki Collegium for Advanced Studies. He was educated in theology and comparative religion at the University of Helsinki, Finland. He earned his PhD in 1993 with a thesis on Buddhist mysticism. Since then he has dedicated himself to the study of cognition and religion. He has published numerous scholarly papers, and his books include *How Religion Works: Towards a New Cognitive Science of Religion* (2001) and *Magic, Miracles, and Religion: A Scientist's Perspective* (2004).

Rebekah Richert is a developmental psychologist who has published widely on children's developing concepts of God. She is currently conducting experimental research at Queen's University Belfast in collaboration with Professor Harvey Whitehouse and at Harvard in collaboration with Professor Paul Harris, funded by the National Science Foundation.

Jason Slone is an assistant professor of comparative religion at the University of Findlay, Ohio. He is particularly interested in the ways that online cognitive reasoning strategies constrain religious thought across cultures, systems, and eras. His recent book, *Theological Incorrectness: Why Religious People Believe What They Shouldn't* (2004), uses cognitive theories to explain why "folk" beliefs stray from theological creeds in the Buddhist cultures of Southeast Asia and the Protestant Christian cultures of the United States. He is also the editor of *Religion and Cognition: A Reader* (2005).

Jesper Sørensen is associate professor in the Department of the Study of Religion, University of Southern Denmark, and from 2005 an international fellow at the Institute of Cognition and Culture at Queen's University Belfast. He received his PhD in 2001 at University of Aarhus after defending his thesis entitled *Essence, Schema and Ritual Action: Towards a Cognitive Theory of Magic*. He is interested in ritual studies in general and the study of magic in particular, and in how cognition and culture interact in religious behavior.

Emma Stewart is currently writing her PhD thesis after eighteen months of ethnographic fieldwork in Belem, Northern Brazil. Her research investigates the explanatory potential of various mechanisms proposed by current cognitive theories of religion in the transmission of Afro-Brazilian spirit-possession cults.

Todd Tremlin has taught in the Department of Comparative Religion at Western Michigan University, Kalamazoo, Michigan, and in the Department of Religious Studies at Michigan State University, Lansing, Michigan. He holds master's degrees from Western Michigan University and Cornerstone University and received his PhD in comparative religion from Western Michigan University. His writing has appeared in several periodicals, including the

Journal of Cognition and Culture. His first book, *Divine Minds: The Cognitive Foundations of God and Religion,* is currently in preparation.

Harvey Whitehouse is professor of anthropology and director of the Institute of Cognition and Culture at Queen's University Belfast. A specialist in Melanesian religion, he carried out two years of ethnographic fieldwork in New Britain, Papua New Guinea, in the late eighties as part of his PhD research at Cambridge University. After a three-year research fellowship at Cambridge (1990–1993), he was appointed to a lectureship at Queen's. In recent years, he has focused his energies on the development of collaborative programs of research on cognition and culture. He is currently the principal grant holder of a British Academy Networks Project on "modes of religiosity" and in 2003 was appointed to a British Academy Research Readership. He is also coeditor, with Luther H. Martin, of the AltaMira Cognitive Science of Religion Series. His previous books include *Inside the Cult: Religious Innovation and Transmission in Papua New Guinea* (1995), *Arguments and Icons: Divergent Modes of Religiosity* (2000), and *Modes of Religiosity: A Cognitive Theory of Religious Transmission* (2004).